The LOVE Command in the New Testament

The LOVE Command in the New Testament

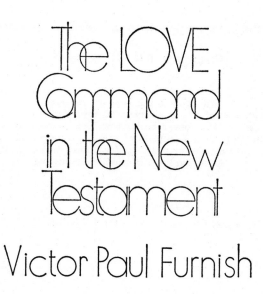

Victor Paul Furnish

Abingdon Press
Nashville and New York

THE LOVE COMMAND IN THE NEW TESTAMENT

Copyright © 1972 by Abingdon Press

ISBN 0-687-22809-3

Library of Congress Catalog Card Number: 75-172814

MANUFACTURED BY THE PARTHENON PRESS AT
NASHVILLE, TENNESSEE, UNITED STATES OF AMERICA

TO
JODY, BRIANNA RUTH, REBECCA JOANN

In whose company I have
found a special *kairos*
for love (Galatians 6:10)

ACKNOWLEDGMENTS

It is not only appropriate but necessary that the prefatory words in any book about the love command in the New Testament should be words of acknowledgment. The topic itself is so vast and it touches so sensitively and significantly on so many other profound New Testament themes, that the investigator must first of all acknowledge his own inability ever to do it justice. Just as surely must he acknowledge his indebtedness to all those who before him have traversed the same terrain, recorded and interpreted their findings, and thereby made yet further exploration possible and meaningful. The scholarly literature is as vast, if not always as profound and important, as the topic itself, and the books and articles cited in the footnotes give a fair sampling of the kind of previous work which has helped to guide and inform my own study. Where possible I have cited and quoted English translations of works from other languages, and I have made my own translations where none existed. Ancient authors are cited according to "The Loeb Classical Library" edition when there is such; otherwise the source is given. In many instances quotations from the New Testament follow my own translation, but I have regularly consulted and compared, and sometimes quoted, the *Revised Standard Version* (*RSV*), the *New English Bible* (*NEB*), and the *Jerusalem Bible* (*JB*).

The topic of this investigation was first suggested to me during the course of a conversation with Professor Günther Bornkamm at his home on the Bahofweg in Heidelberg, in 1964. It would, however, be presumptuous for me to suggest, or even to allow the impression to be gained, that the results of my work accord in any degree with what he had in mind. Indeed, the project has turned out rather differently from what I myself had first envisioned. At the same time, it will be apparent that Professor Bornkamm's work on the love command, particularly in the Synoptic Gospels and in Paul's letters, has helped to give shape and scope to my own studies.

It is also a pleasure to acknowledge here the constant and able assistance of the staff of Bridwell Library, as well as the encouragement of numerous colleagues on the faculty of Perkins School of Theology. Two of these, Professor Frederick S. Carney and Mr. William Longsworth, have materially assisted by referring me to some of the literature in the field of Christian ethics where ideas pertinent to my topic have been developed. My concluding suggestions (pp. 195-218) have been formulated with greater clarity because of their probing questions and comments.

The entire manuscript was skillfully transformed into typescript by Mrs. Bonnie Jordan whose patience and goodwill withstood seemingly endless additions and revisions. No less vital for the eventual completion of my work was my wife's frequent query, born of genuine interest, if also sometimes of a little impatience, "How's the book?" Finally, others must answer that.

CONTENTS

ABBREVIATIONS

AB	The Anchor Bible Commentary
ABR	Australian Biblical Review
AThR	Anglican Theological Review
BEvTh	Beiträge zur evangelischen Theologie
BHTh	Beiträge zur historischen Theologie
BZ	Biblische Zeitschrift
BZNW	Beihefte zur Zeitschrift für die neutestament-liche Wissenschaft
EvTh	Evangelische Theologie
ExT	The Expository Times
FRLANT	Forschungen zur Religion und Literatur des Alten und Neuen Testaments
HNT	Handbuch zum Neuen Testament, begr. von H. Lietzmann
HNTC	Harper's New Testament Commentaries
HThR	The Harvard Theological Review

ICC	The International Critical Commentary of the Holy Scripture of the Old and New Testaments
IntB	The Interpreter's Bible, 12 vols., 1951-57, ed. G. A. Buttrick *et al.*
IntDB	The Interpreter's Dictionary of the Bible: An Illustrated Encyclopedia, 4 vols., 1962, ed. G. A. Buttrick *et al.*
JB	The Jerusalem Bible, 1966
JBL	The Journal of Biblical Literature
JR	The Journal of Religion
JThCh	Journal for Theology and the Church
JThSt	The Journal of Theological Studies
KuD	Kerygma und Dogma
KEK	Kritisch-exegetischer Kommentar über das Neue Testament, begr. von H. A. W. Meyer
LCC	The Loeb Classical Library
LXX	The Septuagint, ed. A. Rahlfs
MNTC	The Moffatt New Testament Commentary
NEB	The New English Bible, 1970
NT	Novum Testamentum
NTD	Das Neue Testament Deutsch
NTS	New Testament Studies
RB	Revue Biblique
RSV	The Holy Bible: Revised Standard Version, 1952
SJTh	The Scottish Journal of Theology
Scot Per	Scottish Periodical
StTh	Studia Theologica
Test. [*XII Patr.*]	The Testaments of the Twelve Patriarchs
ThD	Theological Dictionary of the New Testament, ed. G. Kittel *et al.*, English trans. and ed. G. W. Bromiley, 1964 ff.
ThHNT	Theologischer Handkommentar zum Neuen Testament
ThStK	Theologische Studien und Kritiken
ThT	Theology Today
ThWB	Theologisches Wörterbuch zum Neuen Testament, hg. von G. Kittel *et al.*, 1933 ff.

ThZ	Theologische Zeitschrift
ZEE	Zeitschrift für evangelische Ethik
ZNW	Zeitschrift für die neutestamentliche Wissenschaft
ZSystTh	Zeitschrift für systematische Theologie
ZThK	Zeitschrift für Theologie und Kirche

INTRODUCTION

In the 1920s the great Japanese Christian and humanitarian, Toyohiko Kagawa, published a book entitled *Love: The Law of Life.*[1] One chapter was devoted to love and the neighbor and was composed largely of reflections on his visit to Jane Addams' "Hull House" in the Chicago slums. "Settlement work" as conceived and practiced half a century ago would doubtless be an insufficient, even naïve, response to the seething unrest of our central cities in the latter half of the twentieth century. But Kagawa's comment on the motivation to and meaning of social work in his day retains, both in its simplicity of expression and in its specificity of reference, an authentic Christian word about the love ethic. "The fundamental spirit of settlement work," he wrote, "is kindness to neighbors. It is just helping a man as a neighbor because he is in trouble right beside you."[2] Then he

[1] Trans. J. Fullerton Gressitt (Philadelphia: John C. Winston Co., 1929).
[2] *Ibid.,* p. 226.

goes on, "When I asked Miss Addams for reports of her work, she replied that there were none. 'I don't make reports,' she said, 'because the work is my own.' " [3]

Although these words may sound quaint and naïve in a day when moral issues and social problems are—or at least are understood to be—vastly more complex, even recent, highly sophisticated interpreters of love must write of their subject finally in very elemental ways. The historian of religion, G. van der Leeuw, who sees love as "the basic experience in [all] religion . . . ," [4] suggests that "love may be described as an attempt to force oneself into the place of the other. . . ." [5] The psychiatrist, Karl Menninger, describes love as the experience of "pleasure in proximity, a desire for fuller knowledge of one another, a yearning for mutual identification and personality fusion." This, he says, is expressed in our efforts "to be understood, and by indulging the less imperious longing to understand." [6] And the theologian, Gerhard Ebeling, though in the diction of formal theology, says something about love strikingly similar to Kagawa's simple words about the meaning of "settlement work": "The demand to love our neighbor is simply true, i.e. expresses what is demanded by the reality of human relations as everyone has occasion to experience it." [7]

The simplicity and concreteness of these twentieth-century comments on love put them in the company of the biblical injunction to "love your neighbor as yourself," which in its formulation also is deceptively simple and disturbingly concrete. This command in the so-called "Holiness Code" (Lev. 19:18) is one component of the Great Commandment ascribed to Jesus (Matt. 22:39; Mark 12:31; Luke 10:27; cf. Matt. 5:43; 19:19) and is also employed by Paul (Rom. 13:9; Gal. 5:14), by the writer of James (2:8), in the Didache (1:2; 2:7), and in Barnabas (19:

---

[3] *Ibid.,* p. 227.

[4] *Religion in Essence and Manifestation,* 2 vols., trans. J. E. Turner (New York: Harper & Row [Torchbooks], 1963), p. 509.

[5] *Ibid.,* p. 49.

[6] With Jeanetta Lyle Menninger, *Love Against Hate* (New York: Harcourt, Brace & Co., 1952), p. 272.

[7] "Theology and the Evidentness of the Ethical," trans. J. Leitch in *JThCh* II (1965): 113.

5).[8] In later writers the double commandment as such is often quoted, usually with reference to its promulgation by Jesus (Clement of Alexandria, *Stromata* II.xv; IV.iii; Tertullian, *An Answer to the Jews*, II; *Against Marcion*, V.viii; *On the Resurrection of the Flesh*, IX; *On Fasting*, II; Origen, *De Principiis*, II.ii), although at least twice Tertullian cites only the second half (Lev. 19:18; see *Against Marcion*, V.xiv; *On the Apparel of Women*, II.ii).

The centrality of this commandment in Christian teaching of the first and second centuries (whether or not the Leviticus text is specifically used) is attested not only by Christian writers who consistently stress the love imperative, but also by ancient pagan testimony to the actual life of love they observed as characteristic of the early Christian congregations. Tertullian's reference to such testimony is famous: pagans who note the brotherly care of Christians for one another exclaim in surprise and admiration, "Look . . . how they love one another . . ." (*Apology*, XXXIX, 7). Further pagan testimony to Christian love is ascribed by Minucius Felix (late second century) to Q. Caecilius Natalis, who is represented, however, as misunderstanding the love of Christians for one another as a vile abomination: "They fall in love almost before they are acquainted . . ." (ix, 2).

A less quoted but even more impressive report of how the life of the earliest church was animated by concrete deeds of brotherly love is present in one of the works of the non-Christian writer, Lucian of Samosata (A.D. 125-190). One of Lucian's essays concerns a certain Cynic philosopher named Proteus (d. A.D. 165) who, for a time, espoused Christianity and went by the name "Peregrinus." Lucian regarded this man as a first-class charlatan —before, during, and after his Christian period. Whether or not Lucian was correct in his judgment, Lucian's account of Peregrinus' Christian period and his relations during that time with fellow Christians gives us—from a non-Christian writer—valuable information about what brotherly love meant in the second-

[8] Whether the cited passages in Did. and Barn. are dependent upon the formulation of the double commandment found in the Synoptic Gospels is disputed. For the case against this, see Helmut Köster, *Synoptische Überlieferung bei den apostolischen Vätern*, Texte und Untersuchungen, 65 (Berlin: Akademie-Verlag, 1957): 134, 170-72.

century church. Lucian reports that, at one point, Peregrinus was imprisoned in Syria for being a Christian (probably about A.D. 150), and then testifies that other Christians, "regarding the incident as a calamity, left nothing undone in the effort to rescue him." When this proved impossible, they ministered to him by other means, "not in any casual way but with zeal." Widows, orphans, and church officials visited him in prison, brought meals to him, and read aloud to him from the Scriptures. Even from the cities of Asia Christians came to help Peregrinus in both spiritual and material ways. "They show incredible speed," writes Lucian, "whenever any such public action is taken." For "their first lawgiver [i.e. Jesus] persuaded them that they are all brothers of one another. . . ." [9]

There is no need to belabor further the obvious point that the love ethic is a crucial aspect of both the literature and the life of earliest Christianity. There may be some need, however, to justify yet *another* investigation of this topic. In addition to countless articles, chapters, and monographs on specialized aspects of the love ethic in earliest Christianity, there have been three major works published in our century, in English, German, and French respectively: James Moffatt's *Love in the New Testament*,[10] Viktor Warnach's *Agape. Die Liebe als Grundmotiv der neutestamentlichen Theologie*,[11] and Ceslaus Spicq's *Agapè dans le Nouveau Testament: Analyse des Textes*.[12] Each of these, in its own way, makes valuable contributions to our topic, but each seeks to cut a broad swathe through *all* aspects of "love" in the New Testament and none focuses as such on the love command. Moreover, Moffatt's book—which was not, in the first place, intended to be more than a very general discussion of the topic —needs to be updated in the light of subsequent New Testament

----

[9] "The Passing of Peregrinus," pp. 11 ff. in Vol. V of *Lucian of Samosata* (*LCC*, trans. A. W. Harmon). I have altered the translation slightly.

[10] London: Hodder & Stoughton, 1929.

[11] Düsseldorf: Patmos-Verlag, 1951.

[12] *Études Bibliques*, 3 vols. (Paris: Librairie Lecoffre, 1958-59). An English translation (St. Louis and London: B. Herder Book Co., 1963-66) by Sister Marie Aquinas McNamara and Sister Mary Honoria Richter re-arranges slightly the contents of the French edition and omits virtually all technical footnotes. I shall cite the English text where possible, but occasionally references will have to be to the French edition only.

scholarship. And the more recent studies of Warnach and Spicq (both Roman Catholics) are not sufficiently critical in method to avoid what many Protestant *and* Roman Catholic interpreters would now regard to be an unjustified homogenization of differing perspectives and emphases within the New Testament itself.

The objective of this present study is considerably more limited than that which guided Moffatt, Warnach, and Spicq. It focuses on the love *ethic,* the love *command,* what the New Testament teaches and otherwise reflects about earliest Christainity's view of loving one's brother, one's neighbor, and one's enemy. God's love for man and man's love for God are discussed only insofar as New Testament writers themselves directly relate these to the love ethic. In two respects, however, this investigation seeks to provide a somewhat broader view of the earliest Christian love ethic than is available in most of the specialized studies. For one thing, attention is given to each of the New Testament writers, and also to certain other Christian literature of the first two centuries, in an effort to trace and define the *various ways* the love command has been received, interpreted, and applied. Most previous studies have either harmonized the various points of view (e.g. Warnach, Spicq), dealt only incidentally with the variety of positions (e.g. Moffatt), or else sought to impose a schematized construct upon the evidence without a sufficiently careful historical, literary, and theological assessment of the evidence. A provocative, but finally unsatisfactory essay by Carl Heinz Ratschow falls into this latter category.[13] His contention is that, while Jesus freed the Old Testament command to love the neighbor from the restrictive circumference of God's *electing* love and thus interpreted "neighbor" to include those outside the covenant community, successive Christian writers—Paul, John, Ignatius—moved increasingly back toward a limited application of the love commandment.[14] This kind of schematization, in my view, makes too many generalizations on the basis of

---

[13] "Agape, Nächstenliebe und Bruderliebe," *ZSystTh* **XXI** (1950): 160-82.
[14] *Ibid.*, esp. pp. 171-72, 173-74, 175, 176. Similar views are expressed by Hugh Montefiore, "Thou Shalt Love the Neighbour as Thyself," *NT* **V** (1962): 157-70, and—respecting the Johannine literature—by John Knox, *The Ethic of Jesus in the Teaching of the Church: Its Authority and Relevance* (Nashville: Abingdon Press, 1961), pp. 95-96.

too little careful exegetical work, and does not inquire seriously enough into the ever-changing needs and crises in the life of the church which required its preachers and teachers to articulate the tradition in ever new ways and to emphasize different kinds of things. The present study tries to take account of these factors and to develop its picture of the love ethic in earliest Christianity on a solid exegetical basis.

My further intention here is to examine the *full context* in which each writer employs and applies the love commandment. One of the fatal weaknesses of Spicq's *magnum opus* is his failure at just this point. He focuses his attention so exclusively on passages where the *word* "love" occurs, that he constantly ignores many other texts which reflect just as much, or even more, about a given writer's view of the meaning and requirements of love in the Christian life. In this regard it must be stressed that the "full context" of the love command in any given source must include the way it is theologically grounded and construed, the way it is illustrated and applied, and its place in relation to other ethical commands and norms.

One further introductory remark is in order. Too often discussions of the Christian gospel of love have been oriented almost entirely in relation to the Greek vocable agape, which is—admittedly—the most common New Testament word and the most characteristic early Christian word for "love." I have already suggested, however, that preoccupation with texts where the *word* "love" happens to appear fatally restricts one's view of the love ethic in earliest Christianity. Moreover, agape is by no means the *only* word for love even in the New Testament. And, finally, it is no longer possible to hold that especially the noun agape is so uniquely Christian that it always and everywhere carries a particular freight of meaning and of theological significance. My study, therefore, does not proceed with the kind of philological orientation characteristic of so many earlier works, especially Spicq's. It proceeds, rather, upon the basis of the conviction that agape—or any other word for love—not only contributes to the total meaning of the context in which it is employed, but, just as importantly, receives meaning from that context. A priori judgments about the meaning of the various words for love hinder rather than help the exegetical enterprise. In an Appendix I have sought to provide some perspective on the philological situation regarding love in the New Testament. But finally, the meaning of the love command in earliest Christianity has to be based on much broader considerations.

I
JESUS' COMMANDMENTS TO LOVE

It would seem to be obvious that the teaching of Jesus himself must be the starting point for an investigation of the love command in earliest Christianity. But it is equally clear that Jesus' teaching is accessible only in the traditions preserved and interpreted in the church's own teaching and preaching, and presented finally in the faith documents we know as "Gospels." Therefore, it is not with "Jesus in history" but with "Jesus in the Gospels" that our study must commence, whereupon it becomes immediately apparent that each of the evangelists has received and formulated Jesus' teachings on love in a distinctive way. Fortunately, however, careful literary-critical and form-historical analysis of the parallel materials used by the Synoptic writers[1] provides some degree of control over our written sources and thus some clues as to particular points which may be presumed to be derived ultimately from the teaching of the historical Jesus. It must be emphasized, nevertheless, that whatever fleeting glimpses of Jesus' own words may come, will come as by-products of our exegesis which, as such, can only be of texts which are already *interpreting* Jesus' teaching in the light of the Easter faith.

Thus, with particular reference to the love ethic, we are confronted from the very outset of this study with a fact which shall become increasingly clear as it proceeds: the Christian gospel of love cannot be distilled into some universal proposition or commandment, but can only be grasped in its concreteness as it impinges upon specific relationships and situations in history. The Gospels do not constitute a literary museum for the mere display of Jesus' commandments as if those in and of themselves had some time- and space-transcending validity. The gospels do not just *exhibit* Jesus' teaching, but rather receive, transmit, and apply it in specific ways relevant to the needs of the church in the writers' own times. Thereby they demonstrate their faithfulness to one of the most crucial aspects of Jesus' teaching: that it did not consist of the mere promulgation or exposition of general truths, values, and rules, but was rather a call, a summons, a command addressed to specific persons in actual situations. And so there is no golden nugget—or Golden Rule!—which can be singled out as the essence of the love ethic in earliest Christianity. This would be the case even if we could with full certainty reclaim Jesus' own words about love. For while the church did indeed (probably in dependence upon Jesus' own teaching) sometimes offer succinct formulations of the gospel's love imperative, these are consistently adapted and addressed to meet particular issues involving Christians.

Two of these formulations will serve very well to open our

---

[1] Throughout I shall refer to these writers as "Matthew," "Mark," and "Luke" respectively, although I do not believe the traditional view of authorship can in any case be substantiated. I regard the Synoptic Gospels as having been written in the last two or three decades of the first century for variously located churches.

study, the so-called "double commandment" to love God and the neighbor which is present in all three of the Synoptic Gospels, and the more radical commandment present in Matthew and Luke to love even one's enemy. These are important texts for several reasons. First, they are frequently cited or otherwise employed in other Christian writings of the first two centuries. Second, there can be little doubt but that the command to love even the enemy goes back to the teaching of Jesus himself, and it is at least possible that the specific coupling of two Old Testament texts (Deut. 6:5 and Lev. 19:18) to form the "double command-ment" was also an element of his teaching. And finally, the varied use of these teachings of Jesus by the Synoptic evangelists illustrates the point that the early church did not just passively *receive* but actively *appropriated* the teaching of the one whom they had come to confess as Christ and as Lord.

The Great Commandment

Introductory Observations

According to both Matthew and Mark Jesus, during the last week of his life, in Jerusalem, upon being questioned formulates the so-called "double commandment" concerning love to God and love to neighbor (Matt. 22:34-40; Mark 12:28-34). In both gospels the pericope immediately follows Jesus' response to the Sadducees about resurrection and immediately precedes Jesus' words about the Davidic sonship.

The corresponding point in the Lucan passion story does not have this formulation of the double commandment. Instead, in Luke the pericopes about resurrection (20:27-40) and Davidic sonship (20:41-44) stand side by side. That Luke's tradition did in fact originally include the double commandment between these two pericopes is probable, however.[2] For the Lucan con-

[2] See Hermann Binder, "Das Gleichnis vom barmherzigen Samariter," *ThZ* XV (1959): 176-77.

clusion to the resurrection pericope ("And in answer to him some of the scribes said, 'Teacher, you have spoken well,' " 20:39) seems to make use of the formulations with which Mark has opened and concluded his account of the double commandment ("And one of the scribes, when he came up, heard them disputing, saw that he answered them well, and asked him . . . ," 12:28a; "And the scribe said to him, '[You answer] well, Teacher,' " 12:32a). Moreover, Luke 20:40 ("for they no longer dared to ask him a thing") makes use of the idea of Mark 12:34b ("and no one dared any longer to ask him [any question]").

In Luke, the double commandment itself occurs much earlier (10:25-28), in the midst of Jesus' journey to Jerusalem (see 9:51, 57 ff.). Whereas in Matthew and Mark the commandment pericope is tied at least formally to what precedes (in both cases a series of questions is being addressed to Jesus, and the question about the greatest commandment is introduced by a reference to Jesus' excellent fielding of other questions), in Luke such formal ties with the context are missing. Furthermore, the preceding material has been presented as Jesus' private teaching to his disciples (Luke 10:23), and we are thus quite unprepared for the sudden arising of a "lawyer" with a question (vs. 25). It should also be noted that in Luke the double commandment is closely linked with the parable of the "Good Samaritan" (10:29-37), the two together thus forming a single topical unit. The many other variations among our sources are best identified and assessed in the course of a more detailed consideration of each Synoptic version of the Great Commandment.

The Marcan Version, 12:28-34

Since, if Luke's attached parable is excluded, Mark's version of the Commandment is the longest of the three, it will be useful to examine it first. There are two points at which the Marcan pericope is extended: in vs. 29 Jesus cites the *Shema* (Deut. 6:4), and in vss. 32-33 the questioner affirms Jesus' answer, repeats it, and in fact adds to it (vs. 33b).

The reference to Jesus' impressive response to the Sadducees' questioning (vs. 28a) is doubtless an editorial link with the preceding pericope forged by the evangelist himself.[3] While the questions put to Jesus by the Sadducees had been formulated with hostile intent, there is no hint of hostility as the scribe puts his own question about the "chief commandment." The scribe is portrayed as coming to Jesus sincerely impressed with this teacher's ability to answer difficult questions, and before he goes away he not only affirms Jesus' response to *his* question (vss. 32-33) but is himself commended by Jesus (vs. 34). The form of the story is that of the typical (rabbinic) scholastic dialogue.[4]

The scribe's question is simply stated and is by no means an unusual one for a Jew to ask: "What is the chief commandment?" (vs. 28b). Rabbis were constantly asked to summarize the 613 commandments (365 negative, 248 positive) of the law and willingly replied, although with varying answers.[5] A distinctive feature of Mark's version of Jesus' reply is the citation of the *Shema* from Deut. 6:4—the confession of faith repeated twice daily by the pious Jew and regarded as fundamental for the devout life. The repetition of this confession of faith in the one God by the scribe himself later in the pericope (vs. 32) shows that the affirmation is not just intended as an introduction to Jesus' answer, but as a vital part of it. As we shall see, it is not without significance that in this Marcan version, affirmation of the *one* God who is "Lord" is inseparably a part of "the chief commandment."

The scribe's original question to Jesus had been, literally, concerning the "first" of all commandments. But in reply Jesus offers both a "first" (vss. 29-30) and a "second" (vs. 31a) commandment. There is no attempt, explicit or implicit, to justify this, and the sequential "first-second," as well as the "than *these*" in vs. 31b helps give each commandment a distinct identity. In effect, then, the scribe is being told that no *one* commandment

[3] So, e.g., R. Bultmann, *The History of the Synoptic Tradition*, trans. John Marsh (New York: Harper & Row, 1963), p. 22.

[4] Bultmann, *ibid.*, 51, 54, 55; G. Bornkamm, "Das Doppelgebot der Liebe," *Neutestamentliche Studien für Rudolf Bultmann*, 2nd ed., BZNW 21 (Berlin: A. Töpelmann, 1957): 85.

[5] See George Foot Moore, *Judaism in the First Centuries of the Christian Era: The Age of the Tannaim*, II (Cambridge: Harvard University Press, 1932): 83.

can be marked as "first," but that these two together (love of the one God and love of one's neighbor) constitute the essence of the law. I have on occasion heard Christian ministers criticize Christian social action on the grounds that the church's real business is "religious," for Jesus' "first" commandment is to love *God,* and one's duty to love the neighbor is only secondary. But this interpretation of the Great Commandment is entirely excluded by the context here. The two commands *together* are set over against all other requirements of the law: "There is no other commandment greater than these" (vs. 31b). The "second" commandment is not "of second importance." It is, simply, the second of two mentioned as together comprising the "chief" commandment about which the scribe had initially inquired. "The union of the singular 'no other commandment' and the plural 'than these' maintains the distinction between the two precepts, but puts both of them into a special category." [6] One may compare, for form at least, the famous dictum of Simeon the Just (3rd century B.C.): "Upon three things the world standeth; upon Torah, upon Worship and upon the showing of kindness." [7] These items are not *ranked,* but *listed,* and as in the double commandment of Mark 12:29-31a the components are of equal and related importance.

It is noteworthy that, apart from the Synoptic formulations of the double commandment, the command of Deut. 6:5 to "love the Lord your God" is not cited by New Testament writers. In fact, there is only one other Synoptic passage which speaks at all of man's love for God (Luke 11:42: the Pharisees "neglect justice and the love of God"), and the idea appears only rarely elsewhere in the New Testament (e.g., Rom. 8:28; I Cor. 2:9; 8:3; 16:22; Eph. 6:24; I John 4:20-21). [8] Ordinarily man's proper relationship to God is described in other ways (to "believe," to "know," to "obey," etc.), so it would seem that the citation of Deut. 6:5 has its point principally if not exclusively in relation

[6] Spicq, *Agape in the New Testament,* I: 64.

[7] Aboth I, 2, trans. R. Travers Herford in *Pirke Aboth, The Ethics of the Talmud: Sayings of the Fathers,* 3rd ed. reprinted (New York: Schocken Books, 1962).

[8] See D. E. Nineham, *The Gospel of St. Mark,* The Pelican Gospel Commentaries (London: Penguin Books, 1963), p. 325.

to the subsequent quotation of Lev. 19:18 to love the neighbor as one's self. It may well be, as Asher Finkel has suggested, that this combination of texts is an example of an ancient Pharisaic hermeneutical procedure.[9] By the "analogy of words" two or more scriptural texts could be brought together and conjointly interpreted. Thus, because in these two texts the same word is used to command *love* for God (Deut. 6:5) and *love* for the neighbor (Lev. 19:18), the commands themselves are regarded as analogous and are combined and interpreted as one.

It is best to defer until a later point our comments on the significance of this striking juxtaposition of commands to love God *and* one's neighbor.[10] For in Mark's version, the effect of the scribe's response to Jesus' promulgation of the Great Commandment is to accentuate the monotheistic confession with which Jesus had begun: "[You answer] well, Teacher. In truth have you said that he is One and there is none but he" (vs. 32). As Bornkamm points out, in the scribe's recapitulation of Jesus' answer the affirmation of the one God gains independent status, so that the division is not so much between a "first" and "second" commandment (the enumeration is itself dropped in the scribe's recapitulation) as it is between the *Shema* on the one hand (vs. 32b) and the Great Commandment on the other (vs. 33a).[11] Moreover, in reformulating Jesus' answer the scribe proceeds to introduce an entirely new element. The Great Commandment is now deliberately and emphatically assessed as "much more [important] than all whole burnt offerings and sacrifices" (vs. 33b). In fact, then, the original formulation has been restated in such a way as to interpret and extend its meaning. This interpretation is in turn approved by Jesus who, according to the evangelist, judges the scribe to have spoken "wisely" and to be close to the kingdom of God (vs. 34a).[12]

[9] *The Pharisees and the Teacher of Nazareth. A Study of Their Background, Their Halachic and Midrashic Teachings, the Similarities and Differences,* Arbeiten zur Geschichte des späteren Judentums und des Urchristentums, IV (Leiden: E. J. Brill, 1964): 174.

[10] See below, pp. 62-63.

[11] "Das Doppelgebot der Liebe," p. 87.

[12] "You are not far from the kingdom of God" is an example of the rhetorical device, *litotes,* understatement for the sake of emphasis. Thus, the meaning is unqualifiedly affirmative: the scribe is said to belong to the

It should now be clear that the Marcan version of the Great Commandment has its own special point and meaning, revealed best in the scribe's response which is in turn given Jesus' own imprimatur in the closing verse of the passage. The overall point is just this: What is important for true religion is belief in and worship of the one God and obedience to the moral law, not religious ceremony or cultic performance. Bornkamm's analysis of the passage brings this meaning out very well,[13] and he shows how a number of linguistic details serve to confirm it. Thus, the Marcan version of Deut. 6:5 (vs. 30) substitutes for the LXX's, "with all your *might* [δυνάμεως]," the phrase, "with all your *mind* [διανοίας]," which is then interpreted (in the scribe's recapitulation of the command, vs. 33) to mean, "with all your *understanding* [συνέσεως]." These words, plus the good Greek formula employed in vs. 32, "In truth have you said [ἐπ' ἀληθείας εἶπες]," and the word "wisely" [νουνεχῶς] in vs. 34a (used only here in the whole New Testament) give the Marcan version a decidedly rationalistic aspect.[14] When the distinctively rationalistic vocabulary here is coupled with the emphasis upon the oneness of God (vss. 29, 32), the result is material which would have particular merit and meaning within the context of Hellenistic-Jewish and Christian apologetic, directed against Greek polytheism.[15] Moreover, when the double commandment to love God and the neighbor is specifically set over against the cultic requirements of "whole burnt offerings and sacrifices" (vs. 33), another typically anti-pagan motif emerges.[16] In the

---

Kingdom. Many commentators find it impossible to reconcile the conception of one's "being near" the kingdom of God with the more usual New Testament conception of the Kingdom's "coming." But I think it is unwarranted to extract from the phrase "not far from the kingdom of God" any intentional picture of a pilgrim "on the way" to some static kingdom. The point could very well be that the scribe, because he recognizes the meaning of "true religion," stands to inherit and enter into the Kingdom when it finally comes. For discussions, see, e.g., Bornkamm, *ibid.*, pp. 90-91 and Vincent Taylor, *The Gospel According to St. Mark* (London: Macmillan & Co., 1952), pp. 489-90.

[13] "Das Doppelgebot der Liebe," pp. 85-92.
[14] *Ibid.*, pp. 88-89.
[15] *Ibid.*, pp. 86-88, 91.
[16] Cf. Aristeas 234, cited by Bornkamm, *ibid.*, p. 89, n. 17.

prophets and in Jesus' teaching such criticism is also directed against the Jewish cult itself.

In summary, then, the Marcan version of the Great Commandment has been formulated for apologetic purposes. Its usefulness in early Christian missionary preaching is evident: There is One God. You must love him and your neighbor. Obedience to his will is more important than the performance of cultic ritual. Except for apparent Marcan editorial work in introducing (vs. 28a) and concluding (vs. 34b) the scene, neither the content nor the style of this passage exhibits peculiarly Marcan elements. The probability is that this particular adaptation and application of the double commandment were achieved already before Mark and taken over by him.[17] This tradition as we have it in Mark focuses neither upon the meaning of *love* nor upon the meaning of who the *neighbor* is who is to be loved. Nor do we have here any special concern for emphasizing or defining the relationship between love for God and love for the neighbor. What is emphasized, doubtless for apologetic-missionary purposes, is the necessary connection between belief in the one God and obedience to the moral (as contrasted with the cultic) law.

The Matthean Version, 22:34-40

There are several notable differences between the Marcan and Matthean versions of the Great Commandment. First, in Matthew the questioner is not described as "one of the scribes" but as a "lawyer" from among the Pharisees (Matt. 22:35). Moreover, his question is presented to Jesus as a challenge, indeed with outright hostile intent: "and [he] asked a question . . . in order to test him" (vs. 35). Also in Matthew the question itself is differently formulated. The lawyer asks not for the "first" (i.e., the "chief") commandment, but for the "great" commandment, and in so doing specific mention is made of the law: "Teacher, which is the great commandment in the law?" (vs. 36 RSV). Not once is there direct reference to "the law" in the Marcan version (perhaps due to the apologetic intention of the tradition Mark em-

---

[17] So also Bornkamm, *ibid.*, p. 92.

ploys). Jesus' response to his questioner also varies in Matthew: no use is made of Deut. 6:4 (the confession that God is one), Mark's fourth phrase describing the proper love of God ("with all your strength," Mark 12:30) is not present, and the preposition used to introduce these phrases is not ἐκ (ἐξ) as in Mark and the LXX, but ἐν.[18] Perhaps most significant is the apparent concern in Matthew's version to emphasize the relatedness of the two commands to love God and the neighbor (vss. 38-39a). To love God is underscored as the "great and first commandment," but then the "second" is said to be "like" it, which quite apparently means *equal* to it in importance. Moreover, in summary the Matthean version links the two commandments together as those upon which "all the law and the prophet depend" (vs. 40). Finally, in contrast to Mark the questioner does not respond to Jesus and is not commended by him, and there is no distinction drawn here between the double commandment and the cultic law. Whereas Mark's version is correctly described as a "scholastic dialogue," Matthew's falls clearly into the category of a "controversy story"—a form which would actually fit the Marcan context better than the form Mark has.[19]

The evangelist's own editorial hand is more often apparent in Matthew than in Mark, and an examination of his use of the traditional material helps to show what kind of "controversy" is implicit in this Matthean version. In Matthew as in Mark the

[18] Krister Stendahl points out that Matthew's form of Deut. 6:5 therefore retains the "three tones" of the *Shema* which both the Hebrew and Greek Old Testaments also enshrine (*The School of St. Matthew and Its Use of the Old Testament*, American ed. [Philadelphia: Fortress Press, 1968], p. 75). But, as Stendahl observes, it can hardly be supposed that any form of the *Shema* in which two of the member phrases contained the synonyms "heart" and "mind" (Matthew) was actually used and thus known to the evangelists. The Matthean text, then, looks like a revision of Mark's—the last of Mark's four phrases having been dropped in order to achieve the traditional "three tones" (Stendahl, *ibid.*, pp. 75-76; also Georg Strecker, *Der Weg der Gerechtigkeit: Untersuchung zur Theologie des Matthäus*, FRLANT 82 [Göttingen: Vandenhoeck & Ruprecht, 1962]: 25). Actually, Mark's *third* phrase should have been dropped, then Matthew's text would have conformed to the LXX (A text), save for "strength" (ἰσχύς) instead of "might" (δύναμις) and the preposition ἐν instead of ἐκ (ἐξ). Matthew's ἐν represents the Hebrew b‛ and is the only way in which Matthew seems to be dependent upon the Masoretic Text (Strecker, *ibid.*).

[19] Cf. Taylor, *The Gospel According to St. Mark*, p. 485.

introductory formulation is obviously editorial. The mention of Pharisees (vs. 34) and of the hostility of the questioner toward Jesus (vs. 35) helps to set the stage for the polemic which follows in chap. 23.[20] The evangelist's redaction is also, and most obviously,[21] present at the conclusion of the pericope. Of course there is nothing in Matthew corresponding to the scribe's response to and commendation by Jesus in Mark. But neither is there anything in Matthew corresponding to the Marcan editorial conclusion to the whole scene, "And no longer did anyone dare ask him a question" (Mark 12:34b). Instead, Matthew's version concludes with a comment about the significance of the double commandment, "Everything in the Law and the prophets hangs on these two commandments" (vs. 40 NEB). Although this comment is ascribed to Jesus, it contains the characteristically Matthean conception of "the law and the prophets," present also in Matt. 5:17 ("Think not that I have come to abolish the law and the prophets," RSV) and, with reference to the "Golden Rule," in 7:12 ("for this is the law and the prophets," RSV).[22]

From this Matthean comment on the Great Commandment it may be seen in what sense the evangelist understands the lawyer's question to have been posed as a challenge to Jesus. The real question on the lawyer's "hidden agenda" is whether Jesus accepts all the statutes of the Torah as of equal importance. Jesus' singling out of two commandments as "great" is interpreted by Matthew (vs. 40) as a negative response, whereby Jesus is set over against Judaism.[23] In contrast with both Mark and Luke, this Matthean version contains no hint of agreement or accord between Jesus and his questioner on the point at issue, which is: the right interpretation of the law.

In Matthew, then, and in clear contrast to Mark, there is an emphasis upon the double commandment *itself* and upon its im-

[20] Willoughby C. Allen, *A Critical and Exegetical Commentary on the Gospel According to St. Matthew, ICC* (New York: Charles Scribner's Sons, 1907), p. 240.

[21] See Bultmann, *History of the Synoptic Tradition,* p. 90.

[22] On the Matthean character of this phrase, see Strecker, *Der Weg der Gerechtigkeit,* p. 60 and n. 7.

[23] See Gerhard Barth, "Matthew's Understanding of the Law," *Tradition and Interpretation in Matthew,* by G. Bornkamm et al., trans. Percy Scott (Philadelphia: Westminster Press, 1963), p. 78.

portance as the key to the right interpretation of the whole law. The abruptness of Mark's *two* commandments when *one* had been asked for is somewhat overcome in Matthew where it is made clear beyond question that the "second" is of the same rank as the first, is "like it" (vs. 39a).[24] Matthew's understanding of the meaning of this double commandment is given, as we have seen, in the redactional comment in vs. 40: it is the essence of the law and therefore the key to its meaning. This evangelist is fond of summaries of the law's essence, and among these can be listed his use of the "Golden Rule" (7:12), of scriptural citations (Hos. 6:6 cited in 9:13a and 12:7; perhaps Mic. 6:8 lies behind the formulation of 23:33), and of a dominical epigram (9:13b).[25] But for Matthew the most important epitomization of the law is clearly the double commandment to love God and the neighbor.[26]

What precisely does it mean to say the whole law and the prophets "hang" or "depend" on the two commandments of Deut. 6:5 and Lev. 19:18? The equivalent Hebrew idiom as employed by the rabbis meant that from a given scriptural passage a "Halakah" or general moral principle could be derived exegetically.[27] Thus, Bar Qappara (*Berakoth* 63a): "What is the smallest portion of Scripture on which all the regulations of the Torah hang . . . ? In all thy ways remember him. . . ." And *Hagigah* 1.8: "The Halakoth concerning the Sabbath . . . are like mountains which hang on a hair . . . , for there is little Scripture to support them but many Halakoth." [28] If Matthew is employing the idiom in this way, then his point is that from the two key commandments identified by Jesus all the other statutes of the law can be deduced, that these two *contain* all the others. But, as Gerhard Barth observes, if this were the evangelist's meaning, there would be no reason for the controversial posture that both the lawyer's question and the abrupt ending of the pericope presuppose. Moreover, considerable force would be drained from

[24] See Taylor, *The Gospel According to St. Mark*, p. 487. For a discussion of ὁμοία ("like"), see Spicq, *Agape in the New Testament*, I: 28-29.

[25] See Bornkamm, "Das Doppelgebot der Liebe," p. 93.

[26] See below, pp. 74-84.

[27] G. Barth, "Matthew's Understanding of the Law," p. 77.

[28] Cited *ibid.*, p. 77, n. 1.

the emphasis on these two commandments constituting what is "great" and "first" in the law. For Matthew, it would appear, these two commandments do not just *contain* or *spawn* the law, but *constitute* it, or better, provide the decisive word about its *meaning* and thus enable its correct interpretation.[29]

The Lucan Version, 10:25-37

The evangelist's own editorial activity can be detected at a number of points in the Lucan version of the Great Commandment. As noted earlier, this evangelist has placed the whole pericope at a much earlier point in the Gospel narrative and has integrated it with the parable of the Good Samartian.[30] There are some commentators who, on this account, follow T. W. Manson's lead in arguing that Luke 10:25-28 is not at all a parallel to the Great Commandment in Matthew and Mark, "but refers to a different occasion." [31] The interior formulation of the pericope is indeed rather different from the other two versions we have considered, but, I think, not so radically different as to demand hypothesizing a second occasion. Even the different locus of the

---

[29] I do not see that either the immediate or the extended context of the Great Commandment in Matthew supports Spicq's conclusion that the intention is to identify love as the motive and force by which one obeys all the commandments: "The emphasis is on interior cohesion; whatever a Christian does because of a particular commandment he will do in the name of the love which impels him" (*Agape in the New Testament*, I: 44). With the Great Commandment one may compare the criticism of the Pharisees in 23:23 that they neglect "justice, mercy, and faith." The Lucan parallel (11:42) has "justice and the love of God" which sounds even more like the double injunction of the Great Commandment pericope. But again, Matthew stresses the contrast between these "weightier matters of the law" (Luke has no such reference) and the legalistic preoccupations of the Pharisees.

[30] Among those who believe the joining of commandment and parable is Luke's own work are Bultmann, *History of the Synoptic Tradition*, p. 178 and Binder, "Das Gleichnis vom barmherzigen Samariter," pp. 176, 178.

[31] C. E. B. Cranfield, *The Gospel According to St. Mark*, Cambridge Greek Testament Commentary, 3rd impression (Cambridge: At the University Press, 1966), p. 376. The most notable exponent of this view is Joachim Jeremias, *The Parables of Jesus*, rev. ed., trans. S. H. Hooke (New York: Charles Scribner's Sons, 1963), p. 202. See also Cranfield's article, "The Good Samaritan" (Luke 10:25-37)," *ThT* XI (1954-55): 368-72.

Commandment in the Gospel narrative can perhaps be explained by Luke's interest in placing yet another encounter with a would-be disciple (see Luke 9: 57-62; 10: 38-42) into the cycle of events which comprise Jesus' journey to Jerusalem.[32] There are numerous other Lucan touches evident in these verses (beginning with the "And behold" of vs. 25 [33]), but these may be noted as we examine the passage in more detail.

In Luke's version as in Matthew's, Jesus' questioner is a lawyer who addresses him as "Teacher" and seeks to "test" him (vs. 25). So here again the material is in the form of a controversy story. The lawyer's question, however, reads differently in Luke, for he makes no request concerning the "chief" or "great" commandment (as in Mark and Matthew respectively). Instead, his question is: "Teacher, what shall I do to inherit eternal life?" (*RSV*). The question, "What shall I do . . . ?" is here formulated in a distinctively Lucan way (τί ποιήσας;) present also in 18: 18 where the Matthean and Marcan parallels use a different Greek formulation (τί ποιήσω;).[34] Indeed, the "ruler's" question in 18: 18 is exactly that of the lawyer in 10: 25, and the two pericopes may be compared to good advantage.

From Luke 18: 18 ff. and its parallels it is clear that "inheriting eternal life" (vss. 18, 30) is but another expression for what that story elsewhere terms "entering the kingdom of God" (vss. 24, 25, 29*b*) and being "saved" (vs. 26). In effect, then, the question, "What shall I do to inherit eternal life?" is *the* most important question of all for a Jew (or Christian) to ask. Note Jesus' answer which (in Luke and Mark) begins by affirming what the questioner should himself already know ("You know the commandments . . . ," vs. 20), and proceeds to enumerate some of

[32] For discussions of the significance of this journey in Luke, see, e.g., Hans Conzelmann, *The Theology of St. Luke*, trans. G. Buswell (London: Faber and Faber, 1960), pp. 60-73, and William C. Robinson, Jr., *Der Weg des Herrn: Studien zur Geschichte und Eschatologie im Lukas-Evangelium*, Theologische Forschung, 36 (Hamburg-Bergstedt: Herbert Reich, 1964): 39-43.

[33] See Rudolf Schnackenburg, *The Moral Teaching of the New Testament*, trans. J. Holland-Smith and W. J. O'Hara (London: Burns & Oates, 1965), p. 92, n. 3; Binder, "Das Gleichnis vom barmherzigen Samariter," p. 176.

[34] Schnackenburg, *The Moral Teaching of the New Testament*.

them from the Decalogue.[35] Jesus subsequently insists that formal obedience to the statutes is not meaningful apart from a total, radical commitment to them. And for this wealthy ruler that is possible only when he is freed from those things in his life to which he is now most firmly attached (vs. 22). Nevertheless, the initial exchange makes it clear that the hope for inheriting eternal life (entering the Kingdom, being saved) is closely connected with the concept of obedience to the commandments. Therefore, the question put by Luke's lawyer in 10:25 is not so different, after all, from the question as formulated in Matthew and in Mark. For there the question about the greatest commandment is finally the question about what kind of obedience leads to life (the Kingdom, salvation).

In Luke 10:26 Jesus responds to his interrogator with two related counter questions.[36] To begin with, the lawyer is referred to the contents of the law, to what is written there. In contrast with both Matthew and Luke, no question is raised, either by the lawyer or by Jesus, about the most important *commandment* of the law. This is perhaps another instance of Lucan redaction for, as Conzelmann has pointed out, this evangelist's tendency throughout his Gospel is to avoid the word "commandment." [37] Jesus' next counter question is probably also a Lucan formulation since it employs the Greek interrogative particle in a good Hellenistic way to mean "What . . . ?" and not in accord with the Semitic, "How is it possible that . . . ?" [38] Thus, the question of what the law contains is now extended into the question about the law's interpretation, "What is your reading of it?" (*NEB*).[39]

One of the most remarkable features of this Lucan version appears in vs. 27 where it is the lawyer and not Jesus himself

---

[35] The Matthean parallel, 19:16 ff., is significantly different from the Marcan and Lucan versions and will require attention in its own right in another connection. See below, pp. 74-75.

[36] This is a familiar feature of controversy stories (Bultmann, *History of the Synoptic Tradition*, p. 51). See also Jesus' counter questions in Luke 18:19 and Mark 10:18 (Binder, "Das Gleichnis vom barmherzigen Samariter," p. 177, n. 6).

[37] *The Theology of St. Luke*, p. 160, n. 1.

[38] Schnackenburg, *The Moral Teaching*, p. 92, n. 3.

[39] This translation (or that of *JB*, "What do you read there?") is more accurate than *RSV*'s, "How do you read?"

who formulates the Great Commandment to love God and the neighbor. As in Mark, but in contrast to Matthew and the LXX, four phrases rather than three are used to describe the means by which one ought to love God: [40] with heart, soul, strength, and mind. More significant, however, is the closeness with which the two commandments of Deut. 6:5 and Lev. 19:18 have been identified. Not only is any enumeration of them as "first" and "second" entirely lacking; just one occurrence of the verb "you shall love" governs the *two* commands, which are joined by the simple conjunction "and." [41] In this way the two commands really do become just one, and there is no need for the sort of explicit indication of their equality to be found in Matthew's "A second is like it" (22:39).

The fact that in Luke this Great Commandment is actually formulated by the questioner and not by Jesus himself has sometimes been used to argue that we do indeed have here an incident distinct from that reported in Matt. 22 and Mark 12. Thus, it is suggested, in response to Jesus' counter questions the lawyer gives the answer Jesus has himself previously offered: the sum of the law and of its meaning is to love God and the neighbor.[42] It is much more likely, however, that here again one may see an instance of Luke's redaction. The evangelist's joining of the Good Samaritan parable to this Great Commandment pericope shows that he is using the material to *exhort* his readers. The climax of the whole unit comes in the admonition of vs. 37 to "go and do as [the Samaritan] did" (*NEB*). This hortatory note has been injected already into the dialogue preceding the parable when, after commending the lawyer's answer, Jesus challenges him to "*do* this" (vs. 28). It is therefore probable that this exhortation, unparalleled in either the Matthean or Marcan version, stands here in Luke by virtue of the evangelist's own editorial activity. Confirmation of this may be found in a demonstrably

---

[40] But the last two of these stand in the reverse order from Mark's version, and two different Greek prepositions are used to introduce the phrases.

[41] See Georg Eichholz, *Jesus Christus und der Nächste: Eine Auslegung des Gleichnisses vom barmherzigen Samariter*, Biblische Studien, 9 (Neukirchen: Verlag der Buchhandlung des Erziehungsvereins, 1952): 21.

[42] See, e.g., T. W. Manson, *The Sayings of Jesus* (London: SCM Press, 1949), p. 260.

Lucan expression present in the introduction to this admonition. In approving the lawyer's response to his challenge Jesus says: "You have answered *rightly*." Luke's fondness for this particular form of commendation may be seen by comparing 7:43 (without parallels), "You have judged *rightly*," and 20:21, "You are speaking and teaching *rightly*." [43] Elsewhere in the New Testament this adverb (ὀρθῶς) occurs only in Mark 7:35, and there with another meaning, to speak "without (physical) impediment" (*RSV* and *NEB*, "plainly"; *JB*, "clearly"). With some confidence, then, we may conclude that Luke himself has recast the traditional material so as to have Jesus' *questioner* formulate the Great Commandment. But this only shows that for Luke the "punch line" in the dialogue comes not in the formulation of the Commandment as such (as in Matthew), but in Jesus' urging the lawyer to *do* what he himself acknowledges to be the essence of the law. In sum, it would appear to be better to regard the Lucan version as formed in accord with the evangelist's own concerns and emphases, therefore not necessarily as the earliest version of the Great Commandment pericope.[44]

The close connection Luke effects between this dialogue and Jesus' parable of the Good Samaritan does not just illustrate, but in fact provides an important clue to this evangelist's use of the Great Commandment. The controversial element inherent in the lawyer's original inquiry of Jesus (vs. 25) is only temporarily subdued by Jesus' commendatory word in vs. 28a. The controversy resurfaces when, apparently in order to blunt the force of Jesus' exhortation in vs. 28b, and perhaps also in order

---

[43] In Luke 20:21 the expression "You are speaking and teaching rightly" replaces "Teacher, we know that you are true" in Matthew (22:16) and Mark (12:14). Jesus' commendation of the scribe in Mark 12:34 uses the word "wisely" which, as we have seen, is due probably to the pre-Marcan employment of the pericope in missionary preaching. Schnackenburg (*The Moral Teaching*, p. 92, n. 3) also lists the ὀρθῶς of Luke 10:28 as a mark of the evangelist himself.

[44] M. Goguel, among others, regards the Lucan version as earliest, and argues further that the evolving tradition "re-enforced the authority of 'the Summary of the Law' by putting it into the mouth of Jesus. This shows the growing importance given to the law in Christian life by the second generation" (*The Primitive Church*, trans. H. C. Snape [New York: The Macmillan Co., 1964], p. 489).

to present himself as a close and earnest student of the law,[45] the lawyer challenges Jesus with another question: "And just who *is* my neighbor?" (vs. 29). The controversy is thus resumed in a question which, judging from what its context here reveals about Luke's own views, must have seemed like pure casuistry to the evangelist himself.[46] In this context of controversy, the comment that in asking his second question the lawyer seeks to "justify himself" is quite understandable. It is unnecessary and unwarranted to resort to a conjecture about a literal *historical* context, as Jeremias does when he suggests that the lawyer "is excusing himself for asking Jesus, although he knows what Jesus thinks." [47]

Jesus responds to the lawyer's new question with a parable (vss. 30-35). A man (that he is a Jew is presumed) is set upon and wounded by brigands as he travels from Jerusalem to Jericho.[48] He languishes half dead by the roadside and is ignored first by a priest, then by a Levite. But a passing Samaritan has compassion and stops. He dresses his wounds, takes him to shelter, cares for him, and even provides for the care to continue after his own departure.[49] The point of this parable (which, in fact, is an example story) is clear enough, and by a further question directed to the lawyer he himself is challenged to articulate it. "Which of these three has been shown to be a neighbor of the man who fell among thieves?" (vs. 36). The answer can only be, "The one who performed an act of mercy to him" (vs. 37a). Thus it is left for Jesus to function not just as a rabbi—instructing his questioner in the law and interpreting it for him—but as a prophetic and, certainly in Luke's own view, a sovereign command-er: "You go and perform in the same manner!" (vs. 37b).

[45] Cf. J. Weiss, cited by John Martin Creed, *The Gospel According to St. Luke* (London: Macmillan & Co., 1930), p. 152: "the desire for sharp definition is genuinely rabbinic."

[46] Binder, "Das Gleichnis vom barmherzigen Samariter," p. 177.

[47] *The Parables of Jesus,* p. 202.

[48] Is the comment that the brigands "laid blows upon him" (vs. 30), found again in Acts 16:23 (in the story of the imprisonment of Paul and Silas in Philippi), another Lucan expression?

[49] Some commentators have emphasized the similarity of this parable to the story of Oded in II Chron. 28:1-15. See, e.g., Frank H. Wilkinson, "Oded: Proto-Type of the Good Samaritan," *ExT* LXIX (1957): 94.

Many different interpretations of this apparently simple parable have been proposed. B. Gerhardsson, for instance, argues that the Samaritan is really a Christ figure. He observes that there is an etymological relationship between the Hebrew word for "shepherd" (rō'eh) and the Hebrew word for which the Greek word "neighbor" is a translation (rē'ah). Gerhardsson therefore interprets the parable as a reference to Jesus, the true shepherd, who ministers to Israel (the wounded Jew) in a way Israel's own religious leaders (the priest and the Levite) do not.[50] Another type of christological interpretation of this parable has been proposed by Hermann Binder who believes the central figure is the wounded man himself, not the Samaritan. In this reading of the parable the wounded man represents, in his half-dead, cultically impure state, the Jesus who is despised and spurned by the religious leaders of Judaism (priest and Levite), who are concerned most of all for their own ritual cleanliness.[51]

Yet another possibility in approaching this parable is to concentrate on the apparent discrepancy between the lawyer's question, "And just who is my neighbor?" (which inquires after the *object* of neighborliness) and Jesus' answer (deduced from the parable by the lawyer himself) which has to do with the *subject* of the neighborliness: "The one who performed an act of mercy [was neighbor to the wounded man]." In this case the point would be that the original question is unanswerable and shouldn't even have been asked.[52] Jesus then corrects the question by urging the questioner to consider his *own* responsibility; his concern should not be for who *the neighbor* is, but for who *he himself* is in relation to the neighbor (any neighbor).[53]

[50] For a discussion of Gerhardsson's interpretation, see Robert W. Funk, *Language, Hermeneutic, and Word of God: The Problem of Language in the New Testament and Contemporary Theology* (New York: Harper & Row, 1966), pp. 206 ff.

[51] "Das Gleichnis vom barmherzigen Samariter," pp. 190-91. Cf. the brief remarks of Alan Richardson, *An Introduction to the Theology of the New Testament* (London: SCM Press, 1958), p. 137.

[52] So, e.g., T. W. Manson, *The Sayings of Jesus*, p. 261.

[53] Cf. the remarks of E. Fuchs, "Was heisst: 'Du sollst deinen Nächsten lieben wie dich selbst'?" reprinted in his *Gesammelte Aufsätze*, II (Tübingen: J. C. B. Mohr [Paul Siebeck], 1960): 7-8, and also those of G. Bornkamm in *Jesus of Nazareth*, trans. I. and F. McLuskey with J. M. Robinson (New York: Harper & Bros., 1960), p. 113.

Perhaps the most familiar interpretation, however, is the one which stresses the admittedly remarkable fact that, in this parable, it is a *Samaritan* who renders aid to a *Jew* and who thus receives commendation for being a neighbor. The effect of this for a Jew in Jesus' day would have been roughly analogous to the effect on a modern Jew, were a similar story told about an Israeli citizen ignored by passing Israeli officials but aided by a passing Arab. Thus, although one might recognize a certain formal discrepancy between the lawyer's question and the way the parable is told (we might have expected the *wounded man* to be a Samaritan and his rescuer a Jew), the question is nevertheless clearly answered: the command to love the neighbor breaks down all barriers which divide men. Neighbor love means helping the man who needs help, regardless of who he is in relation to oneself: "Be prepared to abandon presuppositions." [54]

In view of such diverse approaches to the parable, one has to find his own way into its meaning. But no matter what one's interpretation, certain basic features of the parable command attention. It is important, clearly, that a *Samaritan* is the one whose action is commended, precisely in contrast to two pious Jews who show no compassion for their helpless kinsman. It is also striking that, as in the "introduction" to the parable Jesus responded to a question about eternal life with his own counter questions, so now following the presentation of the parable Jesus again turns the lawyer's question (vs. 29b) back to him (vs. 36). There are, however, two differences from the way the earlier repartee had developed. First, Jesus now asks the man to answer, not on the basis of what the law says, but on the basis of what Jesus' parable would indicate. And second, the lawyer's question about whom he is required to love as neighbor is converted into the question about what kind of action constitutes neighborly love.

There are yet other features of the parable which require attention. For instance, the great detail with which the parable speaks of the wounded man's condition, and then especially the detail with which the Samaritan's ministrations are portrayed.

[54] Norman Perrin, *Rediscovering the Teaching of Jesus* (New York: Harper & Row, 1967), p. 124.

The Samaritan's assistance is described in two related ways. Within the parable itself the narrator speaks of his actions as rooted in his *compassion* (vs. 33), and then in response to Jesus' question the lawyer describes the Samaritan's deed as an act of *mercy* (vs. 37).[55] Finally, this parabolic example story concludes with a forceful exhortation to the lawyer to "Go and do as he did" (vs. 37 *NEB*). This is more than a mere repetition of the corresponding exhortation which had followed the formulation of the Great Commandment (vs. 28). The earlier one has to do with obedience to the law as epitomized by the double commandment to love God and the neighbor. But now the lawyer has before him not only the law, but a dramatic illustration of what obedience to that law actually involves, indeed actually *must* involve for *him*.

This survey of the distinctive and striking features of Luke 10:25-37 reveals a most interesting thing about the Lucan juxtaposition of double commandment and parable. If we seriously take the two together, as the evangelist obviously intends that we should, we must recognize a significant change in the lawyer's position vis-à-vis Jesus. The passage begins with Jesus being challenged (vs. 25) but ends with his challenger being challenged by him (vss. 36-37). The discussion moves from theological (theoretical, hermeneutical) questions about the law and its interpretation to practical, ethical questions about obedience to it. That is, as the exchange develops, the fact of the questioner's being a *lawyer*, a student and interpreter of the law, is less and less important, and his being simply *a man to whom the law lays claim* becomes more and more important. One crucial turning point is Jesus' reformulation of the lawyer's question about the meaning of "neighbor." Not only is the question now directed by Jesus to the realm of actual experience (Jesus' parable) rather than to the law; even more significantly Jesus now directs attention away from the question about what *status* qualifies one to be called "neighbor," and toward the question of what kind of *deeds* qualify as an authentic expression of a neighbor's love. It is often said that the lawyer's question about neighbor as

---

[55] The two Greek expressions are, respectively, ἐσπλαγχνίσθη (vs. 33) and τὸ ἔλεος (vs. 37), with which one may compare Luke 1:78, "by the compassionate mercy of our God" (διὰ σπλάγχνα ἐλέους θεοῦ ἡμῶν).

object has been converted into a question about neighbor as subject, and formally this is quite true. But the actual *meaning* of this is that the lawyer himself is drawn into the dialogue in a new way. No longer can he hide behind his casuistic questions regarding the scope—he really means the *limits*—of the concept "neighbor." Finally he is forced to assess the meaning of neighbor love in very concrete terms, and thus at last to feel the effect of the Great Commandment in his own life as a man under God's law.

The change of focus from a casuistic to a concrete question is partly reflected in and enabled by the fascinating details included in the parable, especially the detail with which the Samaritan's actions are described: moved by compassion he cleanses and soothes the man's wounds with oil and wine and bandages them; he transports him to an inn and attends him there until the next day. Then we are told exactly how much money is left with the innkeeper and precisely what additional provisions are made for the wounded man's convalescence. The effect of all this is to show that loving the neighbor means serving him in his concrete need, so that the "legal" question becomes an urgently practical one. There is in this respect a certain discrepancy between the two traditional units (Commandment and parable) which Luke has joined together here. The first defines love in terms of obedience to a commandment, the second as compassionate response to encountered need. But we should not make too much of this discrepancy, for the evangelist's evident intention in joining Commandment and parable together is simply to illustrate and concretize the meaning of neighbor love. In Luke's version the lawyer is not challenged to understand the law according to some new principle of interpretation (he himself has formulated the Great Commandment), but actually to *do* the law by performing, like the Samaritan, concrete acts of mercy.[56]

So far our reading of the parable has not taken into account the important point that it was a Samaritan, not the priest or Levite, who had compassion and helped the injured Jew. Had the

[56] Spicq makes some similar remarks about the passage, *Agape in the New Testament*, I: 110, 111-12, 117.

"loving neighbor" himself been a Jew, everything said so far about the parable would remain true. But introduction of a *Samaritan* (in Jewish eyes no better than a Gentile) adds a further dimension. For one thing it is significant that the parable describes the helper and not the victim as a Samaritan. This enables the lawyer (or any hearer or reader of the parable) to identify immediately with the "certain man" going down to Jericho (vs. 30). Depiction of another human being in trouble almost invariably exerts an empathetic "tug" hard to resist. One's own deepest experiences or fears of personal adversity are called up almost instantaneously, so there is very little difficulty identifying with the hapless victim of calamity. Thus, Luke's lawyer is immediately stripped of his scholarly credentials and finds himself lying along the roadside as that "certain man," desperate and helpless.[57]

At the same time, identifying the *helper* as a Samaritan enables a surprising and shocking contrast to be drawn between him and the Jewish officials who "passed by on the other side." Whether the intention is that we should regard the priest and Levite as wanting to avoid ritual contamination, as some interpreters hold, must be left an open question. It is more important that they *do not* give assistance and that one of the hated Samaritans *does*. Thus, the parable teaches that what counts is not just knowledge of the law (the five books of the law were commonly recognized by Jews and Samaritans) but an obedience to the law of love so complete that where love is operative all the artificial barriers of race, nation, and religion are broken down.

In sum, the parable can effectively engage the lawyer to whom it is addressed because he can instantaneously identify with the plight of the robbers' victim. From the point of view of one who is himself the object of another's love he is brought to the insight that obedience to the law involves concrete deeds of mercy. Moreover, "the Samaritan is he whom the victim does not, could not expect would help, indeed does not want help from." [58] The parable declares that obedience in love establishes relationships

---

[57] Cf. Bornkamm, *Jesus of Nazareth*, pp. 112-13; Jeremias, *The Parables of Jesus*, p. 205; Funk, *Language, Hermeneutic, and Word of God*, pp. 212, 219.

[58] Funk, *Language, Hermeneutic, and Word of God*, p. 213.

where none were conceivable or possible before. Thus, the problem of "neighbor" is not one of definition but of performance, and where there is performance, where one's deeds are moved and shaped by love, there is neither time nor reason to ask, "*Who* is my neighbor?" As Ernst Fuchs perceptively notes, while the rabbis emphasized the *periphery* of the circle within which neighbor love should be operative and discussed the problem of a longer or shorter radius, this parable stresses the *midpoint* of that circle (love) and allows the periphery to extend endlessly outward.[59] Concrete deeds of love, not casuistic definitions of love's limits, should be of concern. This interpretation of the parable accords well with the hortatory formulas within which the whole passage has been framed: "Do this and you will live" (vs. 28b); "Go and do as he did" (vs. 37b).

On Loving One's Enemies

Matthew 5:43-48

The command to love one's enemies stands in Matthew's Gospel as the last of the six antitheses in the "Sermon on the Mount" and reaches its climax in the exhortation to imitate God in being "perfect." There are no parallels to this material in Mark, but there are in Luke, and those will deserve study in their own right.

Here, as in the Great Commandment pericope, we can see Matthew's editorial formulation and adaptation of traditional material. There is, for instance, widespread scholarly agreement that this sixth antithesis at least (and perhaps the whole series) has been constructed by the evangelist.[60] The first half of the

---

[59] "Was heisst: 'Du sollst deinen Nächsten lieben wie dich selbst'?" p. 5.

[60] See, e.g., Bultmann, *History of the Synoptic Tradition*, p. 148; Herbert Braun, *Spätjüdisch-häretischer und frühchristlicher Radikalismus: Jesus von Nazareth und die essenische Qumransekte*, BHTh 24 (Tübingen: J. C. B. Mohr [Paul Siebeck], 1957), II: 7, n. 2; Strecker, *Der Weg der Gerechtigkeit*, p. 24, n. 5; cf. G. Barth, "Matthew's Understanding of the Law," p. 93.

formulation makes use of Lev. 19:18, but with two differences from the citation of that verse in the Great Commandment. First, the "as yourself" is omitted. Second, and more importantly, the words, "and shall hate your enemy" are added as if they, too, stood in the Old Testament text. But they do not stand in Lev. 19:18, nor anywhere else in the Old Testament.[61] In an attempt to account for the added phrase in Matt. 5:43, the Jewish scholar I. Abrahams long ago appealed to the exegetical method of R. Ishmael (late first century, A.D.). Abrahams, following Schechter, suggested that all Matthean antitheses, but especially this final one, make use of a similar exegetical procedure. R. Ishmael would say repeatedly, "The text reads so and so. I *hear* from it so and so: *but* other texts prove that this is not its true meaning. . . ."[62] Accordingly, the point of Matt. 5:43-44 would be that the command to love the neighbor may be and usually is *understood* ("heard," vs. 43) to imply that one "hates [the] enemy," but other texts—in this instance the command to perfection quoted in vs. 48 (cf. Lev. 19:2 and Deut. 18:13)—prove that the real meaning is something different.[63]

Since Abrahams wrote, however, a second (though possibly related) explanation of Matt. 5:43 has become possible with the discovery of the Jewish sectarian literature from Qumran. Thus, in IQS i.9-10 the members of the community are admonished to "love all the sons of light, each according to his lot among the council of God, but to hate all the sons of darkness, each accord-

---

[61] Although God's hatred of his enemies is mentioned frequently in the Old Testament, and those who hate God are viewed as Israel's enemies and thus outside the circle envisioned by the love commandment. Relevant texts are cited by O. J. F. Seitz, "Love Your Enemies," *NTS* XVI (1969): 44. Cf. Spicq, *Agapè dans le Nouveau Testament*, I: 17-19.

[62] "The Freedom of the Synagogue," *Studies in Pharisaism and the Gospels*, 1st series (1917) (New York: KTAV reprints, 1967), p. 16. Cf. the remarks of Paul Fiebig concerning R. Akiba's exegesis of Lev. 19:18 ("Jesu Worte über die Feindesliebe im Zusammenhang mit den wichtigsten rabbinischen Parallelen erläutert," *ThStK* XCI [1918]: 33).

[63] Contrast the comments on Matt. 5:43-44 of another Jewish writer who, before Abrahams, insisted that the concept of hating the enemy is "a fine example of deliberate invention," a falsification of the old law into an "un-Jewish sentence" (Gerald Friedlander, *The Jewish Sources of the Sermon on the Mount* [New York: KTAV reprints, 1969; first published in 1911], pp. 69, 70).

ing to his guilt in the vengeance of God." [64] Here is clear evidence that there was current in Palestinian Judaism, shortly before Jesus' day, a counsel to "hate" one's enemies. Whether Jesus and his followers knew this in its legal form, perhaps directly from Qumran,[65] as a targumic interpretation and therefore as part of the Jewish catechism[66] or as some "popular maxim or partisan rallying cry," [67] the fact is such teaching was abroad in their day and the issue raised in Matt. 5:43 is not a hypothetical one.[68]

What does the word "enemy" mean in this passage? In the LXX the word may refer to Gentiles when they are at war among themselves or when they are personal enemies of one another in daily life; to Gentiles as enemies of Israel, or to those within Israel itself who are enemies of the pious; or to *God's* enemies.[69] In the Synoptic Gospels there are instances where the word is used of enemies of Israel: Luke 1:71, 74 (spoken by John the Baptist's father) and Luke 19:43 (Jesus' lament over Jerusalem): "Your enemies will cast up a bank about you and surround you . . ." (*RSV*). Elsewhere in Luke the term apparently designates enemies of God (19:27), while in Acts 13:10 Paul charges Elymas with being an "enemy" of righteousness.

In Matt. 5:43-44 "enemies" is parallel with "those who per-

[64] Quoted from Seitz, "Love Your Enemies," p. 50, who lists other relevant Qumran passages as well, *ibid.*, n. 51. For a discussion of "brotherly love" at Qumran, see Helmer Ringgren, *The Faith of Qumran: Theology of the Dead Sea Scrolls*, trans. E. T. Sander (Philadelphia: Fortress Press, 1963), pp. 137-39.

[65] Braun, *Radikalismus*, II: 58, 135; W. D. Davies, *The Setting of the Sermon on the Mount* (Cambridge: At the University Press, 1964), pp. 245-48. Cf. Seitz, "Love Your Enemies," p. 51.

[66] Stendahl, *The School of St. Matthew*, p. 137; Morton Smith, "Mt. v, 43: Hate Thine Enemy," *HThR* XLV (1952): 72.

[67] Seitz, "Love Your Enemies," p. 51—who leaves the question more or less open.

[68] Strecker believes the dualistic context of the Qumran command to hate "the sons of darkness" and the absence of other apparent relationships between Matthew and Qumran, make it unlikely that Qumran teaching is behind Matt. 5:43. But he does acknowledge the possibility that the added words may reflect general Jewish teaching or targumic or catechetical teaching. He regards it as most probable, however, that the formulation is simply part of the evangelist's redactional work (*Der Weg der Gerechtigkeit*, n. 2 on pp. 24-25).

[69] See W. Foerster, *ThD* II: 812.

secute you" (vs. 44b), while in the Lucan version it parallels those who "hate you" (6:27) and who "curse" and "abuse" you (vs. 28). Further connotations of the concept "enemy" may be derived from the analogous use of the words "evil" and "unjust" in Matt. 5:45, and from the idea of "those who *do not* love you," the implied opposite of "those who love you," vs. 46. Correspondingly, we may say that the concept of "neighbor" is colored here by such words as "good," "righteous" (vs. 45), "those who love you" (vs. 46), and "brethren" (vs. 47).[70] Thus it seems clear that the "enemies" envisioned in both Synoptic versions of the commandment are those who oppose God's people (and therefore also God), and whose opposition is expressed in direct, personal ways: as persecution, cursing, abuse.[71] Thus, 5:43-44 is couched in such a way as to present one interpretation of the law (to love your neighbor implies hating your enemy), and then immediately to reject that interpretation ("But I say to you. . . .") in favor of another (". . . *love* your enemies"). Even if it be argued that one must reckon here with the Semitic idiom whereby "to hate" means "to love less," [72] the rejection of the first cited interpretation is just as complete and emphatic.

It must be remembered that this whole section of Matthew's "Sermon" stands under the heading of 5:20 which urges that one's righteousness "exceed" that of the scribes and the Pharisees. Love of enemies is thus a further distinguishing mark of the higher righteousness and of Christian discipleship. The point is made specifically in vss. 46, 47 when it is pointed out that even the tax collectors and the Gentiles *return* love to friends. But it should also be noted that in Matthew the concept of a higher righteousness is connected with sayings about *fulfilling* the law, not abolishing it (5:17-19). With only one exception,[73] the antitheses do not reject the law, but only the way the law is usually interpreted.[74]

[70] Cf. Spicq, *Agape in the New Testament*, I: 10.
[71] See also Schnackenburg, *The Moral Teaching*, p. 104, and Foerster, *ThD* II: 814.
[72] See, for instance, note "n" to Matt. 5:43 in *JB*.
[73] On this, see below, p. 56.
[74] G. Barth, "Matthew's Understanding of the Law," pp. 93-94.

What does this command to "love your enemies" actually mean, as we have it in Matthew? Spicq, characteristically, seeks an answer by first noting that the word for love used here is ἀγαπᾶν, the verb related to *agape*, not φιλεῖν, the verb related to *philia*. He holds that agape "means to show respect and kindness" but does not involve the reciprocal, friendly love denoted by *philia*.[75] Spicq also finds it significant that this formulation omits the phrase "as yourself" from Lev. 19:18 and later speaks of the objective of becoming "sons of your Father" (vs. 45).

When we limit our affection to our brothers or to our neighbors, we can love them "as ourselves" because our love for them is an extension of our love for ourselves; it is the same kind of love we have for ourselves. When it becomes necessary to love those who are disagreeable or even dangerous, we can desire their good and love them truly only if we have a higher inspiration: "in order to be sons of our Father who is in heaven." [76]

This view must be challenged at two points. First, Spicq's belief that the two different Greek verbs representing, respectively, agapic and filial love can be always and everywhere sharply differentiated is not tenable. Evidence particularly apt for the concept of loving one's enemies is present in Epictetus' description of the true Cynic as the ideal "moral man." He is one, says Epictetus (*ca.* A.D. 50-138), who "must needs be flogged like an ass, and while he is being flogged he must love the men who flog him, as though he were the father or brother of them all." [77] Not only is love of enemies conceived here after the model of family love (i.e., real affection, paternal and fraternal), but the verb used is φιλεῖν not ἀγαπᾶν. Thus, Spicq's notion that φιλεῖν cannot be used with respect to love of enemies is refuted, and with it his hard and fast distinction between *agape* and *philia*. R. Joly has further demonstrated that, over the course of several centuries, ἀγαπᾶν came more and to replace φιλεῖν as the common

[75] *Agape in the New Testament*, I: 11.
[76] *Ibid.*, p. 12.
[77] III, xxii.54, cited by Robert Joly, *Le vocabulaire chrétien de l'amour est-il original?* Φιλεῖν *et* Ἀγαπᾶν *dans le grec antique* (Bruxelles: Presses Univ. de Bruxelles, 1968), p. 52 and n. 20.

49

word for love.[78] Therefore, the mere fact that the Greek verb for *agapic* love is the one used in the New Testament commandment to "love your enemies" does not exclude the possibility that something like "friendship" or "affection" may also be involved. Moreover, if the lexical distinction Spicq alleges is valid, then the verb φιλεῖν ought to have been employed in Matt. 5:46 where the reference is clearly to reciprocal, "friendly" love. As it is, the verb there is ἀγαπᾶν, just as in vs. 44!

In the second place, Spicq is surely reading too much into the fact that "as yourself" is missing from the quotation of Lev. 19: 18 in vs. 43. Where it *does* occur (in the original Old Testament commandment and in all New Testament citations of it except the present one) it is not part of the command per se, as if the admonition were to "Love your neighbor and love yourself." In the command self love is *presumed* as the "natural condition" of man, and he is commanded to love the neighbor *as he already loves himself without any need to be commanded to do so.* As several commentators have pointed out,[79] the best exegesis of "as yourself" comes in the parable of the Good Samaritan which artfully causes each hearer of the parable to identify himself with the hapless victim by the roadside. Finding himself in that place, one really discovers what "as yourself" means. It means that the neighbor can be no more avoided than one's own self, that the neighbor is as present and as real as one's own ego.[80] The point of the phrase is not, as Spicq would have it, that our love for neighbors is to be an "extension" of self love and of the "same kind." Rather, the point is that the neighbor must be no less an object of our loving concern than our own life inevitably is. There is certainly no hint in Matt. 5:43 ff. that anything less is being said about loving one's enemies. Thus it is unwarranted to say that the "as yourself" has been omitted for theological reasons. There is a better and a much simpler *rhetorical* explanation. Retention of "as yourself" after "You shall love your neigh-

---

[78] For a discussion of the whole lexicographical situation, see the Appendix, below, pp. 219-31, where the pertinent references to Joly's investigation appear.

[79] E.g., Bornkamm, *Jesus of Nazareth*, p. 113.

[80] See Kierkegaard's fine comments on this quoted by Bornkamm, *ibid.*, pp. 113-14.

bor" would throw out of kilter the rhetorical balance between the text ("You shall love your neighbor") and its commonly accepted corollary ("You shall hate your enemy"). Matt. 5:43 as it stands (without the "as yourself") brings both the text and the alleged corollary into sharp focus and lends rhetorical force to the rejection of the corollary which comes in vs. 44.

Contextual and not lexical considerations should be paramount as we try to determine the meaning of the command to "love your enemies" in Matthew. The parallel admonition (vs. 44b) is to "pray" for them, but this itself requires interpretation. Is one to pray that they be forgiven? Or punished? Forgiveness is not a topic in this particular passage, and the idea of punishment for one's enemies would collide head-on with both the command to love them (vs. 44) and the reference to God's mercy (vs. 45). Perhaps, as W. C. Allen suggests, there is some clue in vs. 47 which notes that even the Gentiles "salute" their own brethren.[81] Originally a salute was an embrace upon meeting, a visible sign of a warm personal relationship. Although the salute became in time simply a verbal greeting, its significance as a token of friendship was retained.[82] In the ancient world, to "salute" or "greet" someone meant to affirm his existence as a person and in relation to oneself.[83] Accordingly, the context in Matthew[84] of the command to love one's enemies suggests that such love would mean acknowledging their presence and the bond that exists between oneself and them by virtue of sharing together in the beneficence and the mercy of God.

The imperative to love your enemies is given its objective and its ground in vs. 45: that you might become a son of your heavenly Father whose providential care encompasses the evil and the unjust as well as the good and the just—that is, his "enemies" as well as those who love him. Taken together, then, vss. 44-45 are strikingly parallel to Matthew's seventh beatitude, "Blessed are the peacemakers, for they shall be called sons of

[81] *A Critical and Exegetical Commentary on the Gospel According to S. Matthew*, p. 55.

[82] See H. Windisch, *ThD* I: 497, 499.

[83] Cf. II John 10-11 which suggests that a greeting (χαίρειν) could even mean *identifying oneself with* another person's life and work.

[84] It is possible that vss. 46-47 are secondary to the saying of vss. 44b-45 (so Braun, *Radikalismus*, II: 91, n. 2).

51

God" (5:9 *RSV*). And the juxtaposition of a commandment to love (vs. 44) with a reference to becoming God's sons is not unlike the juxtaposition of admonitions to love God and love the neighbor found in the Great Commandment.[85] Moreover, the charge to dispose oneself toward enemies in accord with God's action toward his enemies contributes to the meaning of the climactic admonition to "be perfect" as God himself is perfect (vs. 48).

From one point of view the reference to God's granting sun and rain even to his enemies might appear to suggest that these were not benefits specifically *intended* for them, but were received only because God chose not to withhold such benefits from "the just" who are also, with the unjust, in the world. In this case love of enemies wouldn't need to involve much more than *toleration* of their presence.[86] But such a meaning is excluded because of the clear intentionality inherent in the preceding command to "love your enemies," which now the reference to God's providence is meant to support. Moreover, in Judaism and in earliest Christianity God's providential care is understood to be exercised with great intentionality, as in the *Wisdom of Solomon*: "But thou, our God, art kind and true, patient, and ruling all things in mercy. For even if we sin we are thine, knowing thy power" (15:1-2 *RSV*).

In the remaining verses of the passage, vss. 46-48, we must reckon with the evangelist's further editorial work. Vss. 46-47 [87] relate the commandment to love one's enemies to the requirement for disciples to exhibit a higher righteousness (5:20). The true disciples' conduct is contrasted with that of the despised tax collectors (probably Jewish employees of the chief collectors[88]) and the hated Gentiles. To the original grounding of the commandment in God's love of his own "enemies" (vs. 45) there is now added a second. Even the unrighteous are willing to show

---

[85] See Schnackenburg, *The Moral Teaching*, pp. 104-5.

[86] In this connection it should be noted that the word "makes" in vs. 45 (*RSV, NEB; JB* uses "causes") represents no word in the Greek text, but only the apparently transitive force of the verb. Thus, "he causes his sun to rise . . . ," etc.

[87] See above, n. 84.

[88] B. J. Bamberger, *IntDB*, R-Z, p. 522.

love where it is reciprocated. The righteous must do better than that.

The admonition in vs. 48 to be perfect as God is perfect accords with the thought of vss. 44-45, but in addition looks back over the whole series of commandments which began in vs. 21. This charge to "be perfect" recapitulates them all, one effect of which is to accentuate the whole of the sixth antithesis (vss. 43-47) and thus to present love of one's enemies as the crowning instance of true righteousness.[89] Vs. 48 is doubtless modeled on Lev. 19:2, "You shall be holy, for I the Lord your God am holy," although Deut. 18:13 should also be noted, for in the LXX the same Greek word is used (τέλειος) as in Matt. 5:49: "You shall be *perfect* before the Lord your God."

What does the admonition to be "perfect" mean? In the rabbinic midrash on Ps. 119:1, Deut. 18:13 is interpreted as a reference to man's moral purity, so that "perfect" would mean "spotless" or "faultless." [90] But this is not the case in Matthew. Indeed, most commentators are agreed that "perfect" in Matt. 5:48 is the evangelist's own word.[91] It is used in no other Synoptic Gospel, not even in the Lucan parallel to this vs. (which has "merciful"). The other Matthean occurrence is in 19:21 where Jesus' final exhortation to the rich young man is to go and sell his possessions if he would be "perfect." As Stendahl has pointed out, in 19:18 ff. the order of the commandments is the same as in the antitheses of 5:21 ff.: on murder, adultery, false witness, and love (although Matt. 5 also includes commandments on divorce and on retaliation, and Matt. 19 mentions also theft and parental honor). In both passages the listed commandments are climaxed by an appeal to be "perfect." [92]

There is also a material relationship between the meaning of *perfection* in these two passages. In chap. 19 the man is told that keeping the commandments is not sufficient if he wants to be per-

[89] See G. Barth, "Matthew's Understanding of the Law," p. 80.

[90] G. Delling, *ThWB* VIII: 75, n. 36. Deut. 18:13 is also interpreted this way by the *RSV* translators, "You shall be *blameless* before the Lord your God."

[91] See G. Barth, "Matthew's Understanding of the Law," p. 97, n. 1; Schnackenburg, *The Moral Teaching*, p. 108; Strecker, *Der Weg der Gerechtigkeit*, p. 141, n. 2; Creed, *The Gospel According to St. Luke*, p. 96.

[92] *The School of St. Matthew*, p. 137.

fect. That requires something extra, a total giving of himself unto obedience, not just perfunctory obedience to statutes. Similarly, in chap. 5 the perfection commanded is understood to be the "more" (vs. 47) demanded of those who would have their righteousness exceed that of the scribes and Pharisees (vs. 20) who are righteous, but nothing "more" than righteous.[93] In both instances the evangelist conceives of perfection as a totality of obedience which goes beyond formal adherence to the law, and which expresses itself in concrete ways toward men. Nor can it be accidental that the climactic appeal of each passage, drawn from Lev. 19:18, is the command to love—the neighbor (19:19b) and even the enemy (5:43-44). For Matthew true righteousness consists of the sort of total, radical obedience to God which is not only best epitomized but also uniquely called forth by the commandment to love.[94]

Luke 6:27-36

Luke's version of the command to love one's enemies and of the context in which it was given differs from Matthew's in numerous respects, and in this version as in the other we must reckon often with the possibility of the evangelist's own editorial work. Whereas in Matthew the importance of the command for the evangelist is shown by the way he has formulated it into the sixth and climactic antithesis, in Luke the command is given prominence in another way. Here in Luke's "Sermon on the Plain" it stands as Jesus' first direct commandment, and is preceded only by the introductory "blessings" and "woes" (vss. 20-26).[95] The Lucan introduction to the commandment ("But

[93] Cf. Strecker, *Der Weg der Gerechtigkeit,* p. 141; G. Barth, "Matthew's Understanding of the Law," p. 97 and n. 2.

[94] Cf. the *JB* translation of Deut. 18:13, "You must be entirely faithful to Yahweh your God." Spicq's comment on Matt. 5:48 shows that he has not grasped the vital connection between the true righteousness, love, and perfection in Matthean theology: "Verse 48 formulates [Jesus' concept of morality] positively as an interior perfection of the same completely spiritual nature as God's perfection" (*Agape in the New Testament,* I: 15).

[95] See also Spicq, *Agape in the New Testament,* I: 78-79, although he has so stressed the importance of the love commandment in Luke that he undervalues its importance for Matthew.

rather, to you I say . . . ," vs. 27) is at least as strongly adversative as Matt. 5:44 where the love commandment is specifically antithetical to the preceding "Hate your enemies." [96] But there are no antitheses in Luke, so the adversative construction is apparently related to the preceding "woes" (vss. 24-26) which are in effect prohibited actions. In contrast, now, "to you who stand ready to receive God's blessings [vss. 20-23], the word is —'Love your enemies. . . .'" This commandment is not offered as an interpretation of Lev. 19:18 but is, as it were, a free standing word of the Lord himself. It is followed by three auxiliary commands which seem intended to elucidate the meaning of this love. In these subsequent admonitions one's "enemies" are identified as those who hate, curse, and abuse, and it is suggested that loving them means doing good to them, blessing them, and praying for them. It has been argued that the parallelism here is evidence that Luke's version of this commandment is earlier than Matthew's.[97] But it is more likely that we have, instead, the evangelist's own stylized adaptation of the tradition. W. C. van Unnik has shown that the two different Greek expressions for "doing good" employed here (in vs. 27 and in vss. 33, 35 respectively) would have provided for Greek readers, in quite familiar Hellenistic phrases, a picture of the "concrete, active character of this love." [98] This remains, to be sure, a very general way of talking about what love does. But it shows that for Luke loving the enemy means more than tolerating him. It means serving him and thus affirming him. Similarly, in earliest Christianity to "bless" and "pray for" enemies would not have been regarded as vague and vapid exercises. They would not have been regarded as pious ways of *avoiding* specific acts of kindness to the enemy, but ways—along *with* good deeds—of actually being kind to him.

In vss. 29-30 four more commands are presented, in pairs of two and, in contrast with the initial commands (vss. 27-28), second person *singular* rather than plural in form. These incorpo-

[96] Luke: ἀλλὰ ὑμῖν λέγω; Matthew: ἐγὼ δὲ λέγω ὑμῖν.

[97] Seitz, "Love Your Enemies," p. 44.

[98] "Die Motivierung der Feindesliebe in Lukas VI 32-35", NT VIII (1966): 298. The verb ἀγαθοποιεῖν used in vss. 33, 35 (and also in vs. 9) appears in no other Gospel, although the expression καλῶς ποιεῖν in vs. 27 is also used at Matt. 12:12 and Mark 7:37.

rate material which in Matthew comprises the fifth antithesis (5:38-42), although there are numerous differences.[99] Most significantly, the sharp polemic of the Matthean antithesis is absent from Luke. Matthew has so formulated the material as to have Jesus overthrowing a particular commandment of the law itself, not just an interpretation of it.[100] Specifically it is the *lex talionis* which is rejected. This was not observed literally even in Jesus' day, except as the phrase "life for life" in Exod. 21:23 was applied in criminal law.[101] But "an eye for an eye" was part of the private law and signified "the claim to accurate, nicely calculated compensation," especially in cases of insult and character defamation.[102] Whereas in Matthew the teaching on nonretaliation assumes a polemical form in opposition to Jewish practice, in Luke the teaching is presented as a further positive example of what is involved in loving one's enemies. Love means forgoing the luxury of spiteful vengeance or calculated retaliation. It busies itself only with doing good. The appended exhortation to give generously to anyone who begs (vs. 30*a*) does not fit the topic of nonretaliation very well, and the concluding charge to seek no recovery of stolen goods (vs. 30*b*) is only slightly more apt. But Luke apparently intends the composite effect of these four commandments to be a vivid portrayal of the radical extent of Christian love.

In a recapitulation of these commandments Luke incorporates next his version of the so-called "Golden Rule" (vs. 31) which, in Matthew, comes at a later point in the Sermon (7:12). The clue to Matthew's understanding and use of the Golden Rule is in the concluding phrase of the Matthean form, "for this is the law and the prophets," a demonstrably Matthean expression.[103]

---

[99] In Luke there is no citation of Exod. 21:24 (Matt. 5:38), no generalized introductory command not to resist evil (Matt. 5:39*a*), no specification of the *right* cheek (Matt. 5:39*b*), no idea that one's clothing has been claimed in *court* (Matt. 5:40), and no command to go a second mile if impressed to go one (Matt. 5:41). And instead of the Matthean command to be generous to those who seek to borrow money (5:42*a*) Luke charges that one should not seek to recover stolen goods.

[100] See G. Barth, "Matthew's Understanding of the Law," p. 94.

[101] D. Daube, *The New Testament and Rabbinic Judaism* (London: The Athlone Press, 1956), pp. 254-56, 258.

[102] *Ibid.*, p. 258.

[103] See above, p. 32.

He uses the same phrase with reference to the Great Commandment (22:40), and there can be no doubt but that, for Matthew, the Golden Rule represents the same demands present in the injunction to love God and the neighbor. This description of the Rule as the sum of "the law and the prophets" also links Matt. 7:12 with the earlier polemic against lawlessness, where Jesus' support of "the law and the prophets" had been stressed (5:17-19). Subsequent materials (5:21–7:11) are so arranged as to define and describe the higher righteousness which Jesus' followers should attain (5:20), and then to conclude and epitomize these teachings Matthew employs the Golden Rule (7:12). The introductory "Therefore" (RSV: "So") of 7:12 is only understandable in this way,[104] and the whole verse should be separated from 7:7-11 and printed as a summarizing paragraph for the whole Sermon so far (as in NEB and JB).

In Luke 6:31 the Golden Rule has no such clearly definable place within the context, and it is much more simply formulated: "Treat others as you would like them to treat you" (NEB and JB). Obviously, the evangelist does intend this to be further illustrative of love's requirements, but it is not otherwise closely linked with what precedes or follows. It is separated from vss. 29-30 by virtue of its return (cf. vss. 27, 28) to the second person plural and from vss. 32 ff. by virtue of what it says.[105] Indeed, the command to "treat others as you would like them to treat you" seems to presuppose the kind of eagerness for reciprocity in moral conduct which vss. 32 ff. go on to condemn.[106] It would appear best, therefore, to read the Golden Rule in Luke as a separate counsel only generally illustrative of the love command in vs. 27.[107]

[104] G. Barth, "Matthew's Understanding of the Law," p. 73 and n. 1; see also pp. 79-80.
[105] Although RSV, NEB, and JB all incorporate vs. 31 into the same paragraph with vss. 29-30, and JB extends the paragraph even through vs. 35.
[106] Albrecht Dihle, Die goldene Regel. Eine Einführung in die Geschichte der antiken und frühchristlichen Vulgärethik, Studienhefte zur Altertumswissenschaft, 7 (Göttingen: Vandenhoeck & Ruprecht, 1962): 113.
[107] Dihle (ibid., pp. 113-14) proposes to read vs. 31 as an indicative rather than imperative sentence, and thus as introductory to vss. 32 ff. Thus: "You do [in fact] treat others as you would like them to treat you. [But] if you

In vss. 32-34 (which parallel Matt. 5:46-47) the command
to love one's enemies is directly supported by means of a criticism
of the commonly practiced "reciprocity ethic." [108] The point is
that one's actions toward others should *not* be shaped by what he
has received or can expect or hope to receive from them. In
Luke 14:12-14 (without parallel in Matthew or Mark) the teaching is the same: dinner invitations which go to those who may be
expected to reciprocate are meaningless. When those who cannot
repay are invited, the host will be blessed at the last day. In
6:32-35 Luke has so edited the material as to make the point
unambiguously clear to Gentile readers. For instance, the thrice
intoned question, "What sort of *credit* is it . . . ?" (if you love
those who love you, vs. 32; if you do good to those who do good
to you, vs. 33; if you lend to those from whom you can make a
profit, vs. 34), makes use of the word regularly employed by
Hellenistic ethicists to designate the return for his good deeds a
moral man might properly expect.[109] The expression, "to do
good" (vss. 27, 33, 35) is also employed in such contexts,[110]
and it is not unusual for Greek writers to discuss the subject of
lending (vs. 34) in connection with a reciprocity ethic.[111] All
these elements are present only in Luke's version and probably
represent his own redactional work.[112] Luke's substitution of
references to "sinners" (vss. 32, 33, 34) for Matthew's "tax col-

---

love those who love you . . . ," etc. There is no grammatical reason why
vs. 31 could not be translated as an indicative, but there are two other
difficulties with Dihle's suggestion. First, if his interpretation were correct
one would normally expect vs. 32 to begin, "But if" (εἰ δέ) or, "But rather"
(ἀλλά) instead of with the simple conjunction "And" (καί). Second, the
Golden Rule was so widely employed in earliest Christian preaching and
teaching (see Dihle's own list, p. 107) that—failing some clear repudiation of
it—one is almost compelled to interpret vs. 31 in the imperative mood.
Luke's first readers almost certainly would have.

[108] This has been ably shown by van Unnik, "Die Motivierung der
Feindesliebe in Lukas VI 32-35," pp. 284-300.

[109] *Ibid.*, p. 296.

[110] See above, p. 55.

[111] van Unnik, "Die Motivierung der Feindesliebe," pp. 298-99. It should
also be noted, however, that Hellenistic-Jewish parenesis could regard willingness to lend as a form of mercy, e.g., Sirach 29:1-2: "He that shows
mercy will lend to his neighbor. . . . Lend to your neighbor in the time
of his need . . ." (*RSV*). Of course here, too, the presumption is that the
"neighbor" will eventually have no "need" and be in a position to reciprocate.

[112] *Ibid.*

lectors" and "Gentiles" (5:46, 47) is also probably an accommodation to Gentile readers.

The criticism of the Greek concern for reciprocity in doing good is concluded in vs. 35 which represents the transference to this position of the thought of Matt. 5:45. One can love even his enemies (from whom nothing good can be expected in return) because there is a greater "reward" than anything men can bestow. That reward is, to be "sons of the Most High." And that means, in turn, to be conformed to his way, which is to show kindness even to those who are ungrateful and evil. The admonition to "be perfect" which in Matthew concludes one whole section of the sermon has a parallel in Luke 6:36. In fact Luke's wording, "Be *merciful*, even as your Father is merciful" (*RSV*), is probably traditional.[113] But here in Luke this admonition does not (*contra*, e.g., *RSV* and *NEB*) conclude the unit on loving one's enemies. Rather, it opens a new section (see *JB*) by introducing the admonitions of vss. 37-38 to pass no judgment on others.[114] This does not mean that vs. 36 *leaves* the thought of the preceding verses, yet it is clear that it does lead the way into a "further development" of the theme of love.[115]

Love in Jesus' Teachings

We have seen that the Synoptic evangelists variously interpret and apply the traditional double commandment to love God and one's neighbor. In Mark there is a missionary-apologetic concern to contrast obedience to the moral law with cultic performance and to link morality with belief in one God. In Matthew

---

[113] See above, p. 53 and n. 91. Bultmann, however, regards the Matthean version as traditional, "changed by Luke to make a transition to the following section" (*Jesus and the Word*, trans. L. P. Smith and E. H. Lantero [New York: Charles Scribner's Sons, 1934], p. 119).

[114] Note the initial "And" (καὶ) in vs. 37 which binds it closely to vs. 36. See Creed, *The Gospel According to St. Luke*, p. 95; Gilmour, *IntB*, VIII: 122.

[115] Alfred Plummer, *A Critical and Exegetical Commentary on the Gospel According to St. Luke*, 5th ed., *ICC* (New York: Charles Scribner's Sons, 1902), p. 189.

there is a polemical thrust with stress on the double commandment as such as the key to the interpretation of the whole law.
And in Luke the hortatory note is paramount. There the double
commandment is already known by Jesus' questioner, and Jesus'
function in the dialogue is to urge obedience to the command.
The attached parable of the Good Samaritan then further con-
cretizes and accentuates the meaning of neighborly love. We have
also noted the ways in which Matthew and Luke have used the
traditional material about loving one's enemies. In Matthew
there is again a polemical intent—to refute the idea that the command to love one's neighbor implies the command, or at least the
permission, to hate one's enemy. Loving the enemy is, moreover, a vital aspect of what Matthew thinks of as the "higher
righteousness" required of Christians. In Luke there is notable
concern to emphasize the practical implications of the command,
and the polemical element in Luke's version of the material is
not aimed at wrong interpretations of the Jewish law, but at the
widespread Hellenistic reciprocity ethic according to which one
shows kindness to those who show kindness in return.

It is universally acknowledged that the Synoptic parables—
excluding certain obvious redactional adaptations and interpretations—put us in touch with the teaching of Jesus himself. Thus,
in the parable of the Good Samaritan we may be reasonably
confident we have some indication of Jesus' own view of the
meaning of love in the relationships between persons. It is only
accidental that the word "love" does not actually appear in the
parable. Jesus here presents an effective picture of love at work,
concretely serving a neighbor in his need. Moreover, neighborly
love is shown to transcend what otherwise appear to be obvious
and logical cultural, religious, and ethnic barriers. Jesus does
not seek to define "neighbor" as if a class of neighbors could
somehow be distinguished from a class of "non-neighbors." Instead, he offers the parable to exemplify the character and extent
of neighborly love, and to urge its performance. Already in this
parable we may see the radical dimensions of Jesus' teachings
on love. Love is not just an attitude but a way of life. Love requires the real expenditure of one's time, effort, and resources.
And love is not guided in its course, like an antiballistic missile,
by something inherently attractive in its object. It is empowered

and guided, rather, by its own inherent rightness as a response to human need.

There is hardly any less certainty that the command to love one's enemies also comes from Jesus himself. It is but a more formal and explicit articulation of one crucial point made by the parable. Thus, Bultmann classifies Jesus' words about loving enemies among those sayings where "if anywhere we can find what is characteristic of the preaching of Jesus." [116] He is joined in this judgment by Herbert Braun who usually tends to be even more hesitant to speak with certainty about Jesus' teaching.[117] In spite of certain differences, the Matthean and Lucan versions of this teaching agree in two vital respects. They both present the command to love one's enemies as a direct charge from Jesus himself, and they both present a theological basis for this: God himself shows kindness to those who despise him (Matt. 5:45; Luke 6:35c). Given the redactional character of the Matthean antitheses, it may be that Luke's presentation of the sayings on nonretaliation (6:29) as secondary to, and in a sense illustrative of, the love command is more original than the simple juxtaposition of these two topics in Matthew. In any case, the Lucan arrangement may be commended as the proper interpretation of Jesus' words on nonretaliation. They are not to be viewed as counsels for the formation of a utopian society, but as a challenge to those who await God's own coming and Rule to stand free from evil, not to be caught up in it by allowing one's life to be preoccupied with personal retaliation. Jesus' preaching focuses not on one's own honor or personal justice, but on the sovereign claim of God. The first question is not, "To what am I entitled?" but, "By what, or by whom, is my life ultimately claimed?"

Here it may be noted that the earliest New Testament formulation of Jesus' teaching on loving enemies is probably to be found in Paul, Rom. 12:14: "Bless those who persecute you; bless and do not curse them" (*RSV*). The contrast here between blessing and cursing one's persecutors ties this Pauline form of the teaching to the Matthean interpretation that loving one's persecutors

---

[116] *History of the Synoptic Tradition*, p. 105.
[117] *Radikalismus*, II: 91, n. 2. See also P. Fiebig, "Jesu Worte über die Feindesliebe," pp. 41, 61, 63.

involves willingness to "salute" them on the street (5:47). But even more particularly, it suggests that the Lucan formulation, "Bless those who curse you" (6:28) antedates Matthew's, "Pray for those who persecute you" (5:44). There is a further echo of this teaching in I Cor. 4:12 when, with reference to the apostolic style of life, Paul says, "When we are reviled, we bless; when we are persecuted, we endure."

It remains for us to consider whether also the Great Commandment can be numbered among Jesus' own teachings. Bultmann is one who doubts that the scene (he refers especially to Mark) contains even a "historical reminiscence" of Jesus— except perhaps "in the sense that it gave fitting expression to [Jesus'] spiritual attitude." [118] Indeed, our analysis of the parallel versions of the Commandment has shown that its setting was variously portrayed and that the Commandment itself was variously employed. At the same time, one could well expect that Jesus, like other rabbis of his time, would have been asked occasionally to summarize the law in some appropriate fashion. There are several near-contemporary Jewish summaries of the law which, like the Great Commandment ascribed to Jesus, juxtapose commands to love God and one's fellows.[119] Nowhere else, however, is there the specific coupling of the two texts from Deut. 6:5 and Lev. 19:18 which we find attributed to Jesus by the traditions employed in the Synoptic Gospels.

In short, while we cannot with certainty ascribe the formulation of the Great Commandment to Jesus himself, there is no compelling reason for doubting that some such summary was formulated by Jesus, although it then receives varied interpretations and adaptations in the tradition, both oral and written. Moreover, the emphasis upon loving one's neighbor conforms to what we know about Jesus' teaching from such materials as the Good Samaritan parable, the command to love even the enemy, and various scattered sayings on forgiveness and refraining from the judgment of others.

It is significant that this so-called "double commandment"

---

[118] *History of the Synoptic Tradition*, p. 55.

[119] See, e.g., *Test. XII Patr.*, Issachar 5:1-2; 7:2-7; Zebulun 5:1; Dan 5: 1-3; Benjamin 3:1-5; Sifré on Deut. 32:39; Philo, *Spec. Leg.* II, 63.

joins closely together love of God and love of neighbor. Each of the Synoptic evangelists in his own way stresses the equal importance and interrelation of these two. Loving the neighbor is no less an act of obedience than loving God and is part of the *total* response to the sovereign claim of God under which man stands. One's response to God—setting aside self-will, renouncing one's own claims—is to be paradigmatic for one's relation to his neighbor.[120]

Finally, we must seek to identify what is most characteristic of Jesus' teachings on love and to discover whether there may even be something distinctive about them. Sometimes the "Golden Rule" (Matt. 7:12; Luke 6:31) is singled out as the epitome of Jesus' teaching respecting one's duty to his neighbor.[121] It has also been held that the *positive* formulation of this Rule is a significant departure from the *negative* formulation found in other ancient sources, and is one of the distinctive features of Jesus' ethic.[122] But in fact the positive formulation of this Rule *is* present outside of and prior to Jesus' teaching, as Dihle has shown in his valuable monograph on the subject.[123] In its origin the "Golden Rule" is a bit of practical folk wisdom of the Greeks, from them taken over into Judaism, and subsequently into Christian teaching.[124]

Dihle has also demonstrated that basic to *both* the positive

[120] Bultmann, *Jesus and the Word*, p. 114.
[121] So Ernest F. Scott, *The Ethical Teaching of Jesus* (New York: The Macmillan Co., 1924), p. 85.
[122] *Ibid.*, p. 20. Also Plummer, *A Critical and Exegetical Commentary*, p. 186; G. B. Caird, *The Gospel of St. Luke*, The Pelican Gospel Commentaries (Baltimore: Penguin Books, 1963), p. 104. Most famous of the negative formulations is R. Hillel's response to a request to summarize the law while standing on one leg: "What is hateful to you, do not to your fellow. That is the whole law and all the rest is commentary" (bShab. 31a). See also Tobit 4:15: "And what you hate, do not do to anyone." Also Aristeas 207; Sirach 31:15; *Test.* Shimeon 4:7; Gad 6; and from among later rabbis, Aboth II, 14, 16; Aboth R. Nathan XV, 1. Further, Philo, according to Eusebius, *Praep.* viii.7 (cited by Bultmann, *History of the Synoptic Tradition*, p. 103, n. 3); Isocrates, Nicocles 61; and Confucius (cited by Creed, *The Gospel According to St. Luke*, p. 94).
[123] *Die goldene Regel*, p. 10. Among the instances cited is Isocrates, Nicocles 49 (4th century B.C.): "You should be such in your dealings with others as you expect me to be in my dealings with you."
[124] See Dihle's excellent survey of this history, *ibid.*, pp. 80-108.

and negative formulations is a reciprocity or retribution ethic. In and of itself, then, the "Golden Rule" enshrines exactly that kind of measured justice, tit-for-tat, supported by the Jewish *lex talionis* and so contradictory of what we otherwise know about the teaching of Jesus. Thus there is truth in Bultmann's description of the Rule as "morality of a naïve egoism," [125] and in Tillich's description of it as "calculating justice" which needs love to be transformed into "creative justice" and thus to be truly "just." [126] In the Gospels precisely this sort of transformation of the Rule has taken place, for in Matthew and Luke it has been given a distinctively Christian context and content: in Matthew as a summary of the love command, and in Luke as one illustration among others of love's work.[127] But this interpretation and application of the Rule must be attributed to the evangelists and not to Jesus himself.

We come much closer to the center of Jesus' ethical teaching in his parable of the Good Samaritan which shows that for him "neighbor" is not a limiting but an inclusive concept, in his command to love one's enemies in which the radical extent of the command to love is made clear beyond question, and perhaps also in the Great Commandment itself which so vitally and explicitly links one's love of God and his love of neighbor. The idea that love ought to be the governing principle in human relationships did not originate with Jesus, and within Judaism one finds yet other teachers who in one way or another single out love (e.g., Lev. 19:18) as the sum of the law's requirements.[128] There are also other instances where the responsibilities to love God and one's neighbor are linked together.[129] But it is first of all in Jesus' preaching that the love command is given a central,

[125] *History of the Synoptic Tradition*, p. 103.

[126] Paul Tillich, "The Golden Rule," in *The New Being* (New York: Charles Scribner's Sons, 1955), p. 32.

[127] See, e.g., the comments of S. E. Johnson, *IntB* VII: 330.

[128] For instance R. Akiba (late first century A.D.), "Love is the greatest general principle in the law" (cited by I. Abrahams, "The Greatest Commandment," in *Studies in Pharisaism and the Gospels*, 1st series, p. 20); R. Eliezer (A.D. 90-130), "Let the honor of thine associate be dear to thee as thine own . . ." (Aboth II, 15).

[129] See n. 119 above.

determinative role as the principle for *interpreting* (not just for arranging) the moral requirements of the whole law.

Moreover, as the context of Jesus' preaching has shown us, his command to love was not restricted to a limited group of friends, associates, or kinsmen. In Lev. 19:18 "neighbor" has only this narrower meaning,[130] and in principle the Judaism of Jesus' day never overthrew the particularity of the concept of "neighbor love." [131] Nor was the situation in any way different in Graeco-Roman society. Even the Stoic ideal of a universal brotherhood was not able to change the deeply ingrained Greek conviction that men are essentially unequal and that one's duties to them are to be appropriate to their status.[132] Especially sharp was the Greek distinction between friends and enemies, "as though the relation of enmity was natural and permanent. . . ." [133] And so, on into Hellenistic times the Greek popular ethic of retaliation,

---

[130] See, e.g., Martin Noth, *Leviticus: A Commentary*, trans. J. E. Anderson (Philadelphia: Westminster Press, 1965), p. 141.

[131] For a balanced discussion of this, see Wilhelm Bousset, *Die Religion des Judentums im späthellenistischen Zeitalter*, 3rd ed. rev. H. Gressmann (4th photomechanically produced ed. with a Foreword by E. Lohse), *HNT* 21 (Tübingen: J. C. B. Mohr [Paul Siebeck], 1966): 134-41. See also Louis Finkelstein, "The Jewish Vision of Human Brotherhood," in Edward J. Jurgi, ed., *Religious Pluralism and World Community*, Studies in the History of Religion, XV (Leiden: E. J. Brill, 1969): 87; P. Kleinert, "Voraussetzungen der neutestamentlichen Lehre von der Liebe," *ThStK* LXXXVI (1913): 6-7; and H. Braun, *Jesus: Der Mann aus Nazareth und seine Zeit* (Themen der Theologie, I), 2nd ed. (Stuttgart: Kreuz-Verlag, 1969): 114-32. Contrary views are expressed by R. T. Herford, *Talmud and Apocrypha* (London: Soncino Press, 1933), p. 146, and Hermann Cohen, "Der Nächste," in *Jüdische Schriften*, I: *Ethische und religiöse Grundfragen* (Berlin: C. A. Schwetschke & Sohn, 1924): 186-87. The exhortation of Lev. 19:33-34 to "love as yourself" also the "stranger," often used as an argument for the broad use of "neighbor" in vs. 18 (e.g. Herford), actually confirms the limitation of the concept in Leviticus. For the "stranger" in vs. 34 is one who actually *lives in* the land (as Israel lived in Egypt, Deut. 10:19); non-Israelites in general, or who are just passing through, are excluded (see J. Fichtner, *ThD* VI: 314-15). And the love enjoined in vss. 33, 34 has to do with refraining from the economic exploitation of dispossessed Israelites or resident non-Israelites (Noth, *Leviticus*, p. 144).

[132] See Glanville Downey, "Who Is My Neighbor? The Greek and Roman Answer," *AThR* XLVII (1965): 12-14.

[133] Lionel Pearson, *Popular Ethics in Ancient Greece* (Stanford: Stanford University Press, 1962), p. 87.

which Aeschylus' chorus represents, lives on: "Requite an enemy with evil" (*Oresteia* 123).[134]

It is Jesus' commandment to *love* the enemy which most of all sets his ethic of love apart from other "love ethics" of antiquity, and which best shows what kind of love is commanded by him. To love God means not only to be obedient to God's commands, as a son obeys his father, but to be *like* him in loving even those who despise us, just as God loves those who have turned against him. The Synoptic evangelists seem to know of no detailed, concrete specifications given by Jesus for *what* love should do in relation to neighbor and enemy.[135] Yet enough is said, especially in Luke's version of the command to love one's enemies (6: 27-36) and in the parable of the Good Samaritan, to show that Jesus and the church after him did not think of love, even when directed toward one's enemies, as only a formal "theological" stance. It is significant that the Synoptics present Jesus as one who "commands" love and not as one who "inspires" it, and from this it is clear that the *command* to love does not involve simple sentimental affection. But it is equally clear that this command involves one's *affirmation* of the other (even the enemy), and that it is therefore something deeper than a merely grudging acknowledgment of his existence. As John Knox has pointed out, Jesus' own teaching "distinguishes between outer behavior and inner attitude and insists that it is precisely a certain inner attitude which God requires." [136] Thus, to love means to show *goodwill* toward others, and that presents us at once with an understanding of love as something sensitive and concretely responsive to other persons and their needs.

To affirm the other person, even when he is my enemy, necessarily carries with it the acknowledgment that his finite presence to me as "an other," that his finite existence, is caught up and bound up with my own finite existence. Just as Jesus' commandment excludes my *hating* him, so the facts of human existence along with the positive command to *love* him exclude my ignoring him. That would be only another form of seeking his annihila-

---

[134] Cited *ibid.*, p. 121. See also Theognis, lines 869-72, and *Odyssey* VI.184-85, also cited by Pearson (p. 87).

[135] See Bultmann, *Jesus and the Word*, p. 94.

[136] *The Ethic of Jesus in the Teaching of the Church*, p. 44.

tion. To affirm him in the love Jesus commands means to be constructively and compassionately extended to him.

It is a further distinction of Jesus' love command that such love does not await, anticipate, or require a response in kind. Again this is clearest in the command to love one's enemy. Such love is not to be conditional upon his repentance or reformation. For this reason, there is a sharp contrast between Jesus' teaching and the ethic inherent in the words of Sophocles' Ajax: "I learnt one need not hate a foe forever;/He may become a friend" (*Ajax* 678-79).[137] Similarly, the Jewish sectarians at Qumran were charged to accept and affirm even those in their midst who had offended—but only *after* the offending brother had repented and himself taken the first steps toward reconciliation.[138] But Jesus' commandment involves no such presuppositions. It presupposes only God's own mercy and love toward his enemies, and one's responsibility to be thus disposed toward his own enemies. There is nothing here about "making the enemy into a friend." Loving him is not proposed as a means of transforming him or of dissolving the issues which may have generated the enmity in the first place. Though such issues remain standing, they are now approached, from one side at least, in ways directed by love. Thereby the whole *relationship* between us is changed, although the enemy remain "the enemy." [139]

Finally, it must be emphasized that in Jesus' teaching the love command is set fully within the context of the eschatological proclamation about the coming Rule of God. By word and by deed Jesus was present to his hearers as the herald of the "kingdom of God." Jesus did not speak of God's Kingdom as a new epoch of human history, but as the institution of God's own

---

[137] Cited by Pearson, *Popular Ethics in Ancient Greece*, p. 193.

[138] See the remarks of William H. Brownlee, "Jesus and Qumran" in *Jesus and the Historian: Written in Honor of Ernest Cadman Colwell*, ed. F. Thomas Trotter (Philadelphia: Westminster Press, 1968), p. 74.

[139] Ratschow, "Agape, Nächstenliebe und Bruderliebe," p. 169; similarly G. Friedrich, "Der Christ und die Moral," ZEE XI (1967): 289. Contrast, however, Cyril C. Richardson's description of the New Testament view of love as involving "an attitude by which we reckon [our enemies] as our equals, as fellow-humans; and, affirming ourselves, we are concerned for their true welfare as children of God. *We love them for what they may become, not for what they are*" ("Love: Greek and Christian," JR XXIII [1943]: 179; my italics).

sovereign power, in judgment and in love. In his preaching the declaration of the imminence of God's Rule involves as its necessary corollary a summons to repentance (e.g., Mark 1:15), to turn and return to God, to reorder one's priorities and to reorient one's whole life. The repeated admonition to "seek first God's Kingdom" is nothing but the command to acknowledge one's dependence upon God by receiving his claim and responding to it.

Jesus' call to repentance in view of the imminence of God's Rule presupposes that God's sovereign power is manifested in his judgment as well as in his claim. The parable tradition and also the sayings tradition reflect the importance of the judgment theme in Jesus' teaching (e.g., Matt. 7:13-14, 24-27; 13:47-50; 24:40-41). But the demand for repentance also, and even more significantly, presupposes God's mercy, love, and forgiveness. The penitent sinner, by his repentance, lays hold upon a salvation which is not simply "reserved" for him, but which in fact is constantly extended to him. A prodigal son is received in love and rejoicing (Luke 15:11 ff.), a shepherd seeks out and finds a single lost sheep (Luke 15:3 ff.), a woman searches through the whole house until one lost coin is recovered (Luke 15:8 ff.), and these are parables of the joy in heaven when a sinner repents (15:7, 10, 21). Indeed, they stress God's initiative in forgiveness and love. Not only is it said that the sheep and the coin are "found"; even the penitent, to whom the loving father has run out with eager compassion (Luke 15:20), can be described as "lost and found" (vs. 32).

All this shows that Jesus' heralding of God's Kingdom is the heralding of the sovereign power and saving purpose of God's love. The Rule of God is the rule of love. Love is the law of life in the Kingdom.[140] To receive Jesus' preaching of God's Rule is to receive the proffer of forgiveness, and to accept the claim inherent in the promise is to allow God's love to qualify one's own life in radical and concrete ways. We have already seen that Jesus' love command is anchored in the assurance that love is God's own way with men. To this it must now be added that,

[140] Correctly, e.g., J. Jeremias, *New Testament Theology: The Proclamation of Jesus,* trans. John Bowden (New York: Charles Scribner's Sons, 1971), pp. 212-13.

because Jesus proclaims the sovereign *Rule* of God, love is in fact regarded as the power and the purpose of God's coming and reign. So in Jesus' teaching, love is not just *commended* as a prudent or noble way of life; it is actually *commanded* as the rule of the Kingdom.

Jesus' love command has, therefore, an eschatological basis and not a simple humanitarian one. It is true that even the humanitarian ethics of the Hellenistic world could upon occasion speak of the need for the good man's total and exclusive commitment to the divine moral purpose for his life. Epictetus, for instance, held that in surrendering one's freedom to God one finds true freedom from the burdens of finite existence (see *Discourses,* IV.i.89-90). But for Epictetus that meant, specifically, *freedom from* other persons. To be "attached to God" is man's greatest security, he said, because it affords him freedom from kinsmen, friends, and enemies alike (*Discourses,* IV.i.91 ff.; cf. IV.v.28-35; *Encheiridion* 1-3; Seneca *Epistles* IX.18, 19).[141] But Jesus' promulgation of the love command as the law of the Kingdom does not allow for this idea of freedom. To belong to the kingdom of God, and even to anticipate its coming, requires that one's devotion to the King be manifested in obedience to his command to love the neighbor, even though he be an "enemy." To be bound to God is to be bound in a love which cares for others and serves them. "Service," not "security," is the watchword of this ethic and the visible expression of the love Jesus commands.

---

[141] The same point, respecting Seneca, is made by J. N. Sevenster, *Paul and Seneca,* Supplements to *Novum Testamentum,* IV (Leiden: E. J. Brill, 1961): 180-83.

II
THE SETTINGS IN THE SYNOPTIC GOSPELS

We have examined so far only two Synoptic pericopes, the Great Commandment and the charge to love one's enemies, but already it has become clear that the individual evangelists (or the traditions they use) have shaped and applied the materials in somewhat different ways. At the same time, we have judged it probable that these particular commandments (and the parable of the Good Samaritan) put us in touch with Jesus' own teaching, and some attempt has been made to interpret Jesus' teachings on love in their own right. It will also prove helpful, however, to examine the wider setting into which Jesus' teachings have been drawn in each of the Synoptic Gospels. Although these evangelists are not the earliest New Testament writers, they are the ones who have most deliberately set themselves the task of interpreting *Jesus'* teachings for the church.

Mark

Mark, unlike the other Synoptic writers, uses no material concerning loving the enemy. We have also seen that this evangelist incorporates into his Gospel a version of the Great Commandment which had been formulated with a missionary-apologetic objective and which did not specifically stress either the centrality or the meaning of the love command itself. Nor does Mark, for his own part, seek to alter that version in ways that would accentuate love as the key to the law's interpretation (Matthew) or as the chief guide for Christian conduct (Luke). In fact, throughout his Gospel he shows far less interest in anything like a "love ethic" than either Matthew or Luke.

The noun *agape* appears nowhere in Mark, and outside the Great Commandment the verb occurs only in 10:21 in the story of the rich young man who came to Jesus wanting to learn the way to eternal life. After the young man had rehearsed the commandments of the law to which he had been devoted, Jesus looked at him and "loved him." There is no parallel to this remark in the Matthean or Lucan versions of this same story, and except for the "beloved disciple" and Lazarus passages in the Fourth Gospel there is no other instance where Jesus is described by an evangelist as "loving" any specific person.[1] Some commentators have attached a measure of theological weight to Mark 10:21. One of these is C. E. B. Cranfield who finds here a love which gives itself helpfully to another "regardless of the worthiness or unworthiness of its object." [2] Another is Adolf Schlatter

[1] On the Johannine passages, see below, pp. 133, 227.
[2] *The Gospel According to St. Mark,* p. 329.

who sees a reference here to God's grace which always precedes and provides the fit context for God's command (vs. 21b).[3] But neither the immediate nor the wider context in Mark supports such a theological meaning. It is more likely that the reference is simply to Jesus' admiration of and affection for his young questioner ("his heart warmed to him," *NEB*)[4] or—in keeping with one secular Greek meaning of the verb—to some kind of cordial physical embrace.[5] Actually more significant for ethics, therefore, are the commands given in vs. 21b to go and sell all his possessions, to give his income to the poor, and then to follow Jesus. The remark that Jesus "loved" the man has no integral theological connection with these admonitions. Jesus' love is not viewed as either enabling the man's obedience or providing a model for it.

Where, then, are we to turn for a "love ethic" in Mark? Since Jesus' healing ministry is so prominent in this Gospel, we may well inquire whether that is regarded by the evangelist as some kind of model for Christian compassion and charity. In fact, however, there is surprisingly little said in this connection about Jesus' compassion. With respect to the leper, some texts of Mark read, "And [Jesus] had compassion" (1:41—not present in the Matthean or Lucan parallels), prompting C. G. Montefiore's words about Jesus' "intense compassion for the outcast" and "a new and exquisite manifestation of the very pity and love which the prophets had demanded." [6] But even if this be the correct reading,[7] this healing, like the others in Mark, is presented mainly

[3] *Die Evangelien nach Markus und Lukas,* Erläuterungen zum Neuen Testament, 2 (Stuttgart: Calwer Verlag, reprinted 1961): 107-8. See also E. Stauffer in *ThD* I: 43.

[4] So Moffatt, *Love in the New Testament,* p. 76; Taylor, *The Gospel According to St. Mark,* p. 428.

[5] So Martin Dibelius, *From Tradition to Gospel,* trans. B. L. Woolf (London: Ivor Nicholson and Watson, 1934), p. 50, n.1; Ernst Lohmeyer, *Das Evangelium des Markus,* 16th ed., KEK 2 (Göttingen: Vandenhoeck & Ruprecht, 1963): 211 and n.2; E. Klostermann, *Das Markusevangelium,* 4th ed. HNT 3 (Tübingen: J. C. B. Mohr [Paul Siebeck], 1950): 102; Nineham, *The Gospel of St. Mark,* p. 275.

[6] Quoted by Nineham, *The Gospel of St. Mark,* pp. 87-88.

[7] Some commentators adopt the variant, "he was angered" (*NEB:* "In warm indignation . . ."): Taylor, *The Gospel According to St. Mark,* p. 187; Cranfield, *The Gospel According to St. Mark,* p. 92; Lohmeyer, *Das Evangelium des Markus,* p. 44.

as a manifestation of Jesus' divine power, not of his compassion. The same can be said about the reference in 8:2 (par. Matt. 15:32) to Jesus' compassion for the hungry crowds.[8] In neither case is Jesus presented as a moral model. In both cases he is the divine Son of God exercising God's power.[9]

There are only two other texts from Mark which bear directly enough on our topic to warrant attention. One of these is the word of 9:50b which has no parallel: "Have salt in yourselves and be at peace with one another." This is evidently Mark's interpretation of the saying in vs. 50a ("Salt is good; but if the salt has lost its saltness, how will you season it?" RSV), and it is designed as the fitting conclusion to the story of the disciples who were preoccupied with who among them was greatest (9:33 ff.).[10] The verb "to be at peace" occurs nowhere else in the Gospels, but it is used by Paul in an admonition which is closely parallel to Mark 9:50b: "Be at peace among yourselves" (I Thess. 5:13 RSV; see also II Cor. 13:11, and cf. Rom. 12:18). But this hortatory formulation represents no particular theme in Mark as a whole, and there is nothing in the immediate or wider context in this Gospel to suggest any deeper meaning for 9:50b than Taylor suggests: "A declaration that the way to peace is a life seasoned as with the astringent qualities of salt, perhaps, as we should say, with common sense. . . ."[11]

Finally, in 11:25 (par. Matt. 6:14) Jesus urges forgiveness "if you have anything against any one" so that the heavenly Father will forgive you. The language probably reflects that of the Lord's Prayer,[12] though the prayer itself is not present in Mark. There

[8] Cf. 6:34 (par. Matt. 14:14) where, however, Jesus' compassion is stirred by seeing the crowd is like "sheep without a shepherd."

[9] In 5:19 Jesus commands the healed Gerasene to go and proclaim that the Lord has "had mercy" on him, but that means only that he has "healed" him and there is nothing in particular implied about the motivation. Similarly, the cries for "mercy" from victims of disease are simply cries for relief from their distress (9:22; 10:47, 48).

[10] Klostermann, Das Markusevangelium, p. 97; Taylor, The Gospel According to St. Mark, p. 414; Cranfield, The Gospel According to St. Mark, p. 316.

[11] The Gospel According to St. Mark, p. 415.

[12] Lohmeyer, Das Evangelium des Markus, p. 239; Taylor, The Gospel According to St. Mark, p. 467.

are impressive Jewish parallels to the thought,[13] and such an idea is also present in the parable of Matt. 18:23-35.[14] The theme, however, is not present elsewhere in Mark.

In sum, we must conclude that the love command and related themes play no great role in Mark's Gospel. This should not be surprising, for this evangelist does not focus on Jesus' teaching (for example, his interpretation of the law) but on his deeds as the divine Son of God and as the suffering Messiah. Nor does Mark stress Jesus' healing ministry as a model for the love, compassion, and active goodwill which might properly characterize the Christian life. Rather, Mark's "ethic" is defined and guided by his concentration upon Jesus' divine presence with men as one who serves them and suffers and dies for them. Consequently, the ethic here is not articulated in terms of obedience to the love command, but in terms of following Jesus as his disciples: serving, suffering, and giving oneself as he served, suffered, and gave himself (8:34-36; 9:35; 10:21, 29-31, 32-45).[15]

Matthew

In contrast with Mark, the love command as such is seen by Matthew to have been a cardinal and formative item in Jesus' teaching. This evangelist regards the love command as the hermeneutical key to the law, the essence of "the law and the prophets," and that which most distinguishes Jesus' teaching from the Pharisaic tradition. This is shown in the way Matthew formulates the Great Commandment and the six antitheses of the "Sermon on the Mount" and puts them into polemical contexts. It is also shown in Matthew's redaction of the story of the man who comes to Jesus asking what he must do to be assured of eternal life (19:16-30).

[13] E.g., Sirach 28:2 cited by Klostermann, *Das Markusevangelium,* p. 119.
[14] See Cranfield, *The Gospel According to St. Mark,* p. 362.
[15] On these themes in Mark, see, e.g., Hans Dieter Betz, *Nachfolge und Nachahmung Jesu Christi im Neuen Testament, BHTh* 37 (Tübingen: J. C. B. Mohr [Paul Siebeck], 1967): 32.

As in the parallel versions (Mark 10:17-31; Luke 18:18-30), so in Matthew certain commandments of the Decalogue are mentioned as Jesus commends obedience to the law as a prerequisite for eternal life. But in Matthew, and only here, the command of Lev. 19:18 to "love your neighbor as yourself" is added to the list (vs. 19b). It is quite true that this one is not singled out as the sum of "the law and the prophets," [16] yet the fact that it is present here at all, attached to the Decalogue of which it is not properly a part, gives it immediate prominence. It also occupies the climactic position in the listing. Apparently Matthew cannot think of what is really important in the law without thinking of the love command which he regards as its epitome. Moreover, the addition of the love command to the list prepares for the climax of the story as a whole. In response to the man's testimony that he has done the law (vs. 20) Jesus points him on to the higher righteousness. If he would be "perfect" (vs. 21, a Matthean concept without parallel in the other versions[17]) he must sell all and give alms to the poor, thus becoming a disciple of Jesus. Here, as in the "Sermon on the Mount" (5:20, 43-48), the evangelist accentuates the need for Christian disciples to achieve "perfection" by practicing the "higher righteousness" indicated preeminently in the command to love the neighbor. We have seen that, within the Sermon, Matthew employs the "Golden Rule" (7:12) to stress the same point.[18]

The close association between the love command and concrete acts of kindness which is implicit in Matthew's redaction of the story of the young man's question about eternal life is evidence of this evangelist's interest in the practical deeds of love. This interest is seen not only in certain materials present also in Luke and/or Mark (7:21-27, cf. Luke 6:46-49 and 13:26-27; 12:50, par. Mark 3:35 and Luke 8:21), but also in materials distinctive to Matthew's sources or redactional work. Matthew alone of the evangelists, when he writes about the endurance which will be required of Christians during the time of lawlessness prior to

---

[16] See the comments of Ernst Lohmeyer, *Das Evangelium des Matthäus*, 3rd ed., ed. W. Schmauck, *KEK* Sonderband (Göttingen: Vandenhoeck & Ruprecht, 1962), pp. 286-87.

[17] On Matthew's view of "perfection," see above, pp. 53-54.

[18] Above, pp. 56-57.

the eschaton, identifies this as remaining obedient to the love command: "and with the increase of lawlessness, love in most men will grow cold; but the man who stands firm to the end will be saved" (24:12-13 JB).[19] In a similar vein John of Patmos writes to the Ephesians, "The love you had at first you have given up" (Rev. 2:4). The context there shows that abandoned love means abandoned *works* of love (vs. 5a). That is certainly also the meaning in Matt. 24:12, just as in Wisdom 3:9; 6:18 remaining faithful in love means remaining true to God (or Wisdom) and obedient to his (her) laws.[20]

There are yet other texts distinctive to Matthew where his concern for love's concrete expression in life is manifest. Upon occasion he uses the word "righteousness" to mean "good deeds" (6:1 JB) and identifies these with such charitable acts as almsgiving (6:2-4). One of the points made in the parable of the two sons is that promises to obey count for nothing and that only the deeds of obedience are important (21:28-32). In a typically polemical mood Matthew's Jesus exhorts that the scribes and Pharisees should be followed in their precepts but not in their works, "since they do not practise what they preach" (23:3 JB). And the final charge the resurrected Lord gives his disciples is to teach all nations to "keep" his commandments. That does not mean just to preserve and cherish them, but to perform them.

Also unique in Matthew is the use of Hos. 6:6, "I desire mercy and not sacrifice" (9:13; 12:7; cf. 23:23). The word "mercy" here represents the LXX's translation of the Hebrew *ḥesed* (*RSV*: "steadfast love"), and the text accords very well with Matthew's view that the essence of "the law and the prophets" is the love commandment, as well as with his stress on its actual performance. Thus, in 9:10-13 this text from Hosea is applied to the matter of Jesus' sitting at table with tax collectors and sinners. The scriptural command to be merciful is seen as clear support for Jesus' entering into fellowship with such "unrighteous" persons,[21] and the typically rabbinical formula with which

[19] See G. Barth, "Matthew's Understanding of the Law," p. 61.

[20] The passages from Wisdom are cited by Spicq, *Agape in the New Testament*, I: 35.

[21] G. Barth, "Matthew's Understanding of the Law," pp. 82-83.

the text is introduced [22] accentuates the earnestness of the appeal. To "go and learn what this means" requires going and *doing* it.

While the theme of forgiveness is hardly present at all in Mark, it is very prominent in Matthew. It is present of course in connection with the Lord's Prayer (6:14-15; cf. Mark 11:25), but then also in the word about forgiving seventy times seven (18:21-22, par. Luke 17:4) and in the parable of the unmerciful servant (18:23-35, without parallel). Matthew also has the related command to refrain from judging others (7:1-5), but he does not include here any specific words about forgiveness such as appear in the Lucan parallel (6:37 ff.). Matthew's beatitudes concerning the "merciful" and the "peacemakers" (5:7, 9, only in Matthew) should also be noted, as well as the radicalization of the law against murder to include even being angry with a brother (5: 21-24). This term "brother" probably has its origin in the church itself,[23] and the commandment as it stands in Matthew reflects the convictions that strife within the church must cease and that the proper service of God requires reconciliation with all the brethren.[24]

The formation of Matthew's teaching material into regulations appropriate for use in church discipline deserves some further comment because sometimes these regulations seem to conflict with the evangelist's otherwise persistent concern that the love command be the guide for all Christian conduct. One example is the teaching of 10:17-25 which includes the counsel to flee one's persecutors (vs. 23; cf. 24:15 ff. and parallels) and thus stands in tension with the commands of 5:38 ff. to love and pray for them. Again, even though Matthew intends the admonition to "endure" (10:22; 24:13) to involve the obedience of love (24:12), there is no indication that he thinks in this connection of loving one's enemies. Clearly, such materials were formulated within a church confronting the daily threat of persecution and the daily facts of misery and hardship. These troubles are interpreted as the signs of the End and of the coming of God's own Rule.

[22] Stendahl, *The School of St. Matthew*, p. 129.

[23] So also Braun, *Radikalismus*, II: 84, n. 2.

[24] Vss. 25-26 (par. Luke 12:57-59) actually raise another point; in these vss. the subject is one's obligations respecting the legal claims another may have against him, not reconciliation in the broader sense.

The evangelist is addressing a church in crisis, on the verge of inner collapse due to steady pressures from without.[25] This is nicely illustrated by Matthew's version of the words about the lost sheep (18:12-14). In contrast with the Lucan parallel (15: 3-7), the concern here is not to bring every sinner to repentance. In Matthew the concern is for backsliding Christians, for those brethren who are in danger of slipping away from the disciplines of faith. Matthew has drawn into this same context instructions about rebuking an errant brother (18:15-17, par. Luke 17:3 which is again quite differently applied). The injured party is told to seek reconciliation by attempting, if need be with the help of a few friends or of the whole congregation, to talk the offending brother into reforming himself. There is no explicit word about love or forgiveness. The restoration of the relationship is not dependent upon acceptance of the offender as he is, but upon his listening to the charges against him and then mending his ways.[26] Although we must understand these disciplinary regulations in the light of the church's critical need to affirm its own identity in the midst of a hostile society, a certain tension between these passages and those on love and forgiveness must be admitted. Here we see how, at a very early stage in its history, the church's gospel of love was in danger of being forgotten or at least momentarily put aside.

In Matthew as in Mark Jesus' "compassion" is occasionally

[25] This is also the context for the word that Jesus has come to bring a sword, not peace (10:34-36, par. Luke 12:51-53). The reference is to the final judgment, and hence this particular passage is not in conflict with Matthew's love ethic, e.g., his beatitude concerning the "peacemakers." On Luke 12:51-53, see below, p. 89.

[26] Note the prominence of the verb "listen" ([παρ-]ἀκούειν) in vss. 15, 16, 17, and compare the stipulated procedure at Qumran: "They shall rebuke one another in truth, humility, and charity. Let no man address his companion with anger, or ill-temper, or obduracy, or with envy prompted by the spirit of wickedness. Let him not hate him . . . , but let him rebuke him on the very same day lest he incur guilt because of him. And furthermore, let no man accuse his companion before the Congregation without having first admonished him in the presence of witnesses" (IQS v. 25–vi.1; quoted from G. Vermes, The Dead Sea Scrolls in English, rev. ed. (Baltimore: Penguin Books, 1965), p. 80. Walter Bauer has also noted the tension between Matt. 18:17 and the evangelist's emphasis on the love commandment ("Das Gebot der Feindesliebe und die alten Christen," ZThK XXVII [1917]: 39-40).

mentioned in connection with his healing (14:14, cf. Mark 6:34; 20:34, without parallel) or with his feeding of the needy (15:32, par. Mark 8:2), but Matthew, too, refrains from elaborating on this compassion of Jesus or offering it as something to be imitated. Distinctive to Matthew is the juxtaposition of the mention of Jesus' compassion for the shepherdless sheep (9:36, par. Mark 6:34) and the commissioning of the Twelve to go out to the "lost sheep" of Israel preaching and healing (9:37–10:8), but the concern is not with the individual Christian's moral life but with the church's mission. For Matthew as for Mark it is much more Jesus' serving and cross-bearing which are commended as the meaning of true discipleship (see 10:37-39, par. Luke 14:26-27; 16:24-26, par. Mark 8:34-37 and Luke 9:23-25; 20:26-28, par. Mark 10:43-45 and Luke 22:26-27). Within a community thus devoted to serving one another, all men are brethren (23:8-10, without parallel).

The dramatic highpoint in Matthew's exposition of the Christian's responsibility to love comes unquestionably in the passage which concludes the last of the five great sections into which this evangelist has drawn his teaching materials, 25:31-46.[27] The passage is peculiar to this Gospel and is one of Matthew's several portrayals of the Last Judgment (others are at 7:21-23; 13:36-43). This is a moving and powerful scene, not because it is portrayed in lurid detail—in this respect there is a noted reserve[28] —but because it leaves rhetoric aside and deals concretely with the meaning of Christian obedience. The word "love" does not once appear in this passage, and there is not even an indirect reference to the Great Commandment. Nevertheless, it offers an unforgettable picture of what love means and of what obedience to the Great Commandment requires.

Some interpreters have taken this passage, largely as it stands, as directly representative of Jesus' own teaching.[29] Such a view

[27] The strategic location of this passage has been pointed out by Robert Maddox, "Who Are the 'Sheep' and the 'Goats'?" *ABR* XIII (1965): 19.

[28] Correctly, Théo Preiss, "The Mystery of the Son of Man," *Life in Christ,* Studies in Biblical Theology 13, trans. H. Knight (London: SCM Press, 1954): 47. However, it is gratuitous to say that such a restrained portrayal "can come from hardly any other source but that of Jesus himself" (*ibid.*).

[29] Preiss, *ibid.;* Jeremias, *The Parables of Jesus,* pp. 206-10.

must necessarily overlook the presence here of numerous Matthean theological interests, especially the emphatically christological orientation of the ethic. As Allen notes, "this splendid ending . . . of the long discourse reads like a Christian homily." [30] J. A. T. Robinson's detailed formal and stylistic analysis of the passage has led him to conclude that the evangelist fused a parable of Jesus with an allegory of the Last Judgment "and then with great skill introduced [some] sayings of Jesus as the ground, upon which the judgment is given." [31] In effect, however, Robinson's study serves only to confirm the conclusion that Matt. 25: 31-46 as we have it is representative of the evangelist's own viewpoint and intentions.

One of the pervasive themes in Matthew is the divine judgment of the church itself. This is very explicit in 13:41, "The Son of man will send his angels, and they will gather *out of his kingdom* all causes of sin and all evildoers . . ." (*RSV*). This is also the meaning of the evangelist's editorial addition to the parable of the marriage feast (22:11-14) where the guest without a proper wedding garment stands for those who are *in* the church but will finally be cast out. This judgment, moreover, will be on the basis of what a man has *done*, a point editorially inserted by Matthew into the passage on discipleship (16:24-28, par. Mark 8:34-9:1 and Luke 9:23-27): "For the Son of man is to come with his angels in the glory of his Father, and then he will repay every man for what he has done" (vs. 27 *RSV*). The context here shows that for this evangelist at least part of what obedience means is devoted discipleship (vss. 24-26).[32] For Matthew, therefore, judgment is not only administered *by* the Lord (at the last day) but *with reference to* the Lord; that is, with reference to a man's relation to Christ as his disciple.[33] In 25:31-46 also we have a picture of the church under judgment at the eschaton, with the division between the righteous and the unrighteous in the kingdom being made according to their service of Christ.

There is much about Matt. 25:31-46 which is matched in Jewish piety. In the Old Testament itself one may read that the proper

---

[30] *A Critical and Exegetical Commentary*, p. 266.
[31] "The 'Parable' of the Sheep and the Goats," *NTS* II (1955-56): 236.
[32] Cf. G. Barth, "Matthew's Understanding of the Law," p. 95.
[33] *Ibid.*, p. 105.

"fast" before God is to free the oppressed, feed the hungry, shelter the homeless, and clothe the naked (Isa. 58:6-8; cf. Ezek. 18:5-10). Such admonitions are also found in later Jewish parenesis (e.g., Tobit 4:16; II Esdras 2:20-23; Sirach 7:32-36; *Test. Joseph* 1:5-6; Slavic Enoch 9 [cf. 42:8; 63]), and in the rabbis. Thus, Sot. f. 14*a*: "In reference to Deut. 13:5 it is asked: How can a man walk after God? . . . But the meaning is that you acquire his properties. Just as God clothes the naked (Gen. 3:21), so must you clothe the naked; as God visits the sick (Gen. 18:1) so do you; as God comforts the mourners (Gen. 25:11) so must you; as God buries the dead (Deut. 34:6) you must do likewise." [34] Therefore, the distinctiveness of Matthew's material is not in the particular acts of charity commended, but in its identification of the Son of man (vs. 31) as "King" (vss. 34, 40) and "Lord" (vss. 37, 44)—that is, as *Christ* the Lord—and in its insistence that he is met in the needy neighbor and served as that neighbor is served.[35] This text goes even beyond the idea expressed in the Midrash (God speaking to Israel): "My children, when you gave food to the poor, I counted it *as though you had given it* to me" (my italics).[36] In Matthew service of the neighbor is not just analogous to the service of God, but it is in itself God's service. The love ethic in Matthew is emphatically christological—not just because *Jesus* commands love, but because the service love renders the neighbor is service to the Lord Christ. Here we have ample New Testament warrant for Luther's continuing insistence that Christ himself may be met in the neighbor.[37]

[34] This and other references are found in Bultmann, *History of the Synoptic Tradition*, p. 124. See also the numerous parallels assembled by A. Wikenhauser, "Die Liebeswerke in dem Gerichtsgemälde Mt. 25:31-46," *BZ* XX (1932): 366-77.

[35] Bultmann, *History of the Synoptic Tradition*, p. 123; Braun, *Radikalismus*, II: 94, n. 2. Cf. Jeremias, *The Parables of Jesus*, p. 208.

[36] *Midrash Tannaim* 15.9, as quoted by Jeremias, *The Parables of Jesus*, p. 207.

[37] See, e.g., Luther's use of this text in his sermons on the Gospel of John, *Luther's Works*, ed. Jaroslav Pelikan (St. Louis: Concordia Publishing House, 1957 ff.), XXII: 519; XXIII: 149. Cf. Ebeling, "Theology and the Evidentness," p. 113: "[The] claim of my fellowman is the claim of Jesus himself." "The man who has no eyes for his fellow's need can have no eyes for the claim of Jesus." Also Preiss finds here "the source and the founda-

Some have proposed to interpret the admonitions of 25:31-46 as directed specifically to Christian leaders concerning their pastoral and didactic functions.[38] The passage can certainly be viewed as including such a concern, but there is nothing that requires us to restrict its meaning in this way. Moreover, such interpretations tend to accord too narrow a meaning to "the least of these my brethren" in vs. 40 and thereby unjustifiably parochialize Matthew's love ethic. Maddox, for instance, wants to punctuate vss. 31-32 so that the first sentence concludes with "all the nations." Then the following sentence, "And he will separate them from one another" would begin a new thought, and "them" would refer just to the leaders of the church, not to "all the nations." [39] But the proposed exegesis is forced even if we accept this punctuation. The first sentence with its reference to "all the nations" is still the introduction to what follows, and it is highly improbable that "them" in the very next sentence suddenly refers to an entirely new group not specifically mentioned. It should also be remembered (and too few commentators on the passage have) that this evangelist believes the End will come only after the church has heeded the Lord's commission to "make disciples of all nations" (28:19): "And this gospel of the kingdom will be preached throughout the whole world, as a testimony to all nations; and then the end will come" (24:14 *RSV;* cf. Mark 13:10). Therefore, in 25:32 "all the nations" gathered before the Son of man must be *evangelized nations,* the worldwide "kingdom" out of which the unrighteous will be separated (13:41).

---

tion of the Christian ethic: henceforth we must see every man and even ourselves no more after the flesh, but in the Son of Man or, as the apostle was to say very logically after the resurrection and exaltation of the Son of Man who had become King and Christ—'in Christ' " ("The Mystery of the Son of Man," p. 58).

[38] Maddox, "Who Are the 'Sheep' and the 'Goats'?" pp. 25 ff.; L. Cope, "Matthew xxv.31-46. 'The Sheep and the Goats' Reinterpreted," *NT* XI (1969): 32-44. Cf. J. R. Michaels who, however, sees a twofold intention here: to exhort Christian missionaries to *become* "poor" and "outcast" in their work and to exhort their hearers to receive them hospitably and charitably ("Apostolic Hardships and Righteous Gentiles," *JBL* LXXXIV [1965]: 27-37).

[39] "Who Are the 'Sheep' and the 'Goats'?" pp. 27-28.

Since this is the scene presupposed, it is futile to debate the question whether "the least of these my brethren" is a reference to Christians only, and not the world at large.[40] In light of Matthew's expectations for the eschaton the question is irrelevant. At that time all men will be within the kingdom in the sense that formally they will have received the gospel. They all stand finally under the claim and the judgment of the gospel of love. But it would be unfair to say that Matthew sees the responsibilities of love to include one's relationships to all men just *because* all men are finally "brethren." Rather, in Matthew it is clear that the love command has universal scope and application because God and his Rule are themselves—finally—universally sovereign. In this great scene of the End, no distinction between believers and unbelievers is relevant. "All the nations" are claimed for God's obedience and love and stand now before his judgment.[41]

Matthew's love ethic finds no better summary than that afforded by these verses. The Christian disciple is summoned to a higher righteousness which consists in his obedience to the commandment to love God and the neighbor. This righteousness is actualized in concrete ministries of mercy to those in need. "Lawlessness" means departing from the way and the deeds of love (24:10-13), for the love command is the key to the law's meaning. Accordingly, in 25:31-46 the unrighteous are such because of the love they have *not* shown, not because of some particular vile deeds they have committed (vs. 45). Significantly, the "righteous" are no less surprised to discover that their service to the needy has been service to Christ, than are the "unrighteous" to discover that they have refused to serve Christ. Love has its full legitimation already in its service of one's fellows; such works of love are not just ways of rendering some

---

[40] See, e.g., Cranfield, "Diakonia in the New Testament," *Service in Christ: Essays Presented to Karl Barth,* ed. J. I. McCord and T. H. L. Parker (Grand Rapids: Eerdmans, 1966), p. 43 (who takes the phrase as a reference to "the needy generally"), and Jeremias, *The Parables of Jesus,* p. 207 (who also interprets it in line with "all the nations," vs. 32).

[41] See Bultmann, *History of the Synoptic Tradition,* pp. 123-24, and Bornkamm, "End-Expectation and Church in Matthew," *Tradition and Interpretation in Matthew,* pp. 23-24.

"higher service" to Christ or God. The Great Commandment is obeyed already as one lives in love with those whom he encounters daily in the world.[42]

Luke-Acts

Luke, like Matthew, is deeply concerned that obedience to the love command should be manifest in very practical deeds of charity and kindness. Unlike Matthew, however, this evangelist does not develop the point so much polemically, in opposition to Pharisaic interpretations of the law, as he does hortatively in relation to the life of the church. His idealized picture in Acts of the church's life really represents his notion of how obedience to the love command could be expected to actualize Christian *koinonia*.[43] The brethren are (to be) devoted to the common good (2:42; cf. 9:31), and this has some practical aspects: they (are to) sell their possessions and share all their resources according to the need of each (2:44-45; 4:32, 34-37) and (are to) stand ready to respond to emergency needs even when they arise among Christians far away (11:28-29). Those who are not willing to share fully with their brethren are warned about the dreadful punishment which will surely befall them as it did Ananias and Sapphira (5:1-11).

We have already seen that Luke's location of the command to love one's enemies at the beginning of Jesus' sermon (Luke 6:27 ff., following the introductory blessings and woes) gives the love ethic a special prominence in Jesus' teaching. Further, in contrast to Matthew, references to Scripture (Lev. 19:18; Exod. 21:21) are missing from the context, so that the love command

[42] Ebeling has some similar remarks on this passage, "Theology and the Evidentness," pp. 112-13, n. 18.

[43] Again, because he is so preoccupied with appearances of the *word, agape,* Spicq's discussion of Luke proceeds without any regard for data from Acts (*Agape in the New Testament,* I: 77-125) where agape terminology happens not to appear. Warnach, on the other hand, has recognized that the picture of the Christian *koinonia* in Acts is part and parcel of the Lucan emphasis on love (*Agape. Die Liebe als Grundmotiv,* pp. 103-5).

is represented as Jesus' own teaching, not just his interpretation of a law already decreed. The same is true in Luke's version of the Great Commandment (10:25-28). The stress there is on the moral content and the practical implications of loving; there is no concern to present the "right interpretation" of the law in opposition to some "wrong interpretation" of it.[44] Luke's chief point comes in the parable of the Good Samaritan which he attaches to the Commandment: one should be obedient in love as the Samaritan was.

This evangelist's practical interest in love and loving service is reflected in yet other ways. For instance, some Jews attest to a centurion's worthiness by identifying him as one who "loves our nation . . . and built us our synagogue" (Luke 7:5 RSV); love is known by what it does. There is no such remark in the Matthean version of the same story (8:5-13). Much more important, however, is Luke's portrayal of Jesus' own ministry as guided from first to last by his having been anointed to "preach the gospel to the poor . . . , to proclaim release to the captives and recovery of sight to the blind, to set at liberty those who are oppressed, to proclaim the acceptable year of the Lord" (RSV). This text from Isaiah read out by Jesus in the Nazareth synagogue at the start of his ministry (Luke 4:16-21) constitutes the charter and program for everything that follows.[45] This definition of his mission is reflected later in the word Jesus sends to John the baptizer in prison: "Go and tell John what you have seen and heard: the blind receive their sight, the lame walk, lepers are cleansed, and the deaf hear, the dead are raised up, the poor have good news preached to them" (7:22 RSV; par. Matt. 11:4-5). And it is still in the evangelist's mind when, in Acts 10:36-38, he has Peter address Cornelius about Jesus' anointing with Holy Spirit and power, and his preaching of the gospel of peace.

Whereas Mark conceives of Jesus' mission in terms of the

[44] Cf. Luke 11:42 where the Pharisees are criticized for neglecting "justice and the love of God" (the double commandment!), but where—unlike Matthew (23:23)—these are not described as the "weightier matters of the law."

[45] See, e.g., Creed, The Gospel According to St. Luke, pp. 65-66; Conzelmann, The Theology of St. Luke, pp. 114, 122, 139.

kerygma of God's sovereign reign and call to decision (Mark 1:15) and sees the cross as the theological center of that kerygma (note the passion predictions beginning at Mark 8:31 and climaxing with the centurion's confession at 15:39), Luke emphasizes much more the practical moral imperative inherent in the kerygma, and focuses not at all on the cross, but on Jesus' ministry to the poor and the outcast. What Jesus in fact does in this Gospel, he commands others to do as well. Jesus' *servant* role, present also in Matthew (20:25-28) and Mark (10:42-45), is given a very particular and practical context in Luke.

Luke is with Matthew and Mark in presenting the requirement to "do good" to those in distress as ample reason for breaking the Sabbath (6:9, par. Matt. 12:12 and Mark 3:4; 13:16 and 14:5, par. Matt. 12:11-12). Even more than Matthew and Mark he stresses almsgiving as a significant instance of doing good. Not only is the rich young man urged to give to the poor (18:22), as in the other Synoptics. Luke (but not Matthew or Mark) uses the same command as the climax of the exhortations to have no anxiety about one's life (12:33-34), and he alone has the story of Zacchaeus whom Jesus commends for giving "half [of his] goods to the poor" and repaying fourfold anyone he has defrauded (19:8-9). Luke also illustrates love's service of the poor in the story of the rich man and Lazarus (16:19-31, without parallel) and in the admonition to invite "the poor, the maimed, the lame, the blind" to one's feasts, not "friends . . . brothers . . . kinsmen or rich neighbors" (14:12-14 RSV, without parallel). In keeping with Luke's earlier criticism of the popular reciprocity ethic (6:32 ff.[46]), the point is made that a dinner invitation is not a beneficent act if it goes to those who may be expected to return the favor. Jeremias notes that Luke has himself adapted the parable of the banquet, which immediately follows in vss. 16-24, to serve as "a hortatory illustration of 14:12-14." This is the significance of the repetition, in vs. 21, of the list of those who are to be invited.[47]

The practicality of the Lucan ethic is further apparent in 6:46-47 (par. Matt. 7:21, 24) which speaks of *doing* what Jesus

[46] See above, pp. 58-59.
[47] *The Parables of Jesus,* pp. 44-45.

commands, and in the exclusively Lucan beatitude of 11:28: "Blessed . . . are those who hear the word of God and observe it." [48] In Acts, moreover, the Christian lady, Tabitha, is described as one "who never tired of doing good or giving in charity" (9:36 JB); Cornelius, the "righteous and God-fearing" centurion (10:22), is described as "doing many acts of charity for the people" (10:2), and Paul is said to have reminded the Ephesian elders how the Lord Jesus declared, "It is more blessed to give than to receive" (20:35 RSV; cf. Luke 6:33-35; 14:12-14).[49]

Another Lucan concern related to the love ethic is for the practice of forgiveness and of restraint in judging one's fellows. Appropriately, words about not judging and about forgiveness follow closely the commandment to love one's enemies (6:36 ff.). The Matthean parallel to these vss. (7:1, 2) not only comes in another context, but makes no mention of forgiveness. The forgiveness theme is also prominent in Luke's story of the sinful woman who anoints Jesus' feet while he sits at table with a Pharisee (7:36-50, esp. vss. 42, 47-49); comparable stories in Matt. 26:6 ff. and Mark 14:3 ff. convey no teaching at all about forgiveness. Also distinctive to Luke is Jesus' prayer from the cross that his persecutors be forgiven (23:34a[50]), to which Stephen's prayer in Acts 7:60 ("Lord, do not hold this sin against them," RSV) is perhaps meant to correspond.[51] Jesus' prayer, however, asks forgiveness on the ground that his opponents[52]

[48] This is perhaps a variant of 8:19-21, par. Matt. 12:46-50 and Mark 3:31-35 (see Creed, *The Gospel According to St. Luke*, p. 162).

[49] There is no known Jewish parallel to this saying, not even Sirach 4:31 (which has to do with repayment of loans; see E. Haenchen, *Die Apostelgeschichte*, 13th ed., KEK 3 [Göttingen: Vandenhoeck & Ruprecht, 1961]: 526-27, n. 5). But Thucydides (II, 97.4) repeats as a Persian maxim, "Give rather than receive," and Seneca (*Epistles* LXXXI, 17) writes: "For anyone who receives a benefit more gladly than he repays it is mistaken" (Haenchen, *ibid.*). The saying in Acts represents the Christianization of a Greek proverb, employed here in a very loosely ordered context (*ibid.*; cf. Conzelmann, *Die Apostelgeschichte*, HNT 7 [Tübingen: J. C. B. Mohr (Paul Siebeck, 1963)]: 119).

[50] There is a textual problem here, however, and some scholars believe the prayer is not an original part of Luke.

[51] Cf. also the prayer of James the Just quoted by Hegesippus (Eusebius, *Church History*, ii.23.16).

[52] Are these the soldiers (so Creed, *The Gospel According to St. Luke*, p. 286; Conzelmann, *The Theology of St. Luke*, p. 89—who refers to vs.

act in ignorance and not on the ground of God's forgiveness or of the love command. There are parallels to this idea of innocence by virtue of ignorance in Greek and Latin literature.[53]

Luke mentions Jesus' compassion just once, in relation to his concern for the widow's son at Nain (7:13). But this evangelist comes closer than any other to an actual commendation of compassion when, in Jesus' parable, the Samaritan is described as being moved by compassion to aid the needy Jew (10:33). The same parable, as we have seen, stresses the universalism of the Christian's responsibility. Luke's concern for this is also served by the story of the Samaritan who, alone of the ten lepers, was grateful for being healed (17:11-19) and by the words, ascribed to Peter, about associating with all men and about God's impartiality (Acts 10:28, 34-36). God's own compassion for even the most alienated of his children is stressed in Jesus' "parable of the prodigal son" which only Luke has (see 15:20).

Finally, it is significant that in Luke Jesus' birth and his climactic entry into Jerusalem at the end of his ministry are both heralded by reference to the "peace" he represents.[54] In Luke 2:14 the angels sing of "glory to God" and of "peace on earth" for God's people; in 19:38 the Palm Sunday throngs sing, "Peace in heaven and glory in the highest!" (*RSV*).[55] Jesus' whole ministry of proclamation and service to the world's needy is conceived in terms of a heavenly peace present, or at least foreshadowed, in the messianic activities of the heavenly King. Therefore, it is not surprising to find Peter summing up Jesus' whole mission as he does in Acts 10:36: "[God] gave the good news

---

35) or the (soldiers and the) Jews (so Plummer, *A Critical and Exegetical Commentary*, p. 531; Caird, *The Gospel of St. Luke*, p. 251—who cites Acts 3:17)?

[53] Creed, *The Gospel According to St. Luke*, p. 286. On the ignorance/guilt motif in Luke-Acts, see Conzelmann, *The Theology of St. Luke*, pp. 90 ff.

[54] The only New Testament writer who uses the word "peace" oftener than Luke is Paul. A number of times the evangelist uses it in accord with Old Testament piety and the *shalom* blessing (Luke 1:79; 2:29; 7:50; 8:48, par. Matt. 5:34; 10:5-6, par. Matt. 10:12-13; 24:36 [D]; Acts 15:33; 16:36). Several other times it has a distinctly political meaning (Luke 14:32; Acts 12:20; 24:2; cf. Luke 19:42). In Luke 11:21, "in peace" describes the security of well-guarded possessions.

[55] See Conzelmann, *The Theology of St. Luke*, n. 4, pp. 75-76.

of peace through Jesus Christ" (*NEB*), or to read that the church was "built up" in such a way by this gospel of peace that it "*had* peace" (Acts 9:31). Perhaps we are given a clue as to Luke's understanding of the meaning of such peace in Stephen's speech. Moses' attempted intervention in an altercation between an Egyptian and a Hebrew (see Exod. 2:11-15*a*) is described as his attempt to "reconcile them unto peace" (Acts 7:26). This evangelist particularly stresses the reconciling outreach to all men of God's love, forgiveness, and compassion, and the importance of the church itself as a community of reconciliation.

Considering Luke's tendency to think of Jesus' message and mission as a "gospel of peace," it is surprising that Luke's beatitudes include none to parallel Matthew's, "Blessed are the peacemakers . . ." (5:9). But even greater surprise may be registered at Luke's inclusion of the saying, "Do you think that I have come to give peace on earth? No, I tell you, but rather division . . ." (Luke 12:51-53, par. Matt. 10:34-36). But this does not really contradict the evangelist's characterization of the gospel as one of "peace." The saying as it continues echoes Jewish predictions of troubles in the last days (e.g., Mic. 7:6; Ethiopic Enoch 100: 2; Sanh. f. 97*a*[56]), and these often include exactly the sort of family divisions mentioned also in Luke. The point in both cases is that the eschaton will mean judgment and a division between the righteous and the unrighteous. In Luke 12:51 ff., therefore, "peace" means naïve complacency, false security, careless inattention to the coming judgment. Nor does Jesus' command to the disciples to buy a sword (Luke 22:36*b*, without parallel) contradict the evangelist's "gospel of peace." In Luke's view, the time of the church for which Jesus is now preparing his disciples is, in contrast to the period of Jesus' own ministry which has now closed, a time of temptation and martyrdom. The context suggests that Luke's addition of a sword to the apostle's equipment for use after Jesus' departure[57] is symbolic of the need for believers to stand firm against temptation.[58]

In summary, Luke views Jesus' whole ministry as a mission to the world's needy, as the effective presence of the gospel of

---

[56] Cited by Bultmann, *History of the Synoptic Tradition*, p. 154.

[57] A sword is not mentioned in 9:3 or 10:4.

[58] Conzelmann, *The Theology of St. Luke*, pp. 81-83.

peace. The command to love is given special prominence in the Sermon on the Plain, and its practical implications for the Christian life are constantly emphasized. It means the compassionate serving of whoever stands in need, active "doing good" even to one's enemies, restraint in judging others, forgiveness, reconciliation, and sharing one's resources with all the brethren in the Christian *koinonia.*

III
PAUL: FAITH ACTIVE IN LOVE

Love and the New Creation

There is no Pauline letter[1] in which the term "love" (almost always *agape*) does not appear and in which exhortations to love do not figure prominently. It is significant, however, that

[1] I regard as indisputably Pauline only the following: Romans, I and II Corinthians, Galatians, Philippians, I Thessalonians, and Philemon. Other New Testament letters which bear the apostle's name are treated separately, below, pp. 118-31.

the Great Commandment as such is not conveyed by Paul, and that his love ethic is not specifically or explicitly oriented in terms of Jesus' own teachings. Rather, in the case of love as in the case of other major themes of his preaching, the apostle's thought is oriented to Jesus' death. His is a theology of the cross. For him the meaning of the cross is articulated in the resurrection gospel, and its power becomes manifest in the believer's own "new creation" in Christ (II Cor. 5:17). Thus, Paul looks to Jesus Christ as the decisive eschatological event, not just as a great teacher of history. In Christ God's sovereign Rule has been initiated, his sovereign claim has been revealed. In Christ's death and resurrection the meaning of the divine promise and command is particularly evident: the promise is new life, the command is to give oneself utterly in the obedience of love.[2]

Paul's preaching of love does not just stand alongside his emphasis on justification by faith but is vitally related to it. To believe in Christ means to belong to him, and to belong to him means to share in his death and in the power of his resurrection. Thereby one's whole life is radically reoriented from sin to righteousness as he is freed from bondage to himself and placed under the truly liberating dominion of God's grace (Rom. 6:4-14; cf. Phil. 3:7-11). These are the ideas which lie behind the apostle's pregnant formulation of the matter in Gal. 2:19-20: "With Christ have I been crucified, and so I live. Yet it is no longer *I*, but *Christ* who lives in me. And this life which I now live in the flesh, I live by faith in the Son of God who loved me and gave himself up for me." The liberating and transforming grace of God is active as love, and Christ's death ("for us," "for our sins") is the decisive actualization of that love in history. In the cross can be seen God's love seeking to reconcile all men unto his sovereign purpose: "God demonstrates his love for us in that while we were still sinners Christ died on our behalf" (Rom. 5:8; cf. Rom 8:34-35, 37). For this reason—again with reference to the Lord's death—Paul can declare that "Christ's love [for us] sustains us, for we are quite convinced

---

[2] Elsewhere I have dealt at some length with Paul's theology, especially as it relates to his ethical teaching (*Theology and Ethics in Paul* [Nashville: Abingdon Press, 1968], pp. 112-206).

of this, that one has died for all, and therefore all have died"
(II Cor. 5:14). God's love "sustains" us because it redeems and
reconciles, and also because it draws believers into the realm
of grace and places them under the command of their sovereign
Lord.[3]

There is also a close connection in Paul's thought between
God's love and God's Spirit: "God's love has been poured out
into our hearts through the Holy Spirit which has been given
to us" (Rom. 5:5); "I beseech you, brethren, by our Lord Jesus
Christ and by the Spirit's love . . ." (Rom. 15:30). The Spirit
is the "first fruits" of the coming age (Rom. 8:23), the "down
payment" on a glorious inheritance (II Cor. 1:22; 5:5). Hence,
the Spirit is the life-giving power of the new age (II Cor. 3:6)
operative already among the believers. Paul's identification of
the Spirit and love shows that for him the power of the new
age is the power of love. For him love is not just an abstract
ideal or one quality among others which make up the Christian
life. *It is the new aeon itself, powerfully present and active in
history.*[4] It is God's own power at work redeeming men, calling
them to obedience and enabling them to obey. It is both a gift
("we live by the Spirit," Gal. 5:25a) and an exhortation ("let
us walk by the Spirit," Gal. 5:25b). It "leads" the believer into
the ways he should go (Gal. 5:18), and the first and all-inclusive
"fruit" of its working is—love (Gal. 5:22). Through the Spirit's
leading in love the man of faith is able to discern what is required

---

[3] For comments on the translation of II Cor. 5:14, see *ibid.*, pp. 167-68. I
do not find the translations of either *NEB* ("the love of Christ leaves us
no choice") or *JB* ("the love of Christ overwhelms us") to be in keeping
with Paul's understanding of God's love met in the cross as at once a
sustaining and a commanding power.

[4] So G. Bornkamm, "The More Excellent Way" in *Early Christian Experience*, trans. P. L. Hammer (New York: Harper & Row, 1969), pp. 188, 189;
also in his essay, "On the Understanding of Christian Worship," *ibid.*, p.
165 (where he cites Käsemann), and in his *Paul*, trans. D. M. G. Stalker
(New York: Harper & Row, 1971), p. 217. Similarly, Heinrich Schlier, "Über
die Liebe, 1 Korinther 13" in *Die Zeit der Kirche: Exegetische Aufsätze
und Vorträge*, 2nd ed. (Freiburg: Verlag Herder, 1958), pp. 192-93; Kurt
Niederwimmer, "Erkennen und Lieben: Gedanken zum Verhältnis von
Gnosis und Agape im ersten Korintherbrief," *KuD* XI (1965): 98, and Kurt
Stalder, *Das Werk des Geistes in der Heiligung bei Paulus* (Zürich: EVZ-
Verlag, 1962), pp. 473-74.

and thus to manifest the righteousness of which the new creation in Christ consists (Phil. 1: 9-11).[5]

The idea that one should love God is not foreign to Paul, but it is neither frequent nor emphasized in his letters.[6] Although he may well have known the tradition which joined Deut. 6: 5 and Lev. 19: 18 together into the Great Commandment, he makes no use of it and cites Lev. 19: 18 only by itself (Rom. 13: 9; Gal. 5: 14). He prefers to speak of man's proper relationship to God in other ways, and wishes always to stress the priority of the divine love for men (Rom. 5: 6-8). But along with this emphasis on God's gift of love there is, as we have begun to see already, a corresponding emphasis on the task of love to which the man in Christ has been called. Man's response to God's love is faith, and faith is first of all obedience in love.[7] No better title for Paul's "theology" can be devised than his own formulation in Gal. 5: 6: "faith active in love." Love is both the context and the content of faith; God's love makes faith possible and man's love gives it visibility and effect in the world. If we remember Paul's close identification of love and Spirit, then we are able to see this theme present also when the Corinthians are reminded that the Spirit was given each of them "for the common good" (I Cor. 12: 7 RSV). Out of their life in the Spirit there are to come visible, practical deeds of love in the Christian community.[8] A similar concern, using similar terminology, is present when the apostle declares that not everything the Christian is free to do enhances the life of the community (I Cor. 6: 12; 10: 23). For Paul, then, love is not just one of the "social virtues."[9] It is the necessary manifestation within Christ's body of the new creation already underway in the working of God's Spirit. Therefore, love

[5] On Phil. 1: 9-11, see my *Theology and Ethics in Paul,* pp. 235-37.

[6] See Rom. 8: 28; I Cor. 2: 9; 8: 3; 16: 22 which (along with II Thess. 3: 5) are discussed briefly by George Johnston, *IntDB,* K-Q, pp. 172-73.

[7] I have discussed the interrelationship of these themes in *Theology and Ethics in Paul,* pp. 181-206.

[8] The phrase in I Cor. 12: 7 is πρὸς τὸ συμφέρον, which need only mean, "that which is useful." But the context shows that Paul refers to what is useful for the whole congregation, hence the appropriateness of the *RSV* translation which I have followed.

[9] So described by Morton Scott Enslin, *The Ethics of Paul* (New York: Harper & Bros., 1930), p. 74.

stands not only in close connection with faith, but also with hope (I Thess. 1:3; 5:8; I Cor. 13:13; Gal. 5:5-6).

Once we have understood the eschatological-christological orientation of Paul's love ethic, we are better able to understand why the apostle is chiefly concerned with the implications of love for life within the Christian community itself. By virtue of its existence as the body of Christ and the *koinonia* of the Spirit (Rom. 12:3-8; I Cor. 12:12-31a; Phil. 2:1-4; cf. 1:5-7, 27) it *must* be sustained and controlled by the divine love, or it will cease to be at all. The gospel calls men to Christ and thereby to one another, and Paul's view of the church's sacraments includes the recognition that they proclaim this twofold nature of the gospel's summons: "For whoever has been baptized into Christ has put Christ on. No one is 'a Jew' or 'a Greek,' 'a slave' or 'a free man,' 'male' or 'female.' For all of you are one in Christ Jesus" (Gal. 3: 27-28); "The cup of blessing over which we say the blessing, is it not a participation in Christ's blood? The loaf which we break, is it not a participation in Christ's body? Just as there is one loaf, so we who are 'many' are 'one body,' for we all share together in the one loaf" (I Cor. 10:16-17).

Repeatedly, Paul urges his congregations to conduct themselves in accord with what they are. Brotherly love should not be regarded as some special virtue requiring an apostolic discourse. If one has received the gospel then he has already received God's love, and with it the command to love his brethren. This is the meaning of Paul's comment that the Thessalonian Christians have already been "taught by God to love one another" (I Thess. 4:9). It is left for them only to "abound" in such love (4:10; cf. Phil. 1:9). As recipients of God's reconciling love in Christ they have become a new creation and thus stand under a divine commission to carry forward love's reconciling work (II Cor. 5:14-21).

Love and the Law

Paul rejects the law as a way of salvation, but he does not reject it as a norm for the conduct of one's life. It remains for him an instrument of God's will and purpose if it is correctly interpreted. For Paul the hermeneutical key to the law is Jesus Christ. Where the law is done on the basis of faith in him, it is truly fulfilled (cf. Rom. 9:32) and becomes in fact "the law of faith" (Rom. 3:27).[10] Twice he links the fulfilling of God's law with love specifically, and in each instance he appeals to the command of Lev. 19:18 to love one's neighbor (Gal. 5:14; Rom. 13: 8-9). These passages and their wider contexts are important enough to deserve special consideration.

Galatians 5-6

In Galatians Paul is addressing Christian congregations where there is real danger that the gospel will be compromised by insistence on compliance with certain formal requirements of the Jewish law such as circumcision. In response the apostle insists that such legalism is in effect a betrayal of the whole gospel (5:2-4). It means clinging to the law as a law of "works" rather than interpreting and keeping it as "the law of faith." For righteousness comes only on the basis of faith, as a gift from God and thus in God's own future (5:5). That means that nothing— neither circumcision nor uncircumcision—counts for anything, but only faith. In Gal. 5:6 Paul writes specifically about faith's "working in love."[11] A little later in this same letter Paul repeats the thought of 5:6 (neither circumcision nor uncircumcision counts for anything), but with a slight variation: what does count, he says in 6:15, is "a new creation." Here we have confirmation that for Paul God's love is the context for faith's working and man's love is its content, and that it is therefore love which is the power of the new age already present. "Faith active in love" is constitutive of "the new creation." That it is also constitutive of the freedom to which one is called by Christ (5:1) is the precise point Paul seeks to make in 5:13-14: "Take

[10] I have discussed this concept in *Theology and Ethics in Paul*, pp. 160-61, 191-94.

[11] Inexplicably the translators of *JB* omit Paul's reference to faith's "working in love"—a major translation disaster for which there is absolutely no textual warrant.

care not to use 'freedom' as an occasion for the indulgence of your own worldly fancies; rather, through love bind yourselves in service to one another. For the whole law has been epitomized in just this one commandment, namely: 'You shall love your neighbor as yourself.'"

As in Matthew's version of the Great Commandment, there is very strong emphasis here upon the reduction of all the statutes of the Jewish law into just one. Paul speaks on the one hand of "the whole law," and on the other hand of "just one commandment" (literally, "one word").[12] The passive voice verb which I have translated "has been epitomized" (literally, "has been fulfilled," cf. *RSV*) is equivalent to the verb "summed up" which Paul uses in Rom. 13:9 (this is quite properly recognized in both *NEB* and *JB*). The law is "the law of faith" when its essence is recognized in the love commandment. We have previously noted the parallelism of Paul's "faith active in love" (Gal. 5:6) and "a new creation" (Gal. 6:15). A third parallel occurs in I Cor. 7:19 where the apostle says that what really matters is "keeping God's commands." Paul is able to make such a claim precisely because for him "God's commands" are summarized in the one commandment of Lev. 19:18. When one is a new creation in Christ he lives by a faith which becomes active in love, and that is what really matters.

It is surprising that Paul here makes no reference to Jesus' teaching and makes no use of the Great Commandment as such. The commandment to "love God" (Deut. 6:5) is not cited here or anywhere else in the Pauline letters. But even more striking is the apostle's formulation here of the paradox of freedom and slavery. In Rom. 6 this paradox is also developed: to be free from sin means to be a slave of God (of righteousness) (vss. 18-22). The "new life of the Spirit" involves a new kind of bondage (Rom. 7:6). In Gal. 5:13-14 this new bondage is identified with one's service of his neighbor. To be bound to Christ means to be bound to one another in a love that cares and that serves.

---

[12] Correctly Otto Merck, *Handeln aus Glauben: Die Motivierungen der paulinischen Ethik*, Marburger Theologische Studien, 5 (Marburg: N. G. Elwert Verlag, 1968): 70; also W. Schrage, *Die konkreten Einzelgebote in der paulinischen Paränese: Ein Beitrag zur neutestamentlichen Ethik* (Gütersloh: Gütersloher Verlagshaus, Gerd Mohn, 1961), p. 232.

The Hellenistic popular philosophers of Paul's day would have found it hard to agree that freedom consists in servant concern for others. Callicles in Plato's *Gorgias* (491E) had long before expressed the common Greek view: "How can a man be happy if he is bound to anybody at all?" Aristotle later defined a free man as one "who exists for himself and not for another" (*Metaphysics* I, 2), and the view was still current in Paul's day, expressed by Epictetus: "I have been set free by God, I know His commands, no one has power any longer to make a slave of me . . ." (*Discourses* IV.vii.16-17).[13] Paul's position is quite the contrary, and it is related both to his conviction that faith is essentially *obedience* and to his insistence that belonging to Christ means belonging to *Christ's whole body*. In Gal. 5:15 he warns his readers that if they "go on fighting one another, tooth and nail, all [they] can expect is mutual destruction" (*NEB*). It is unclear whether Paul is opening a new paragraph or whether this is just a parenthetic warning, perhaps with the general turmoil of the Galatian churches in mind. In either case, the point is graphically made that *not* to be bound together in mutual, upbuilding love is to be bound together in a grisly, mutual annihilation.

In vss. 16-24 Paul explicates further his meaning: "Let me put it like this . . ." (*JB*): when you recognize that the love command conveys the whole point of the law, you will conduct yourself according to the Spirit's guidance. We have seen that Paul regards God's Spirit as the source and substance of love's power in the believer's new life. Now the apostle declares that freedom from the law (viewed apart from faith) comes as one is "led by the Spirit" away from unrighteous works (vss. 18-21) and into that "fruit of the Spirit" which is love (vs. 22). All eight of the "virtues" subsequently enumerated by Paul ("joy, peace, patience, kindness, goodness, faithfulness, gentleness, self-control," vss. 22-23 *RSV*) may be regarded as social manifestations of the believer's radically new (eschatological) life in Christ, "sustained" by his love. As I have pointed out

---

[13] Cited, respectively, by Downey, "Who Is My Neighbor?" p. 15; G. Friedrich, "Freiheit und Liebe im ersten Korintherbrief," *ThZ* XXVI (1970): 85, and Moffatt, *Love in the New Testament,* p. 190.

elsewhere,[14] Paul's description of love in I Cor. 13:4-7 is re-
markably parallel to Gal. 5:22-23: love "rejoices in the truth"
("joy"), it is "patient" ("patience"), it is "kind" ("kindness"),
and it "bears, believes, hopes, and endures all things" ("faithfulness"). Because love is not jealous, boastful, arrogant, or
rude, because it does not push itself forward or harbor resent-
ments, it may be said to be the very essence of "peace, goodness,
gentleness, and self-control." [15]

In Gal. 5:25, 26 Paul has cast his admonitions into the hortatory
subjunctive, so that formally these verses belong together and
are thereby also set apart from the context. They are best regarded as transitional (so in the paragraphing of *RSV* and *JB*),
summing up the argument so far (vs. 25) and yet drawing from
it some practical and timely implications (vs. 26). Since believers
live by the Spirit's presence and power in their midst, they
should allow their lives to be ordered by its guidance, which is
the guidance of love. And love precludes haughtiness, provocative acts, and envy. The discussion is now moved to the operation
of love within the Galatian congregations themselves, to the
relationships of those brethren with "one another." Vs. 26 reminds
us not only of the kinds of vices the apostle has just identified
as "works of the flesh" (vss. 19-21), but also of his warning
about mutual annihilation (vs. 15) and of his comments in
other letters that love prohibits demeaning other persons in order
to exalt oneself, and always requires the genuine affirmation of
others (e.g., Rom. 12:10, 16; I Cor. 13:4-5; Phil. 2:3-4).

Love's work in the church is discussed still more concretely in
6:1-10. For one thing, brethren should be concerned for the
reform and reconciliation of any errant member of their community (vs. 1*a*). They should seek to "set him right" (*NEB*,
JB) with the sort of "gentleness" which is one mark of the
Spirit's directing presence (see 5:23). Perhaps, then, we may
translate the verse: "Brethren, should anyone be found to have
fallen by the wayside, you who claim to be 'led by the Spirit'
ought to set him right with gentleness, according to the Spirit's
guidance." Characteristically, Paul adds the caution that those

[14] *Theology and Ethics in Paul*, p. 88.
[15] Spicq also notes this parallelism, *Agape in the New Testament*, II: 43.

who are responsible for discipline within the congregation should
be on guard respecting their own conduct (vs. 1b; cf. II Cor.
13:5). It may be that he has reference to the errant brother's bad
influence even on those who would correct him; but it is equally
possible that he is concerned lest the act of discipline itself
should not accord with the command to love the brother. This
would infuse a consideration into Paul's instructions on church
discipline which we found lacking in Matthew.[16]

This concern to restore the wayward brother is one instance of
mutual concern which the apostle describes as "bearing one another's burdens" (vs. 2), and I Cor. 12:25-26 affords a good
commentary: "the members [of Christ's body] should manifest
the same care for one another. Thus, if one member suffers, all
the members share that suffering; if one member rejoices, all
the members rejoice with him." This is what Christian obedience
means, for love is the summary commandment of the law. Love
is in fact "the law of Christ" (Gal. 6:2), a concept equivalent
in Paul's thought to "the law of faith" (Rom. 3:27) and to "the
law of the Spirit of life in Christ Jesus" (Rom. 8:2 RSV).[17] Vss.
3, 4 warn about using a brother's failings as an occasion for self-
congratulation—what the Germans call Schadenfreude. Love
does not allow that; love "does not rejoice at wrong" (I Cor.
13:6 RSV). Vs. 5, "For each man will have to bear his own load"
(RSV) does not at all contradict the earlier charge to "bear one
another's burdens," and as if to make this clear Paul has used
two different terms in vss. 2 and 5 (represented by RSV's "burden" and "load" respectively). Brotherly love requires mutual
caring and serving, but the members of the body retain their
individuality and stand always personally responsible under the
sovereign law of Christ. The concept of a Christian community
of love cannot be abstracted from the concrete demands of love
laid upon each of the brethren within it.

The exhortations of Gal. 5–6 are concluded in 6:10. "So then,
as we have opportunity, let us do good to all men, and especially
to those who are of the household of faith" (RSV). This verse is
linked to the preceding one by its repetition of the word καιρός

---

[16] See above, pp. 77-78.
[17] On "the law of Christ," see my Theology and Ethics in Paul, pp. 59-65,
228, 235, and also now Merck, Handeln aus Glauben, pp. 76-77.

—one of the Greek words for "time" (which *RSV* translates in vs. 9 as "season" and in vs. 10 as "opportunity")—and by a common grammatical form. As in the case of 5:25-26 the two verses are set apart formally from their context because the admonitions are expressed in hortatory subjunctives. Moreover, each verse speaks of "doing good," though the Greek phrases are different.[18] Paul cautions against any slackening of one's zeal for doing good, on the grounds that the "time" is coming (the eschaton) when the believers' obedience in love shall find its consummation in God's own Rule of love (vs. 9). It is likely that the word "time" in vs. 10 bears this same eschatological connotation. Since the Christian already in the present stands under the dominion of God's grace (cf. Rom. 6:14) whereby he is a recipient both of God's gift of love and of God's command to love, he already shares in the new creation. Thus, "as we have opportunity" in vs. 10 does not mean: *Whenever*, from time to time, it may be possible to do good, we should do it. It means, rather: *As long as* this present eschatological time continues, it is in fact the time to love, and we should be obedient in love.[19] It is clear from the context that by "doing good" Paul means being obedient in love. This is confirmed by the parallelism of I Cor. 14:1 ("Pursue [the way of] love!") and I Thess. 5:15 ("Pursue [the way of] the good!") as well as by the fact that in Rom. 13:10 Paul can define love negatively as doing no evil to the neighbor. The word "evil" (κακόν) there is the exact antonym of "good" (καλόν) in Gal. 6:9, and the verb (*"does* no evil") is the same as in Gal. 6:10 ("let us *do* good"—in both instances a form of ἐργάζεσθαι).

In Gal. 6:10 as elsewhere Paul stresses the responsibility to

[18] In vs. 9 the idiom ποιεῖν τὸ καλόν is used (as also in Rom. 7:21; II Cor. 13:7, and in Jas. 4:17), while in vs. 10 the phrase is ἐργάζεσθαι τὸ ἀγαθόν (also in Rom. 2:10).

[19] Used with the present or imperfect tense, ὡς can mean "as long as" and most probably does mean this in Gal. 6:10. Cf. W. Bauer, *A Greek-English Lexicon of the New Testament and Other Early Christian Literature*, trans. and ed. W. F. Arndt and F. W. Gingrich (Chicago: University of Chicago Press, 1957), p. 907; F. Blass and A. Debrunner, *A Greek Grammar of the New Testament and Other Early Christian Literature*, rev. Robert W. Funk (Chicago: University of Chicago Press, 1961), § 455 (2). Had Paul wished to say "Whenever we happen to have the chance" (cf. *NEB*'s "as opportunity offers") he would have used ὡς ἄν or ὅταν with the subjunctive. Cf. the remarks of Merck, *Handeln aus Glauben*, pp. 78-79.

manifest love within the church itself (*"especially* to those who are of the household of faith," 6:10*b RSV*). This phrase should not be charged against Paul as if he were here sponsoring a limited view of love's responsibilities.[20] The qualifying phrase does not *restrict* the initial command to love "all men," but rather *applies* the command to the most immediate and urgent instance.[21] If relationships within the church are not guided in love, then there is no hope relationships with outsiders can be so guided, or that the church's witness to the gospel of love can have any effect in the world. The context of Paul's appeal for love at I Thess. 4:9 shows that such a consideration is in the apostle's mind: the internal order of the congregation will "command the respect of outsiders" (vss. 10-12 *RSV*). Elsewhere in I Thessalonians Paul specifically interprets the love command as applying to the Christian's relationships with outsiders as well as to his relations with other Christians. He prays that the Lord will help them "increase and abound in love to one another *and to all men*" (3:12 *RSV*), and later directly charges them to repay no one evil for evil, but to "seek to do good to one another *and to all*" (5:15 *RSV*). Along with these passages we should perhaps also list Phil. 4:5: "Let all men know your forbearance" (*RSV*).[22] But most important of all is Rom. 12 where the love of outsiders, even of one's enemies, is very directly the subject of exhortation. In the wider context of those admonitions Paul again cites Lev. 19:18 as the essence of the law's demand (Rom. 13:8-10).

Romans 12–13

The exhortations of Rom. 12–13 are set within an eschatological framework provided by the opening appeal not to be conformed

[20] For the view that the universalism of Jesus' love command is at least partially restricted by Paul, see H. Montefiore, "Thou Shalt Love," pp. 161-63.

[21] Similarly, Moffatt, *Love in the New Testament*, p. 202 and—especially —Albrecht Oepke, *Der Brief des Paulus an die Galater*, 2nd ed., *ThHNT* 9 (Berlin: Evangelische Verlagsanstalt, 1957): 156. Cf. O. Michel, "Das Gebot der Nächstenliebe in der Verkündigung Jesu: Vier Vorträge, ed. N. Koch (Tübingen: J. C. B. Mohr [Paul Siebeck], 1947), pp. 75-76.

[22] So Schrage, *Die konkreten Einzelgebote*, p. 252.

to the present age (12:1-2) and by the concluding appeal to live
as one who belongs to "the day" of the Lord which is at hand
(13:11-14). The presupposition of these chapters is that those
addressed are participants in the new creation effected by God's
redemptive love and are thereby called to put their lives at his
disposal. In the exhortations here the apostle offers some concrete
instances of faith's "working in love." [23]

The appeals through 12:13 are formulated with thought for
life within the church itself. They are for the community of
faith (vs. 3), the body of Christ (vss. 4-5). The various functions of the members of Christ's body are specified in ways that
echo I Cor. 12:4-11. Prophecy, service, instruction, exhortation,
the contribution of material resources, and charitable deeds are
all mentioned as manifestations of God's "grace" of which believers are recipients (vss. 6-8). The implicit theme here, as in
I Cor. 12, is love. Just as in I Cor. this theme becomes explicit
in chap. 13, so here in Rom. 12 it becomes explicit in vs. 9a which
stands as a sort of introductory heading to the wide-ranging
exhortations which follow: "Let love be genuine" (RSV). Paul
uses the same adjective to describe love in II Cor. 6:6 where he
is writing about the apostolic style of life. That catalog contains
sixteen phrases which may be divided into eight pairs, thereby
linking together "the Holy Spirit, genuine love"—a typical
Pauline association. Considering the whole context of Paul's
preaching, we are quite justified in saying that for him love
is "genuine" when it is rooted in the new life of the Spirit by
which faith is formed and guided, and when it becomes concretely effective in one's conduct.

Specifically, "genuine love" hates evil and clings to the good
(vs. 9b) [24] and manifests itself as "brotherly affection" (vs. 10a
RSV). Paul uses the word φιλαδελφία, "brotherly love," only here

[23] For further comments on the form and framework of these chapters,
and for detailed comments on 12:1-2, see my Theology and Ethics in Paul,
pp. 98-106, 215-16. See now also Merck, Handeln aus Glauben, pp. 157-67;
and Charles H. Talbert, "Tradition and Redaction in Romans XII.9-21," NTS
XVI (1969): 83-94, whose contention that 12:9-21 reflects Semitic ethical
traditions "subjected to redaction in Hellenistic Christianity" (p. 93) does
not materially alter the interpretation of the passage proposed here.

[24] On the virtual equivalence of "the good" and "love" in Paul, see
above, p. 101.

and in I Thess. 4:9, and in the present instance it seems to be identified as a special form of the agape mentioned in vs. 9a.[25] The image of the church as God's family is implicit in vs. 10 which describes brotherly love as a matter of "family affection" (cf. *NEB:* "Let love for our brotherhood breed warmth of mutual affection"). Brotherly love requires caring more for others than for oneself, "in honor preferring one another" (vs. 10b),[26] a common Pauline exhortation. Phil. 2:3 is closely parallel, and again in the midst of his discussion of Christ's body in I Cor. 12 (vss. 22-26) Paul speaks of the greater "honor" due those members who are weakest and most inferior. Cranfield claims that Paul has here gone beyond the commandment of Lev. 19:18 to love one's neighbor "as yourself," and he cites Karl Barth's comment that behind this is the apostle's thought that Christ himself is met in the needy neighbor.[27] But Paul does not hesitate to quote the full text of Lev. 19:18 when he quotes it at all (Gal. 5:14; Rom. 13:9), and it is more likely that his point here is the same as in I Cor. 12:22 ff.: it is precisely the *weaker* members of the community who need the greatest care. We shall encounter a practical instance of this "preferring" the weak when we examine I Cor. 8 and Rom. 14–15.[28]

The next admonitions follow in quick succession through vs. 13 without a break. In this context the appeal to remain "zealous" (vs. 11a) probably refers to brotherly love, just as "zeal" is explicitly coupled with the love and care of Christians for one another in II Cor. 8:7, 8, 16 (cf. Rom. 12:8; Phil. 2:28). Reference to the Spirit (vs. 11b RSV; contrast NEB and JB) is also appropriate in this context, for the Spirit is the medium of God's love among his people (Rom. 5:5) and thus the means by which the Christian's life is lived in love (Gal. 5:22-23, 25). In vs. 11c ("serve the Lord," RSV) some manuscripts read "time" instead of "Lord," and commentators are divided as to which is the correct reading. A good case can be made for "time." Not only is

---

[25] See C. E. B. Cranfield, *A Commentary on Romans 12–13, SJTh* Occasional Papers, 12 (Edinburgh: Oliver & Boyd, 1965): 38.

[26] In support of this translation, see Cranfield, *ibid.*, p. 41. Spicq interprets Paul as saying that each should take the initiative in showing respect to others (*Agape in the New Testament*, II: 201).

[27] *Romans 12–13*, pp. 41-42.

[28] Below, p. 117.

it the "more difficult reading" (thus, not apt to have been substituted for an "easier" text in the course of transmission); it also
stands here in close association with an admonition to rejoice in
hope (vs. 12a). The meaning could be that the present "eschatologically filled time" should be used for brotherly love,[29] essentially the meaning we have already proposed for the same word
"time" in Gal. 6:10. On the other hand, in Greek the phrase
"serving the time" was a familiar idiom expressing *opportunism*
in a negative sense, and it is quite possible to account for the
change from "Lord" to "time" by a simple mechanical error.[30]
In this case, "serving the Lord, rejoicing in hope" might well
have a meaning similar to that of I Cor. 15:58: "always abound-
ing in the work of the Lord [love!], knowing that in the Lord
your labor is not in vain" (*RSV*). That is, one's hope for the
eschatological fulfillment of salvation both issues in and supports
the concrete "labor of love" (I Thess. 1:3) concerning which Paul
is admonishing his readers throughout Rom. 12–13.

The fifth pair of admonitions deals with endurance in tribulation and persistence in prayer (vs. 12), but it is doubtful whether
Paul has prayer for one's enemies specifically in mind.[31] Elsewhere in a context similar to this one (I Thess. 5:12-22) the
apostle's appeal for increasing prayer (vs. 17) has only a most
general reference. The final pair of exhortations here (vs. 13)
deals with particular ecclesial responsibilities: "Contribute to the
needs of the saints; practice hospitality." The first may well refer
to Paul's commitment to gather an offering for Jerusalem from
his Gentile churches, for that is on his mind as he writes this
letter (see 15:25 ff.).[32] The second must refer to a local congregation's responsibility to provide for the needs of traveling

---

[29] Spicq, *Agapè dans le Nouveau Testament*, p. 147 and n. 1. O. Michel also
adopts "time" (*Der Brief an die Römer, KEK*, 12th ed. [Göttingen: Vandenhoeck & Ruprecht, 1963], p. 304). See also K. Barth, *The Epistle to the
Romans*, trans. E. C. Hoskyns (London: Oxford University Press, 1933), pp.
450 (n. 1), 457.

[30] The two Greek words could easily be confused by a copyist: κυρίῳ
("Lord"), καιρῷ ("time"). Thus, Cranfield (*Romans 12–13*, p. 45) and C. K.
Barrett (*A Commentary on the Epistle to the Romans, HNTC* [New York:
Harper & Bros., 1957]: 234, n. 1) both adopt the reading "Lord."

[31] Against Spicq, *Agape in the New Testament*, II: 202-3.

[32] Barrett, however, thinks such a specific reference is unlikely (*Romans*,
p. 240).

preachers and teachers who come to serve them. In spite of Theodoret's interpretation of this command as embracing also non-Christians,[33] it is unlikely that this was Paul's intent. Concern for hospitality in a very specific *ecclesiastical* sense is often present in early Christian literature.[34]

In 12:14-21 the wider range of love's work is developed, beginning with an initial call to "bless" one's persecutors (vs. 14). We have already noted that this is perhaps the earliest version of Jesus' commandment to love one's enemies,[35] although it is again significant that the authority of Jesus is not specifically invoked by Paul. It is not necessary to regard vss. 15-16 as out of place here, momentarily referring again to relationships within the church. Cranfield, for instance, suggests that the exhortation to "rejoice with those who rejoice, weep with those who weep" (vs. 15 RSV) follows logically on vs. 14, "for truly to bless one's persecutors must surely involve readiness to take one's stand beside them as human beings." [36] Then the charge in vs. 16 to "live in concord with one another" may be laid down with a view to the church's witness to those outside.[37] A similar interpretation of these verses is offered by David Daube who, however, stresses the missionary motive and compares the Jewish idea that the missionary "must adopt the customs and mood" of those he wishes to win, and humble himself in relation to them.[38]

In vs. 17a as also in I Thess. 5:15 Paul urges his readers to refrain from returning evil for evil. The parallelism is so close (see also I Peter 3:9) that the apostle may be dependent upon a catechetical tradition akin to that behind Matt. 5:38-39, 44, and Luke 6:29, 35.[39] The rest of vs. 17 reveals Paul's conviction that the gospel ethic summons up and clarifies the deepest and best

---

[33] Cited by Cranfield, *Romans 12–13*, p. 48, n. 1.

[34] On this, see the Appendix, p. 226. Spicq reads too much into the imperatival participle διώκοντες (literally, "pursue") when he interprets Paul to mean that Christians should "even . . . go out looking for travelers . . . to welcome them at home" (*Agape in the New Testament*, II: 203).

[35] See above, pp. 61-62. F. Kattenbusch calls vss. 14, 17-21, "the oldest commentary on Jesus' words" ("Über Feindesliebe im Sinne des Christentums," *ThStK* LXXXIX (1916): 23.

[36] *Romans 12–13*, p. 50 (following K. Barth).

[37] *Ibid.*, p. 52.

[38] *The New Testament and Rabbinic Judaism*, p. 336.

[39] See Cranfield, *Romans 12–13*, p. 54.

106

moral instincts of man: one should "take thought for what is noble in the sight of all" (*RSV;* cf. Rom. 2:14-16; Phil. 4:8; Rom. 14:18).[40] The universalism of the Pauline love ethic is very clear in vs. 18, "Do all you can to live at peace with everyone" (*JB*). Here again, in the light of similar formulations elsewhere (14:19; Matt. 5:9; Mark 9:50; I Thess. 5:13; Heb. 12:14; cf. Ps. 33:15 LXX), we may be in touch with traditional church teaching.

Paul's meaning in vss. 19, 20 is not altogether clear. He begins by urging that vengeance be left to God's own wrath (cf. Lev. 19:18; Deut. 32:35), and that corresponds well enough with similar ideas elsewhere in his letters (e.g., II Cor. 11:15b; Gal. 5:10).[41] But his subsequent use (vs. 20) of Prov. 25:21-22 has given commentators great anguish. What does it mean to say that one heaps fiery coals on his enemy's head when he gives him needed food and drink? Origen and Chrysostom interpreted this to mean that kind deeds would lay an even greater burden of guilt upon the enemy and put him in line for yet greater punishment, whereas Augustine and Jerome took Paul to mean that the enemy could in effect be shamed into repentance.

The debate goes on. William Klassen finds an ancient Egyptian ritual behind the proverb, in which fiery coals "were evidence . . . that repentance had taken place." Thus, Paul's point could be that one should not just wait for God's punishment to come to the enemy, but should use the interim to show him kindness and perhaps make him a friend.[42] This is reminiscent of the view of Augustine and Jerome. On the other hand, Krister Stendahl's position recalls that of Origen and Chrysostom.[43] Stendahl finds the clue in the idea present among the sectarians of Qumran

[40] Cranfield (*ibid.,* pp. 54-55) is correct in rejecting Michel's attempt to read ἐνώπιον πάντων ἀνθρώπων as "*to* all men" (*Römer,* p. 276).

[41] Ratschow ("Agape, Nächstenliebe und Bruderliebe," p. 175) raises a false issue when he suggests that Paul is weakening Jesus' teaching by basing the appeal to refrain from retaliation on God's wrath rather than on his love. For one thing, it is by no means clear that the apostle would regard these two as opposites or even in tension; for another, elsewhere—and more typically—Paul stresses God's love, even for his enemies (e.g., Rom. 5:6-11).

[42] "Coals of Fire: Sign of Repentance or Revenge?" *NTS* IX (1963): 337-50.

[43] "Hate, Non-Retaliation, and Love: IQS x, 17-20 and Rom. 12:19-21," *HThR* LV (1962): 343-55.

that one's leaving vengeance to God is actually a covert way of expressing one's "hatred" for his enemies: "Neither Qumran, nor Paul speak about love for the enemies. The issue is rather how to act when all attempts to avoid conflict with the enemies of God and of his Church have failed (vv. 17 f.)." [44]

Taken by themselves it is difficult to judge whether the Egyptian or Qumranian parallel is more apt. But if one considers the context of these verses in Rom. 12–13, it is impossible to agree with Stendahl that Paul regards good deeds done to enemies as an expression of concealed hatred. As we have seen, all these exhortations stand under the general one to "let love be genuine," and the immediately preceding counsels (vss. 14-18) are clearly intended to show how love should treat outsiders and enemies. Moreover, the section is concluded in vs. 21 with a summary exhortation not to be overcome by evil, but to overcome evil with good—that is, with love. Perhaps, indeed, the most important parallel is the exegesis of Prov. 25:21-22 ascribed to Rabbi Simeon ben Eleazar (ca. A.D. 190): "The evil impulse is like iron which one holds in a flame. So long as it is in the flame one can make of it any implement he pleases. So too the evil impulse: its only remedy is in the words of the Torah, for they are like fire, as it is said, *If thine enemy be hungry, give him bread to eat, and if he be thirsty, give him water to drink: for thou wilt heap coals of fire upon his head, and the Lord will reward thee* (Prov. 25:21-22)—read not *will reward thee . . .* but *will put him at peace with thee . . . .*" [45] Although in this exegesis "the enemy" is interpreted as a metaphor for "the evil impulse," it is noteworthy that the proverb is regarded as aimed at reconciliation (turning evil into good), not at punishment.

Finally, we must consider Paul's explicit citation of Lev. 19:18 in Rom. 13:8-10. Whatever be the precise relation of 13:1-7 to the whole of chaps. 12–13, the admonition of vs. 7 concerning payment of debts provides a formal, if not material, bridge to vss. 8-10. Paul first repeats in a negative form ("Don't owe anything to anyone," vs. 8a) what he had just put positively ("Pay every-

---

[44] *Ibid.*, p. 354.

[45] *The Fathers According to Rabbi Nathan*, "Yale Judaica Series," X, trans. Judah Goldin (New Haven: Yale University Press, 1955): 85.

one what is owed him," vs. 7), but then he proceeds with an important exception: *"except to love one another"* (vs. 8b *RSV*). In this one vital respect the Christian is always a debtor. For Paul, however, this particular debt is not seen to have been incurred because of what one person has done for another. Rather, the obligation to "love one another" inheres in what *God* has done, in the new life he has granted the believer in Christ. In the present verses this thought is expressed by referring to neighbor love as fulfilling the law, that is—as we have seen—"the law of faith" (Rom. 3:27), "the law of the Spirit of life in Christ Jesus" (Rom. 8:2), "the law of Christ" (Gal. 6:2).

Is Paul again in 13:8-10 focusing on love among *Christians* ("love one another")? It may be that the "universal negatives" which open the exhortation ("Don't owe anything to anyone") demand that the rest of the verse also be construed as universally applicable.[46] But one might equally well argue that it is the exhortation to "love one another" which defines the scope of those negatives which, therefore, are not so "universal" after all. The important thing, however, is that the apostle elsewhere (notably, for this context, in 12:14-21) makes it quite clear that the Christian love command does not apply only to intramural relationships, even though he does at times concentrate upon its importance for the life of the church.

The literal meaning of the word in vs. 8b which *RSV* and *NEB* translate as "the neighbor" is "the other." It is sometimes argued that this should be construed as an adjective modifying "law," so that Paul would be saying, "one who loves has fulfilled the other law," namely, the law of God in contrast to some other— perhaps the Roman civil law.[47] But Cranfield has shown that this exegesis is strained,[48] and that "the other" is best read as a noun, here—as elsewhere by Paul—used as a synonym for "the neighbor." A comparison of the other instances of Paul's use of the term (Rom. 2:1; I Cor. 10:24; cf. 10:29; 14:17) shows that

[46] Cranfield, *Romans 12-13*, p. 83 (following T. W. Manson); also Bauer, "Das Gebot der Feindesliebe und die alten Christen," p. 39; Spicq, *Agape in the New Testament*, II: 57.

[47] For this view, see Willi Marxsen, "Der ἕτερος νόμος, Röm. 13:8," *ThZ* XIII (1955): 230 ff.

[48] *Romans 12-13*, pp. 83-84.

for him it does not just refer to "other people" in some vague, general sense, but to those with whom one comes into direct contact.[49]

Whereas in Gal. 5:14 the subject of the verb "fulfilled" is "the whole law," and the verb therefore refers to what epitomizes the law, here in 13:8b the subject of the same verb is "the one who loves." What, in this case, does "has fulfilled" mean? Cranfield argues that the "for" which links vss. 8a, 8b introduces the reason why love always owes a debt: *should* one perfectly love his neighbor he could "fulfill" the law, but that is impossible, so he is required to keep on loving.[50] But "has fulfilled the law" need mean nothing more than "has resolved to do it" (cf. Rom. 2:13 [51]). The one who loves his neighbor shows that he recognizes the law's fundamental commandment and has set himself to obey it.[52] It is not just because the law can never be "perfectly" obeyed that Paul speaks of one's constant obligation to love.[53] There is a more fundamental reason: the Christian stands under the dominion of grace and under a *sovereign* Lord whose commandment to love is in no way limited, either in its inclusiveness or in its duration.

As in Gal. 5:14, so here (vs. 9) Paul quotes Lev. 19:18. The listing of a few commands exemplary of the Decalogue, plus the reference to "any other commandment," serves the same function here as does the reference to "the whole law" in Gal. 5:14. In each case the point is that the law is "summed up" in the love command. Once more the first half of Jesus' double commandment is missing, but, as Spicq points out, the whole of Rom. 12–13 presupposes love for God as fundamental to every imperative of the Christian life (see 12:1-2).[54]

In vs. 10 the subject shifts from "the one who loves" to "love"

---

[49] See Beyer in *ThD* II: 704; Cranfield, *ibid.*
[50] Cranfield, *Romans 12–13*, pp. 84-85.
[51] Cited by Michel, *Römer*, p. 289, n. 2.
[52] See also Barrett, *Romans*, p. 251: "love is not the *completion* but the *performance* of the law."
[53] So Cranfield, *Romans 12–13*, p. 84, whose reference to Rom. 3:20 is not convincing. There the context is different: Paul is asserting that righteousness can never be *achieved* through *works of law*.
[54] *Agape in the New Testament*, II: 58.

itself. This corresponds to the form of I Cor. 13,[55] just as the negatively formulated "Love works no evil to the neighbor" echoes the negative form of I Cor. 13:4b-6a. The formulation in Rom. 13:10 is perhaps influenced by the negative commandments cited in vs. 9,[56] and its effect is to serve as a kind of *litotes,* understatement for the sake of emphasis.[57] The positive exhortation to "do good" to the neighbor is implicit. (Since the subject of vs. 10 is already "love," it would have been a tautology to say, "Love loves the neighbor," and rather weak to say, "Love does good to the neighbor.") Because all the commandments are summed up in Lev. 19:18, one who loves is doing what the law requires, and it may be said, finally, that "love is the fulfilling of the law" (vs. 10b *RSV*). In Greek vs. 10 has a chiastic arrangement: "love" is the first word and also the last word in the sentence—just as it is the first word and the last word Paul has to say about the meaning of the new life in Christ.

Love and Freedom

We have seen that Paul regards the believer as having been *freed from the law* interpreted as a way of salvation, but then also *bound over* in service to the neighbor *by the law* interpreted as the love commandment.[58] For this reason it is often said that the love command is an important restriction of one's freedom, a "conditioning factor in the exercise of Christian liberty." [59] But it is much more accurate to say that Paul regards love as an *act*

[55] On this, see my comments in *Theology and Ethics in Paul,* p. 99.

[56] Cranfield, *Romans 12-13,* p. 86; cf. Spicq, *Agape in the New Testament,* II: 60.

[57] Cf. Spicq, *Agape in the New Testament,* II: 60.

[58] Above, pp. 96-98.

[59] Richard N. Longenecker, *Paul: Apostle of Liberty* (New York: Harper & Row, 1964), p. 202. Cf. George Johnston: "Paul's principle in guiding his converts was that love sets bounds to individual liberty without destroying individual responsibility" (*IntDB,* K-Q, p. 173); similarly, Heinz-Dietrich Wendland, *Ethik des Neuen Testaments: Eine Einführung, NTD Ergänzungsreihe,* 4: Grundrisse zum Neuen Testament (Göttingen: Vandenhoeck & Ruprecht, 1970), p. 57; cf. p. 62.

of freedom. The man in Christ, claimed for service in the realm of grace, is for the first time really free to love, really free to enter into constructive and humanizing relationships with other persons.[60] For Paul, indeed, such expressions as "to be a slave," "to serve," and "to give oneself" can be used as synonyms for "love." [61] The relationship of love and freedom in Paul's thought is best seen in I Cor. 8 and Rom. 14–15.

I Corinthians 8

The problem addressed in this chapter has doubtless been raised by the Corinthians themselves: is it right or wrong for a Christian to eat meat which has been offered in sacrifice to pagan gods? Most of the Corinthians have no scruples about this, apparently, and in introducing the subject Paul quotes their slogan, "We have knowledge" (vs. 1b), namely—vs. 4—that since idols do not really "exist" pagan sacrifice is void and the Christian may eat such meat with impunity. It is their belief in the One God which thus informs their consciences and gives them the freedom to eat (vs. 7). But Paul responds to the Corinthian slogan with one of his own: "Knowledge puffs up, while love builds up" (vs. 1b). The apostle often speaks to the Corinthian "gnostics" about the dangers of being "puffed up." The phrase as he uses it refers not just to the perversion of one's own "spiritual life," but to the perversion of relationships among the brethren, for instance making invidious comparisons (4:6). In contrast love is not "puffed up" (13:4); love "builds up." Again, the reference is not to one's own moral edification but to his relationships with others and thus to the community of faith as a

[60] Cf. Friedrich, "Freiheit und Liebe," p. 95; Peter Stuhlmacher, "Christliche Verantwortung bei Paulus und seinen Schülern," *EvTh* XXVIII (1968): 168, n. 4.

[61] See Schrage, *Die konkreten Einzelgebote*, p. 252, who refers to Gal. 5:13 (cf. I Cor. 9:19) for the first (δουλεύειν), compares II Cor. 8:8 with 8:19-20, and Philem. 13 with Philem. 9 for the second (διακονεῖν), and compares II Cor. 8:8 with 8:5 and Gal. 2:20 with 1:4 for the third. On the subject of love and freedom in Paul's thought, see, in addition to Friedrich's article cited in notes 13 and 60, H. Schlier, "Über das volkommene Gesetz der Freiheit," pp. 193-206 in *Die Zeit der Kirche*.

whole. This is seen in Rom. 15:2 ("Let each of us please the neighbor for his good, to build him up"), and it is confirmed by Paul's pleas in I Cor. 14:3, 4, 5, 12, 17 that spiritual gifts should be used to "build up" the whole congregation. The criterion for evaluating and using such gifts is love (I Cor. 13), for "love builds up." [62]

In the next verses (2-3) Paul declares that true "knowledge" is not man's knowledge of God but God's knowledge of man.[63] Just to "know something" (vs. 2) about God means little. What does have meaning is a relationship to God founded on love (vs. 3a). Already here in the introductory sentences of his discussion it is clear that Paul will insist that true freedom is not rooted in "knowledge," but is both rooted and actualized in love.

Respecting the immediate "theological" question involved, Paul shows that he is firmly on the side of those who feel free to eat pagan idol meat (vss. 4-6). But he is not insensitive to the minority ("some," vs. 7) who do not share their views. He recognizes that their consciences are not informed by the proper knowledge, and therefore he calls them "weak" (vss. 7, 9-12). Their ignorance, however, is ascribed to the long-standing habits of their past lives as pagans (when they did eat such food with a "sense of its . . . consecration," vs. 7 NEB) and not to mere perversity. Whether or not Paul again quotes the Corinthians themselves in vs. 8a,[64] it is definitely his own conclusion that "we lose nothing if we refuse to eat, we gain nothing if we eat" (vs. 8b JB). The thought is parallel to Paul's remarks about circumcision and uncircumcision (7:19; Gal. 5:6; 6:15). Those who have "knowledge" have the freedom to eat without harming their consciences, but this freedom must be exercised discreetly: where their action will mean an offense to the "weak," they

[62] Cf. H. Conzelmann, *Der erste Brief an die Korinther*, KEK (Göttingen: Vandenhoeck & Ruprecht, 1969), p. 167. The ecclesiological application of the "building" metaphor in Paul's ethical teaching is discussed by Philipp Vielhauer, *Oikodome: Das Bild vom Bau in der christlichen Literatur vom Neuen Testament bis Clemens Alexandrinus* (Karlsruhe-Durlach: Verlagsdruckerei Gebr. Tron, 1940), pp. 92-106.

[63] Niederwimmer ("Erkennen und Lieben," pp. 92-94) notes that this is a Pauline theologoumenon rooted in the apostle's Jewish past.

[64] E.g., C. K. Barrett, *The First Epistle to the Corinthians*, HNTC (New York: Harper & Row, 1968), p. 195; Conzelmann believes the words are Paul's own, *Korinther*, p. 175.

should refrain from eating (vs. 9).[65] We may regard this instruction as a practical application of the more general exhortation to employ one's freedom (in this case, one's freedom either *to eat* or *not* to eat) to serve the neighbor (Gal. 5:13-14).

How a weak brother might be injured is indicated in vs. 10 by posing what is obviously an extreme case.[66] If one of the weak sees a brother eating in a pagan temple, he might be moved to follow suit. But because, in retrospect, his "weak conscience" would assess the action to have been wrong, his conscience would have been defiled (cf. vs. 7).[67] Paul gives an ironic twist to his words here, for he again uses the verb to "build up" (cf. vs. 1b). By ignoring the effect of his actions on the weak, he says, the brother who eats is "building him up unto destruction" (*RSV:* "encouraged"). This "building up" is the reverse of that which love seeks.

So far those without knowledge have been referred to as "some" (vs. 7, cf vs. 10) or as the "weak" (vss. 9, 11a). But finally—both climactically and emphatically—Paul refers to "the brother" and "the brethren" (vss. 11b-13). The weak man must always be counted "the brother" because he, too, has been baptized into Christ's death and participates in the new creation (vs. 11b; cf. 12:13; Gal. 3:27-28). To defile a brother's conscience is to violate his integrity as a person "in Christ," and thus to sin against Christ himself (vs. 12). Here is a negative but no less deliberate articulation of what is put positively elsewhere in the New Testament—that in the neighbor one meets Christ himself.[68]

[65] In chap. 9, Paul will write of his own liberty as an apostle (vss. 12 ff.) which he does not flaunt, but which he uses to become "all things to all men" for the sake of the gospel (vss. 22-23).

[66] Archibald Robertson and Alfred Plummer, *First Epistle of St. Paul to the Corinthians,* 2nd ed., *ICC* (Edinburgh: T. & T. Clark, 1914), p. 171.

[67] Most English translations of vs. 10 are misleading insofar as they allow the interpretation that the weak man sins *because* his conscience is "weak," as if "weak conscience" = "weak will." But the context shows that a "weak conscience" is one improperly informed. The meaning here is that the weak brother sins *in spite of* his weak conscience—which will later condemn him. Perhaps Barrett's translation is best: "Will not his conscience, this weak man's conscience, be fortified to eat things sacrificed to idols?" (*Corinthians,* p. 196.)

[68] Paul himself says this positively in Rom. 14:15, 18; see also Matt. 25: 31-46; 10:40; 9:37; Acts 9:4, 5 (Conzelmann, *Korinther,* p. 117, n. 40; Barrett, *Corinthians,* p. 196; Robertson and Plummer, *First Epistle,* p. 173).

The topic of chap. 8 arises again in 10:23 ff. In vs. 23 Paul quotes another Corinthian slogan, "Anything goes!" He had also quoted it in 6:12 and there corrected it by adding, "but not everything is beneficial," and again, "but I am not going to let anything dominate me" (*JB*). The first of these corrections reappears in 10:23, but another is added which particularly fits the context: "not everything builds up." As in chap. 8, the point is that Christian freedom is active in particular historical contexts and within the web of particular human relationships. Thus, "what goes" cannot be abstractly posited but must be contextually defined. How does it affect others? Does it "build them up"? Freedom must be exercised in love, for, like the law, it is fulfilled as it serves the neighbor. Paul states this another way in I Cor. 10: 24: "Nobody should be looking for his own advantage, but everybody for the other man's" (*JB*). Thereby one is not *restricting* his own freedom, but *exercising* it in love.

Romans 14–15

Romans is addressed to a church of which Paul has no first-hand knowledge, and his discussion of "the strong" and "the weak" in 14:1–15:13 reads like a generalized adaptation of a position he had earlier worked out respecting an actual, known situation in Corinth.[69]

In this passage "the weak" appear as vegetarians (14:2) who observe special sacred days (14:5-6), abstain from wine (14:21), and "pass judgment" on those whose practice differs (14:3, 10). Although Paul numbers himself among "the strong" (15:1), he characterizes them as holding "the weak" in contempt (14:3, 10). The apostle's choice of words here seems deliberate: the

[69] Among the indications that this is the case are the following: in Romans Paul has crystallized his references to two differing groups into the phrases "the strong" and "the weak" (οἱ δύνατοι, οἱ ἀδύνατοι, 15:1), whereas in I Cor. 8 neither term had been used ("weak" in I Cor. 8 translates the adjective ἀσθενής, etc.); many of the exhortations in Rom. 14–15 are either directed specifically to *both* groups equally (e.g. 14:3, 5-6) or else are equally applicable to each group (e.g. 15:2 ff.); and Paul employs the concept of "the brother" earlier and oftener in Romans (14:10 ff.).

THE LOVE COMMAND IN THE NEW TESTAMENT

weak "judge" the strong, the strong "despise" the weak.[70] Judgment—as Paul stresses in this same context (14:4, 10-12)—belongs only to God. The weak are therefore pre-empting God's role when they criticize the strong for doing things which they believe God disapproves. Paul customarily associates "despising" with personal repulsion,[71] and his application of the concept to himself in II Cor. 10:10 and Gal. 4:14 is instructive. In spite of his repulsive personal condition the Galatians did not "despise" him; but the Corinthians did regard his personal presence "weak" and his speech "despisable." It is clear why Paul regards the strong as bearing the greater burden for setting right relationships within the church: their negativism toward the weak does not spring from deep, deliberate religious convictions, but from personal, subjective distaste. (Perhaps this reflects the apostle's insight into his own feelings about them!) At the same time, however, the weak are reminded that they should leave judgment to God.

Here, as in I Cor. 8, Paul emphasizes the importance of love as the guiding power in the church's life and the means by which one's freedom in Christ is authentically realized. He thinks first of God's own love, his "accepting" all the brethren despite their varying opinions on matters of food and feasts (14:1, 3b; 15:7). Thus, in God's sight *what is done* is secondary to the motive and the goal. If it is done as an act of obedience and of thanksgiving to God, then it will be received by him (14:5-9). At the same time, however, it must be performed with regard for one's own brethren. There is no real obedience or thanksgiving where one's brother is being injured (14:10 ff.). A play on words in 14:13, using κρίνειν in its two senses, to *judge* and to *decide,* helps Paul make his point: "Let us therefore cease judging one another, but rather make this simple judgment: that no obstacle or stumblingblock be placed in a brother's way" (*NEB*). These words are addressed to the strong: since they know that uncleanness is not something inherent in an *object* but in the

---

[70] However, in 14:13 "judgment" also seems to be associated with the strong.

[71] Six of the nine New Testament occurrences of the word (ἐξουθενεῖν) are in Paul's letters; the remaining three are in Luke-Acts.

person who uses the object (14:14), they should also understand that the person who thinks an object is unclean will be injured if he uses it. Thus, the whole point of I Cor. 8 is recapitulated as Paul writes: "If your brother is being injured by what you eat, you are no longer walking in love. Do not let what you eat cause the ruin of one for whom Christ died" (14:15 RSV; cf. esp. I Cor. 8:1, 11). If, indeed, the strong ignore their weaker brethren, then their own participation in otherwise neutral things will become evil (14:16). Although food and drink do not contradict God's will, neither does their use *constitute* God's Rule. That is constituted, rather, of "righteousness and peace and joy in the Holy Spirit" (14:17 RSV).

To "walk in love" toward the brother is to "serve Christ" himself (14:18), the positive side of what Paul had said negatively in I Cor. 8:12. One's concern should be for "building up" the church into the body of Christ (14:19). To destroy the brother (cf. I Cor. 8:11) is to tear down God's own work (14:20). Finally, then, the one who understands that the gospel sets him free to eat anything, must understand that the gospel has also set him free to care for and serve his brethren. If he flaunts his freedom to eat in such a way as to offend others, then he will have to judge himself (by conscience) in matters which should really remain indifferent (14:22). In 14:23 Paul speaks about the weak brethren, but is addressing his words to the strong. They should remember that a weak brother whose doubts remain but who goes ahead with questionable things is not acting from faith. Because his actions contradict his own view of what God requires, he acts in sin. The charge to the strong concludes in 15:1: they are to "bear" the weaknesses of the weak brethren, a concrete instance of "bearing one another's burdens" and thereby fulfilling "the law of Christ" (Gal. 6:2).

A new paragraph begins in 15:2 as Paul concludes the whole discussion with exhortations equally appropriate for both groups. One should love his neighbor ("please his neighbor for his good," RSV) in order to "build him up" (vs. 2; parallel to I Cor. 10:24). This commandment is given an emphatic christological grounding in 15:3 ("for Christ did not please himself," RSV) and then

117

again in 15:7: "Accept one another as Christ accepted us, to the glory of God" (*NEB*).[72] Thus the discussion ends as it had begun (14:1). It is important that Paul links Christ's "acceptance" closely with his becoming a "servant" (15:8). Just as Christ's love found expression in his service to the Jews in order that the Gentiles also might be won and the two united in the praise of God, so the brethren ought to become servants of one another for the glory of God. The "strong" do not *lose* any of their freedom thereby, but will be *using* it in love and thus affirming the reality of their new life in Christ.

Love in the Deutero-Pauline Letters

It is at least questionable whether Paul himself is the author of II Thessalonians and Colossians, and it is highly unlikely that he wrote Ephesians or any of the Pastoral Epistles. It will be best, therefore, if we examine these separately to see in what ways the Pauline love ethic is continued or lost, interpreted or changed.

II Thessalonians

The Thessalonians are praised, in typical Pauline fashion, for their increasing faith and "love . . . for one another" (1:3), and there are two references in the letter to God's love: "Now may our Lord Jesus Christ himself, and God our Father, who loved us and gave us eternal comfort and good hope through grace, comfort your hearts and establish them in every good work and word" (2:16-17 *RSV*); "May the Lord direct your hearts to the love of God and to the steadfastness of Christ" (3:5 *RSV*). In

---

[72] The *RSV* translation of 14:1 and 15:7 as "welcome" (cf. *JB*: 14:1, "welcome," 15:7, "treat . . . in [a] friendly way") is insipid. Spicq is correct that "accept one another" functions here as "a direct commentary" on the appeal of 14:15 to walk in love toward the brother for whom Christ died (*Agape in the New Testament*, II: 236).

none of these passages, however, is love discussed as such. The remark of 1:3 is in the opening "Thanksgiving" section and is parallel to a similar remark in I Thess. 1:3. The other two instances are in benedictions and thus liturgically phrased. II Thess. 2:16-17 has a parallel in I Thess. 3:11-13, but there it is "love to one another" and not God's love which is mentioned. The prayer of II Thess. 3:5 that the readers be led into God's love and "the steadfastness of Christ" is in accord with the controlling concern in II Thessalonians that Christians remain faithful to the gospel even amid persecution and apostasy. The only other direct reference to love in this letter is also related to its overall theme: there are some who have "refused to love the truth" (2:10 RSV).[73] There is no equivalent expression in any of the letters which may with confidence be assigned to Paul.

A certain Pauline spirit does breathe through the instructions of 3:6-15 concerning discipline within the church. Backsliders are still reckoned as brothers (3:6) and it is specifically emphasized that they should continue to be accepted as brothers, not enemies, even if they do not heed the writer's pleas (vss. 14-15). The counsels to stay away from these people (vss. 6, 14) are not meant to require their expulsion from the community, for they are still the objects of Christian concern: they may yet heed the warning and be shamed—presumably shamed into repenting (vss. 14-15; cf. I Cor. 5–6; II Cor. 7:8-11).

It is true that this letter lacks the usual Pauline emphasis upon the eschatological-christological basis of the community's life as a *koinonia* of the Spirit and of love. It is also true that the references to the divine judgment in 1:5 ff. carry with them a certain vindictive aspect not typical of the apostle.[74] But we must also acknowledge the special problems to which this letter is directed and grant that nothing is said about love directly which contradicts Paul's usual view.

[73] Cf. the reference to those "who do not obey the gospel . . ." in 1:8; the two phrases are equivalent in meaning. In 2:13 a participial form of the verb "to love" is used to describe the brethren as "beloved by the Lord."

[74] This is pointed out by, among others, Herbert Braun, "Zur nachpaulinischen Herkunft des zweiten Thessalonicherbriefes," ZNW XLIV (1952-53): 152-56.

Colossians

In Colossians as in Paul's own letters (if this be regarded as deutero-Pauline) love is a vital, indeed the pivotal aspect of the new life in Christ. The accent is on fraternal love within the church, and a continuing appeal of the letter is that the brethren be "knit together in love" (2:2 *RSV*). Some[75] have translated this *"instructed* in love," for the term can bear this meaning. Moreover, this meaning fits the immediate context quite well, for there is concern here for the readers' "understanding" and "exact knowledge" (see also 1:28; 2:3). In this case Paul's instruction "in love" would be contrasted with the "beguiling speech" of his opponents (2:4); instruction "in love" would be instruction "according to Christ" (2:8).[76]

On the other hand, the meaning "knit together" is clearly present in 2:19 which speaks of Christ, the head of the body, as the one by whom it is "nourished and knit together through its joints and ligaments" (*RSV*). The word "ligaments" occurs again in 3:14 in the singular ("the ligament of perfection") and is a reference to love. Taken together, 2:19 and 3:14 show that in Colossians love is presented as that which binds together the members of Christ's body just as a human body is held together by its ligaments. It is probable that the same idea is intended in 2:2.[77] The prayer is that Christian brethren may be united in love. To "walk in Christ" (2:6; *RSV*: "live") means to "walk" worthy of the Lord (1:10; *RSV*: "lead a life"); the metaphor is Pauline, and we have met it, for instance, in Rom. 14:15 which speaks of "walking in love." This latter phrase is quite in accord with the point of view of Colossians.

The "walking" image is also present in 3:7. Once the believer has put to death his old "way of life" (3:5-7) he lives as one of God's chosen (3:12). Some of the practical moral consequences (requirements) of the new life are listed in vss. 12-13. One must put on "compassion, kindness, lowliness, meekness, and patience, forbearing one another and, if one has a complaint against an-

[75] Including Spicq, *Agape in the New Testament*, II: 249-50.

[76] *Ibid.*, p. 250.

[77] Correctly E. Lohse, *Die Briefe an die Kolosser und an Philemon*, 14th ed., *KEK* 9 (Göttingen: Vandenhoeck & Ruprecht, 1968): 127-28.

other, forgiving each other . . ." (*RSV*). This list, interestingly, deals exclusively with interpersonal relationships, the life of the community. That the church is thus viewed as a *koinonia* of love is made certain by vs. 14: "Above all"—not just as some "crowning virtue," but as the fundamental reality of life within the body of Christ, one is to "put on love," the bond which makes possible that "perfection" in community which, for this writer, is the essence of the new life in Christ (cf. 1:28).

From 3:12 ff. it is apparent that this writer shares the Pauline understanding of love as the power of the new life given in Christ. It is not simply one "virtue" among others. Moreover, the forms it takes within the community of brethren are expressive of the divine love which has brought the church into being: "Just as the Lord has forgiven you, so you also are to do" (vs. 13b). The brethren have been "called" into one body and its peace is "the peace of Christ" himself which will guide its life. The triad familiar to Paul, "faith, love, hope" (I Cor. 13:13; Gal. 5:5-6; I Thess. 1:3) is also present here (1:4-5; cf. esp. Philem. 5 and I Thess. 1:3), and there is a momentary coupling of love and the Spirit in 1:8: Epaphras "has made known to us your love in the Spirit" (*RSV*). But in keeping with the affirmation of 3:1 ff. that the believer has already been "raised with Christ" (which contradicts Rom. 6:3 ff.[78]), the Pauline notion of the Spirit as the "first fruits" and "down payment" of what is to come, and thus the guiding power of the new creation, does not appear at all.[79]

Colossians has nothing specifically to say about *loving* outsiders, but there is an interesting, general counsel about a Christian's conduct toward them in 4:5-6: "Walk in wisdom toward outsiders. . . ." Earlier in the letter much had been said about God's "wisdom" (1:9, 28; 2:3; 3:16),[80] and in one instance it is linked with the "mystery" of Christ which is revealed to the

---

[78] See my discussion of this in *Theology and Ethics in Paul,* pp. 171-76.

[79] Therefore, Spicq reads too much into 1:8 when he finds an "emphasis . . . on the nature of love," as "the authentic charity possessed by the interior man in whom the Holy Spirit lives" (*Agape in the New Testament,* II: 246). There is no further reference to God's Spirit in Colossians; "spirit" is used anthropologically in 2:5.

[80] Lohse correctly links these passages with the admonition of 4:5 (*Die Briefe an die Kolosser und an Philemon,* p. 237).

members of his body as they are knit together in love (2:2-3). To "walk in wisdom" is, then, to let the "peace of Christ" reign in love in one's life (3:14-15), and this will affect one's relationships with outsiders as well as his relationships within the church. A specific, probably frequently encountered instance of the former is cited in 4:6. When asked a question—or offered a challenge—respecting his faith, the Christian should answer graciously and temperately: his speech should be "seasoned with salt" (*RSV*).[81]

Ephesians

Love is emphasized even more in Ephesians than in Colossians, and here it has a place within the writer's view of the primordial unity of God's church. Consequently, love is spoken of exclusively as a way of life within the church itself. Regarding the immoral and the apostate, it is simply said, "Don't have anything to do with them" (5:7). Paul's dialectical eschatology ("we are being saved, we shall be saved" [82]) is no more present here than in Colossians, although this writer does stress, as Colossians did not, the Spirit of God as God's power resident within the community of believers (2:22) as his mighty word (6:17) which makes the church one (4:3-4), strengthens its individual members (3:16) and provides it access to God (2:18; cf. 5:18; 6:18). But there is no clear identification of the power of the Spirit with the power of love, and the operative concept for the Spirit's work is not its "leading" as in Paul, but its "sealing" (in baptism: 1:13; 4:30). While the Spirit is referred to as the medium of revelation (e.g., to the apostles and prophets, 3:5), this is not related to the ordinary Christian's practical conduct.

In Ephesians love is spoken of first of all as the substance of God's own purpose for his people (1:5-7). He "destined" them "in love," bestowing upon them his grace and forgiveness through Christ the Beloved. Here creation and redemption are intimately related, and it is God's purposeful love which moves through

[81] Cf. Mark 9:50 (discussed above, p. 73) where, however, the reference is to relationships within the church.

[82] See my *Theology and Ethics in Paul*, pp. 122-35.

122

them both. God's love has recreated his people by bringing them to life in Christ (2:4-7). Elsewhere in Ephesians love is spoken of primarily as a mode of the Christian's own conduct, but the origin and motive for this love are clearly in the divine purpose and way of love: "And walk in love, as Christ loved us and gave himself up for us . . ." (5:2 *RSV*). As in Paul's own letters, the imperative inheres in the indicative.

Several love passages in Colossians have parallels here. One of the most important of these is in the "code of household responsibilities" which both writers have incorporated into their exhortations. In Colossians husbands had been urged to love their wives (3:19). In keeping with his concern for the church as Christ's body, the author of Ephesians now uses marriage as a metaphor to describe the relationship Christ bears to the church (5:25 ff.). Christ's "love" for his church is mediated through baptism and the word, and its effect is to cleanse and to sanctify (vss. 26-27).[83] Thereby Christ "nourishes" and "cherishes" the church, for it is his own body (vss. 29-30). In returning to exhortation, Gen. 2:24 is cited (vs. 31), and its implication for marriage is specified (vs. 33): since a husband and a wife become one flesh, the husband should love his wife "as himself" and the wife should respect her husband. Although this exhortation is developed on the basis of Gen. 2:24, that text is in effect being used to show what the "as yourself" of Lev. 19:18 (or of Jesus' Great Commandment) can mean in a particular case. In loving their wives husbands love their "own bodies" (vs. 28), for husband and wife are one flesh. Hence, there is more attention given in Ephesians than in Colossians to the meaning of love in marriage, but this is due to the writer's interest in the use of marriage as a metaphor for Christ's relationship of love to his church.

The specifically ecclesial dimensions of love predominate in most of the remaining passages as well, for the church is presented as the indispensable manifestation of the cosmic reconciliation which God has accomplished through Christ's death. In

---

[83] Cf. I Thess. 4:4 where Paul himself had written about taking a wife in "sanctification and honor" according to God's will. Does the writer of Ephesians build on that concept in developing his metaphor in 5:25 ff.?

Christ and thus in his body, the church, all men (Jew and Gentile) find a new identity as "fellow citizens" and "members of the household of God" (2:11-3:6). This unity in Christ is "the mystery" heretofore hidden in God (3:9, 10) but now made plain to those who, by incorporation into Christ's body, have been "rooted and grounded in love" (3:17 RSV). The latter phrase is parallel to "rooted and built up in him and established in the faith" (Col. 2:7 RSV) and therefore an exegesis of it. To be "built up in [Christ]" is taken as meaning, "to be grounded in love," an interpretation which is thoroughly Pauline (e.g., I Cor. 8:1) and also in accord with the perspective of Colossians.[84] Similarly, where Colossians speaks of God making known the "mystery" and of preaching the "wisdom" of the gospel that every man may become "a mature member of Christ's body" (1:27, 28 NEB), Ephesians speaks of knowing "the love of Christ which surpasses knowledge, that you may be filled with all the fullness of God" (3:19 RSV).

In one instance, however, a direct reference to love in Colossians is significantly altered in the Ephesians parallel. The writer of Colossians, after listing a number of community virtues (3: 12-13), had said, "Above all these put on love, which binds everything together in perfect harmony" (3:14 RSV). In Eph. 4:2, four of the same virtues are listed, but instead of being given a special place above and beyond them all, "love" is mentioned only in connection with forbearance: "forbearing one another in love" (RSV).[85] In Ephesians it is not "love" but "peace" which is identified as the essence of the Spirit's working for unity and life within the church: "eager to maintain the unity of the Spirit

---

[84] Spicq, however, seeks the parallel of Eph. 3:17 in Col. 2:2 which he translates as "instructed in love" (*Agape in the New Testament*, II: 260). While it is true that "love" in Eph. 3:17 refers first of all to the divine love by which the believer knows his life to be given and sustained (*ibid.*, p. 261), the ecclesial dimensions of love are also in mind. Moreover, it is going quite beyond the text to say that, according to Eph. 3:17, love's "only activity is contemplation," the movement toward "union with God" (*ibid.*, pp. 267-68). Cf. Warnach, *Agape. Die Liebe als Grundmotiv*, pp. 135-36.

[85] It may be, as Spicq suggests, that this is a christianization of the Stoic principle, "Bear and forbear." In contrast this writer "is not proposing insensitivity or cold resignation, but fraternal loving patience" (*Agape in the New Testament*, II: 270).

in the bond of peace" (4:3 *RSV*). The peace of God is regarded
(perhaps in analogy to the renowned *Pax Romana*) as God's
cosmic Rule which gives unity by joining all things in common
obedience to the divine Sovereign (2:14, 15, 17). In keeping with
this is the rather surprising omission of "love" from the inventory
of the Christian's armor in Eph. 6:13-17. Paul had listed faith,
love, and hope (I Thess. 5:8); for this writer it is truth, righteousness, the "gospel of *peace*," faith, salvation, and the Spirit.
In Colossians there is only the one reference to "Christ's peace"
which rules in the church as a result of the binding love put on
by the members of Christ's body (3:14).

In Ephesians the concept of cosmic peace is also closely associated with love. In relation to God's purpose in creation love
itself has a "cosmic" dimension (1:5), and "peace and love"
stand together in the benediction at 6:23. Moreover, the repeated
exhortations to conduct oneself in love toward others (4:1-3, 15-
16; 4:25–5:2) may be viewed as appeals to make God's peace
manifest within the practical life of the church. Love is the
church's life force (4:16) and shows itself in the openness and
honesty which should characterize relationships among the
brethren: they are to "speak the truth in love" with their "neighbors," for they are one in Christ (4:15, 25).[86]

The appeal of 4:25 to "speak the truth with [one's] neighbor"
opens a series of exhortations which finds its climax in 5:1-2 to
"walk in love" as Christ himself loved. Just as the opening appeal echoes Zech. 8:16 (with the added note that Christians are
members of one another), so the very next one (vs. 26) recalls
Ps. 4:5 (English tr.: 4:4). The *NEB* translation is typical of the
way the verse is often read: "If you are angry, do not let anger
lead you into sin"; that is, anger is human, but it should not be
vented in ways that harm others. But vss. 27, 31 imply that "the
devil" and all anger should be put away completely. Therefore,
the intention must not be to distinguish between "anger" and

---

[86] Spicq apparently takes "the truth" as a reference to "the orthodox
faith" for he interprets "speaking ["professing"] the truth" (4:15) as "living as an authentic believer" (*Agape in the New Testament*, II: 272-73).
Spicq's error here, as so often, is his preoccupation with texts which contain
the *word* "love." In this case it leads him to interpret 4:15 on the basis of
Eph. 3:17 and causes him to overlook the real parallel which is in 4:25.

"sin," but to say (in a paradoxical formulation) that where anger (sin) exists it should be expelled forthwith.[87] In vs. 28 the Decalogue's eighth commandment is given a positive twist: the thief is to become an honest worker (cf. I Thess. 4:11; II Thess. 3:7-12) and even a philanthropist, giving to the needy! Relationships among the brethren are still of concern in vs. 29: one's conversation should always be constructive, only such as to "build up" the body of Christ (cf. 4:15, 25). God's Spirit by which the brethren were "sealed" into Christ at their baptism is honored when malice is purged from their lives and when kindness, compassion, and forgiveness reign in its place (vss. 30-32).

Throughout the hortatory paragraphs of Ephesians the call into a new life of peace and love is grounded in the *Pax Dei* which has already been established in Christ's church; Christians are to "walk worthily" of their calling (4:1). Since membership in Christ's body is membership with one another (4:25) and believers have been forgiven by God in Christ (4:32; 5:2) and are "beloved children" (5:1), to "walk worthily" means to "walk in love" (5:2).

The Pastoral Epistles

The author of I, II Timothy and Titus has little interest in theological discourse and really no patience for it. The polemic he engages in is not developed theologically, and the exhortations which figure so prominently throughout his writing are seldom given an explicit theological basis. What "theology" is present here is rather secondhand. *This writer uses traditional theological ideas but does not himself think theologically.*[88] Even though we should not expect to find a love ethic as such in these epistles, it will be interesting to see to what extent a very prac-

---

[87] See Hans Conzelmann in *Die kleineren Briefe des Apostels Paulus,* 9th ed., *NTD* 8 (Göttingen: Vandenhoeck & Ruprecht, 1962): 181. "Let not the sun go down on your anger" is a Pythagorean saying, in later Christian literature ascribed to Jesus.

[88] See M. Dibelius, *Die Pastoralbriefe,* 3rd ed. rev. H. Conzelmann, *HNT* 13 (Tübingen: J. C. B. Mohr [Paul Siebeck]: 7; F. D. Gealy, *IntB* XI: 364.

tical-minded churchman of the early second century retains and
employs the teaching on love of the apostle he seeks to follow.

A unique feature of the Pastorals is the high frequency of
words for love formed on the Greek root φιλ-, but a study of these
would not take us very far.[89] Nor are the two occurrences of the
verb for *agape* love very helpful (II Tim. 4:8, 10). The phrase
"all who have loved his appearing" (vs. 8 *RSV*) describes Christians who, like Paul (vs. 7), have "kept the faith" and have not
given up hope in Christ's eventual return. In contrast to these
stands unfaithful Demas, who "has loved the present age" (vs.
10).

This writer does not often refer to God's own love, mercy, or
forgiveness; however two passages are worth considering in this
connection. In I Tim. 1:13-16 there is mention of God's mercy
toward Paul himself, "the foremost of sinners" (*RSV*). Here also
are references to the "grace" of the Lord, to the "faith and love"
which are in Christ Jesus, and to his "perfect patience." Titus
3:4-7 speaks more generally of the justifying grace in Jesus
Christ for all believers which is expressive of God's "goodness,"
"philanthropy," and "mercy." It is clear that Titus 3:4-7 is
meant to ground the imperatives which precede (vss. 1-2) and
follow (vss. 8-11).[90]

The most typical and frequent references to love in the Pastorals are in lists of Christian virtues, usually along with "faith"
(I Tim. 2:15; 4:12; 6:11; II Tim. 2:22; 3:10; Titus 2:2).[91] Only
at II Tim. 1:7 does "love" occur in a list from which "faith" is
absent, yet nowhere is there indication that the conjunction of the
ideas, when it does occur, carries any special theological meaning. In these lists "love" invariably stands as simply one among

[89] Most of the instances of these words are listed and discussed in the
Appendix.

[90] The only other passage which speaks directly of the divine love is II
Tim. 1:13 (parallel to I Tim. 1:14): "the faith and love which are in Christ
Jesus" (*RSV*). But the surrounding exhortations to follow Paul's words
(vs. 13) and to "guard the truth" (vs. 14) suggest the primary reference
may be to the love and faithfulness required of one who looks to Christ
Jesus as Savior.

[91] In three of these passages "steadfastness" (ὑπομονή) is also listed (I
Tim. 6:11; II Tim. 3:10; Titus 2:2), thus recalling the triadic formula "faith,
love, hope [ἐλπίς]" we have met in Paul and in Colossians.

127

several desirable characteristics of the Christian life. What Spicq says about the meaning of love in II Tim. 3:10 must—in spite of Spicq's own judgment to the contrary—be said of its meaning *throughout* these lists: "It is no longer the soul of the Christian life as it was in I Corinthians 13, or the résumé and the plenitude of the Law (Rom. 13:10). It has become a 'virtue' among others, almost on the same level as moderation, purity, and patience." [92]

I Tim. 1:5 requires special attention for here, unquestionably, love receives a certain emphasis. Timothy is told that the whole aim of his ministry should be "love which springs from a pure heart, a good conscience, and genuine faith." This charge must be interpreted in accord with the whole teaching of these epistles. Unlike Paul in whose letters "conscience" plays a minor role as a *neutral* faculty for assessing one's own actions, conscience is an important concept here and may be described as either "good" (I Tim. 1:5, 19) and "pure" (I Tim. 3:9; II Tim. 1:3; cf. Titus 1:15) or evil (I Tim. 4:2; Titus 1:15). Moreover, in the Pastorals "faith" means primarily faithfulness to the apostolic tradition, so the adjective "genuine" applied to it has a special meaning (I Tim. 1:5; II Tim. 1:5). Thus, I Tim. 1:5 is only superficially parallel to Gal. 5:6 which speaks of "faith working in love." Paul had understood faith as the believer's response to God's love, the receiving of God's Spirit (the power of the new age) as the guiding power of his new life. For Paul faith was obedience in a radical sense and obedience took shape in love. But now in I Timothy love is said to be dependent upon one's adherence to the apostolic teaching, by means of which one can act with a "pure heart" (also a non-Pauline concept) and a "good conscience." That is, in remaining true to "the faith" the Christian can depend upon his "heart" and "conscience" to show him what love requires.[93]

---

[92] *Agape in the New Testament,* II: 419.

[93] Spicq, who reckons Paul as the author of the Pastorals, has a quite different view of I Tim. 1:5 (*Agapè dans le Nouveau Testament,* III: 14-15). He believes that a catechetical formulation of the double commandment has been used here and that the phrase ἐκ καθαρᾶς καρδίας should not be rendered *"from* a pure heart" (*RSV;* cf. *NEB, JB*) but *"with* a pure heart" as in Jesus' Great Commandment. (The same expression appears in II

Far more important than the concept of love in the Pastorals is the writer's concern for "godliness" (εὐσέβεια).[94] There is no equivalent term in Hebrew, for this is a distinctly Hellenistic concept, the root meaning of which is to show "reverence" and "respect," especially for the various structures of society, for "the establishment." [95] Since, in the Graeco-Roman view, the gods stood behind these social structures and supported them, respect for the structures was at the same time respect for the gods—hence, "piety," "godliness," even "religion." This meaning of the term is well attested in I Tim. 5:4 where the RSV aptly translates it as "religious duty" (to the family). This author's concern for social structures is possible because the Christian eschatological hope is for him only a formal item of faith (e.g. I Tim. 6:14-16). He presumes that history will continue into an indefinite future and that the church must find its place within the social order.[96] I Tim. 2:1-2 shows his position very well. He urges prayers for "all men," including the non-Christian governing authorities, "in order that we may lead a quiet and peaceable life [βίον], in every regard pious and respectful" (cf. 4:7b-8; 6:11—where in summing up his advice the writer refers first of all to the need for "righteousness" and "godliness" [closely related terms in his vocabulary], and only in the second instance to "faith" and "love").

It is this "piety" which should rule the church's interior life

---

Tim. 2:22.) But this one prepositional phrase is exceedingly slender evidence for Spicq's hypothesis, and his exegesis takes no account of the meanings of "heart," "conscience," and "faith" in the Pastorals overall. It is quite arbitrary (even if, for the sake of argument, we grant Paul's authorship of these epistles) to say that I Tim. 1:5 refers to "faculties of the interior man regenerated by the Holy Spirit" (p. 15).

[94] Thirteen of the twenty-two New Testament occurrences of the word group occur here. It is surprising how often this important concept has been overlooked in discussions of the Pastorals. M. Goguel, e.g., never once mentions it in his analysis of this writer's ethic (*The Primitive Church*, pp. 481-84). While Wendland does recognize its importance, he has little to say about its meaning (*Ethik des Neuen Testaments*, p. 96).

[95] See Foerster in *ThWB* VII, esp. pp. 177-78, 181-83.

[96] Stuhlmacher ("Christliche Verantwortung," p. 184) is correct that in the Pastorals the Pauline *eschatological* distinction between the Christian community and outsiders is practically abandoned. The distinction between these two is now defined primarily in doctrinal and moral terms, with respect to *belief* and to *conduct*.

as well. Anger, quarreling, and violence have no place there (I Tim. 2:8; 3:3; Titus 3:2-3). Moreover, godliness requires constructive good deeds (Titus 3:14), and those officially enrolled as "widows" have particular responsibilities in caring for the needy (I Tim. 5:10). Restraint should be practiced in matters of church discipline whether the offender be an official (I Tim. 5:20-22) or a layman (Titus 3:10-11). In the latter case admonition alone is to be administered. If that fails the offending brother is simply to be ignored, on the grounds that he has already, by his factiousness, condemned himself. The brethren are not to judge one another in any final sense, but are to leave that to God, "the righteous judge" (II Tim. 4:8).

Conclusion

By itself a study of the love ethic in these deutero-Pauline materials can neither overthrow nor uphold the judgment that they are not Paul's own. For instance, we should not require that the full Pauline teaching on love present in the seven clearly authentic letters be exhibited in *each* of the letters of doubtful authenticity. In fact it is not. But in Colossians and Ephesians love is still the central content of the gospel's gift and demand. Although it is no longer seen as the power of the new age of which the *Spirit's* presence and guidance are a foretaste, it is regarded still as the life force of Christian community and the substance of Christian moral action. The special circumstances (of persecution, apostasy, heresy) in and for which II Thessalonians was written permit no final assessment of what love means there. The Pastorals do provide sufficient data for some conclusions, however; and the chief of these must be that in them love is not a central ethical concept, but one virtue among several. The church is no longer regarded as an eschatological community in which love operates as the Spirit's powerful presence. It is, rather, an enclave of God's people in the world and in history, trying to be, simultaneously, faithful to the apostolic tradition and respectful of the social order in which it must exist.

None of these writers shows concern, as had Paul himself, for identifying love as the sum of the law; the problem of law and

130

gospel, Jew and Gentile within the church belongs to the past. Only in Ephesians is there somewhat more than a merely formal or passing interest in defining love's gift and demand with reference to the cross: 2:13, 16; 5:2. But even in Ephesians love is understood first of all with reference to the cosmic peace of God. In Colossians love is emphasized as the power of Christ triumphant, risen and reigning, while in the Pastorals, where love plays only a small role anyway, theological and christological sanctions for the ethic are almost entirely lacking.

IV
THE JOHANNINE LITERATURE:
LOVE ONE ANOTHER

The Fourth Gospel

Introductory Observations

Love is an important theme in the Gospel of John, and it is
quite understandable that Jerome would pass on the tradition
that this evangelist in his latter years reduced his whole mes-

sage to the simple command, "My little children, love one another." [1]

This command has deep roots in Johannine theology. Specifically, the relationship between God the Father and Jesus the Son is often described by reference to the Father's love (3:35; 5: 20; 10:17; 15:9; 17:23, 26) which was bestowed upon Jesus "before the foundation of the world" (17:24 *RSV*). Jesus thus "abides" in God's love (15:10) and by doing what God commands him shows his love for the Father (14:31a). This evangelist also speaks of God's love for "the world" (3:16 [2]) and for those within the world who keep his commandments (14:21, 23; 17:23, 26) or—what amounts to the same thing—who "love" the Son (16: 27). Closely related are the passages which mention Jesus' love for "his own," that is, for his disciples (13:1, 34; 14:21; 15:9, 12; cf. 15:10; 17:26). Occasionally there are references to Jesus' love for specific individuals: an unnamed disciple (13:23; 19:26; 20:2), Mary and Martha (11:5), and Lazarus (11:3, 5, 36; cf. 11:11).

In yet another group of passages[3] believers are *commanded* to love. There is no instance in this Gospel of a direct command to "love God," nor are there even the occasional references to man's love for God which are to be found in Paul's letters. On the other hand, the command to love the Son is often present, either explicitly or implicitly (14:15, 21, 23; 15:9, 10; 16:27; cf. 8:42; 14:24, 28), and in view of this evangelist's Christology loving the Son would be tantamount to loving the Father by

[1] Cited by Raymond E. Brown, *The Gospel According to John*, AB 29, 29A (Garden City, N. Y.: Doubleday & Co., 1966, 1970): 607. I regard this Gospel, like the Synoptics, as anonymous. It was written apparently at the end of the first century or very early in the second.

[2] Some (including, recently, Ernst Käsemann, *The Testament of Jesus: A Study of John in the Light of Chapter 17*, trans. G. Krodel [Philadelphia: Fortress Press, 1968], p. 60) contend that this famous affirmation of God's love was formulated in pre-Johannine Christian tradition and that too much weight should not be placed on it when characterizing the evangelist's own view. Even Bultmann, however, identifies the verse directly with the evangelist himself (*The Gospel of John: A Commentary*, trans. G. R. Beasley-Murray et al. [Philadelphia: Westminster Press, 1971], pp. 153-54, notes 1 and 3), and most commentators concur.

[3] For our purposes there is little need to discuss the two instances where the verb ἀγαπᾶν is used *in malam partem*, of man's preferring darkness to light (3:19) and the praise of other men to the praise of God (12:43).

133

whom he has been sent. (Although it is doubtful that chap. 21 was an original part of this Gospel or comes from the same hand, we may also note the dialogue there between Jesus and Peter in which the disciple is asked three times whether he "loves" Jesus, and repeatedly answers that he does, vss. 15-17). There is, finally, a series of emphatic commands to "love one another" (13:34, 35; 15:12, 13, 17) which, of course, are particularly important for the purposes of this present study.

If we pay attention to the Greek words employed for "love" in the above passages, we shall discover that, while the *agape* group is most frequent, the verb one normally thinks of as meaning "friendly love" is also sometimes used. Thus, both words occur, apparently interchangeably, in statements about the Father's love for the Son, God's love for Jesus' disciples, Jesus' love for Lazarus, and Jesus' love for the "beloved disciple." [4] Moreover, both verbs are used in the Jesus-Peter dialogue of 21:15-17. None of the attempts which have been made to draw profound distinctions between these two Johannine words for love can be judged successful. The Johannine usage provides added evidence for the recent lexicographical conclusion that the words could be used as synonyms.[5] Indeed, from 15:12-17 it is apparent that for this evangelist *agape* is precisely that love which links Jesus to his disciples in "friendship." In this Gospel, as elsewhere in the New Testament, our study of the love ethic cannot be tied exclusively to the passages where the term *agape* and its cognates appear.

Any study of the love ethic in the Fourth Gospel will be centered necessarily on the "Farewell Discourses" of chaps. 13–17, for the love commandments as such are all to be found there. In a helpful excursus on the literary genre of these discourses, Raymond Brown has pointed out the many similarities between them and other biblical and postbiblical speeches ascribed to famous men anticipating their own death—a prominent example of which are the *Testaments of the Twelve Patriarchs*.[6] Quite regularly, as Brown indicates, testamentary addresses, like the

---

[4] The instances have been listed by Brown, *The Gospel According to John*, p. 498.

[5] See below, Appendix, pp. 223-27.

[6] *The Gospel According to John*, pp. 598-600, 611.

discourses in John 13–17, contain exhortations to keep the commandments of God, especially the commandment to love one another (e.g., Moses in Deut. 30:16; Abraham in Jub. 20:2; 21:5; 36:3-4) and thus to manifest the unity of the brethren, for example Zebulun (8:5-6) and Joseph (17:3) in *Test. XII Patr.* In the Fourth Gospel Jesus, like the patriarchs of old, is portrayed as preparing his own people (in Jesus' case, his "friends," his disciples) for his imminent departure. He gives them words of counsel and comfort which are designed to strengthen them in his absence and to help them maintain their corporate identity as *his* people even under difficult circumstances. The Johannine commandments to "love one another" are at the very center of the moral and spiritual legacy which is presented in the Farewell Discourses.

The Farewell Commandment

In the first twelve chapters of this Gospel, attention had been focused largely on Jesus as the "light" and "life" of men. Those who follow Jesus had been described as coming out of the darkness into light (3:16-21), out of death into life (5:24). As disciples they "hear" and "abide" in Jesus' word because they know and believe that he is the way to life (5:24; 8:31). From 12:26 it is apparent that this evangelist conceives of discipleship ("following") in rather concrete terms as "serving" Jesus. Just as the writer regards seeing and believing in Jesus as seeing and believing in God himself (12:44-45), so he would surely regard the disciple's service of Jesus as his service of God himself. For what Jesus speaks and does he speaks and does as one sent from God, with God's own authority and in obedience to God's commandment (6:38; 12:49). Since Jesus has been sent on a saving mission to the world, to bring it eternal life (3:16; 12:47), the divine commandment under which that whole mission is conducted can itself be identified quite directly with eternal life: "And I know that his commandment is eternal life" (12:50 RSV). On this note the first half of the Gospel concludes.

It is indicative of this evangelist's understanding of the meaning of eternal life that the second half of his Gospel opens with a scene in which the divine commandment is further accentuated, now in connection with Jesus' love for his own and their responsibility to manifest that love in their lives. The scene for the Farewell Discourses of chaps. 13–17 is set in 13:1-2, but what is most important here is not the information that it is Passover eve and that Jesus is at supper with his disciples. Much more significant is the declaration that Jesus "loved his own who were in the world . . ." (vs. 1 *RSV*). There is a certain parallelism between this verse and the affirmation of 3:16 that the Son's whole saving mission to and in the world was one of love, and there is some point in Spicq's judgment that these two verses together "constitute the theological framework of the Gospel." [7] For now, in these last discourses, Jesus' parting commandment is that the disciples should love one another just as he has loved them.

Significantly, the only extended narrative passage in chaps. 13–17 comes at the very first, in chap. 13 which tells of Jesus' washing his disciples' feet, their response to this surprising action, and Jesus' explanation of it. In a conversation between Jesus and Peter (spokesman for the group) the footwashing is interpreted as a sign of the participation in Jesus to which a disciple is called: "If I do not wash you . . . you are not in fellowship with me" (vs. 8 *NEB*). Subsequently, in Jesus' discourse in vss. 12 ff., his action is commended to the disciples as an "example" for them to follow in their relationships with one another (vss. 14-15). These two interpretations are closely related. Jesus' washing of his disciples' feet is an acted parable—or perhaps we should even say, an *actual instance*—of the divine mission of love for which the Father has sent him. To become a disciple requires, first of all, receiving that love to good effect in one's own life, but then also acknowledging the *commission* it lays upon one to serve in love as the Son has served. Bultmann rightly emphasizes the importance of the formula of vs. 15: "Just as *I* have done *for you*, so also *you* should do. . . ." Jesus has provided not just an ideal model or pattern to be imitated. His action

[7] *Agape in the New Testament,* III: 32.

becomes "exemplary" insofar as his disciples themselves have been served by his love. They are obligated by what they themselves have received.[8] The "following" and "serving" motif we have noted in 12:26 is also present here.[9]

The climax of the whole scene comes in vss. 34, 35 where Jesus, after a somber reference to his imminent departure, leaves with his disciples "a new commandment" which is "to love one another." Whereas Paul and the Synoptic writers consistently use the word "commandment(s)" to refer to the ordinances of the Old Testament law,[10] it is never used in this way by the Fourth Evangelist for whom "the law" as such is only rarely (1:17; cf. 5:39-47) a matter of direct concern. Instead, he uses it, on the one hand, with reference to the commandment from God by which Jesus' whole mission in the world is directed (10:18; 12:49-50; 14:31; 15:10), and on the other hand with reference to the commandment(s) given by Jesus to his disciples (13:34; 14:15, 21; 15:10, 12; cf. 15:17) to love one another.[11] The alternation between the singular ("commandment," 13:34; 15:12) and plural ("commandments," 14:15, 21; 15:10) has little significance. It certainly cannot be taken as reflecting a conviction that the many commandments of the old law are summed up in the one commandment to love, for there is no evidence that this evangelist thinks in those terms.[12] It may be that the plural indicates his consciousness of the need for the one commandment to be radiated "out into the manifoldness of the obedient life,"[13] but it is

[8] *The Gospel of John,* p. 476.

[9] Cf. the remarks by H. D. Betz, *Nachfolge und Nachahmung,* pp. 39-40.

[10] There are no exceptions in Paul; the only exception in the Synoptics is Luke 15:29 where the prodigal's elder brother claims he has obeyed every command given to him by his father.

[11] Once the term is used of human orders—those given by the chief priests and Pharisees that persons knowing Jesus' whereabouts should inform them (11:57).

[12] Thus, I do not understand what E. C. Hoskyns means by, or how his reference to 8:31 is relevant to, his comment on 14:15: "The commandments of the Lord are His, because they are the fulfilment of the Law" (*The Fourth Gospel,* rev. ed., ed. by F. N. Davey [London: Faber and Faber, 1947], p. 458). In a comment on 13:34-35 he suggests that the new commandment is a "supplementation of the old commandment to love the neighbour . . ." (p. 451). Neither comment is true to this evangelist's conception of the "new commandment."

[13] Schrenk in *ThD* II: 554.

137

more likely that the alternation is only an accident of style. The term *logos* ("word") is also used to refer to the command Jesus brings, and the same variation between singular (8: 51-52; 14: 23; 15: 20; 17: 6) and plural (14: 24; cf. 12: 47 where a different Greek term for "words" is used) is present.[14]

Why is the commandment to love one another given in 13: 34 as "a *new* commandment"? It would have been clear enough to the evangelist and his readers that the substance of the command—to love one another—was by no means novel or unheard of: parallels abound in the Old Testament, in the rabbinic traditions, and in other literature of the Graeco-Roman world. Although the adjective is used nowhere else in this Gospel, the conviction is implicit throughout that Jesus' mission—his incarnation, death, and glorification—has instituted and constitutes for believers a decisively *new* situation. As the bearer of the Father's love Jesus has replaced darkness with light and death with life. Thus, the newness of the command to love one another consists in the christological-eschatological context in which it is given. The one who commands such love is the bringer of the new age which makes love possible and meaningful, so the command is that his followers should love *as he has loved them* (vs. 34). The whole scene had been introduced with a declaration of the Son's love for his own (vs. 1), it has emphasized that such love is expressed in selfless service of others (vss. 4 ff.), and now it concludes with a commandment grounded neither in merely prudential considerations nor in Scripture, but solely in the new reality of God's love manifest in the Son. "What is thus an imperative is only made so by an indicative."[15]

To the extent that one sees in the footwashing scene the

---

[14] See Bultmann, *The Gospel of John,* p. 541, n. 4, and Brown, *The Gospel According to John,* p. 641.

[15] Goguel, *The Primitive Church,* p. 465. Cf. Bultmann, *The Gospel of John,* pp. 526-27. Brown is quite correct in describing as "dubious" the view sometimes expressed that the newness of the commandment consists in the replacement of the "as yourself" in Lev. 19:18 with "as I have loved you" (*The Gospel According to John,* p. 613). As we have seen, the Fourth Evangelist is not concerned to define the relationship between the Christian gospel and "the law" per se. Nevertheless, the "as I have loved you" has an important place in this context and does help to define why the love command as given by Jesus can be called "new."

Johannine substitute for the institution of the eucharist which, in the Synoptics, occurs at this last meal, it may also be possible to relate this "new commandment" to the "new covenant" of which the eucharist is said to be the sign and seal (I Cor. 11:25; Luke 22:20 [in some manuscripts]).[16] The concept of "covenant" itself includes the ideas of God's faithfulness to his people and the obligation to obey his commandments which is thereby laid upon the covenant community. Paul's reference to the eucharistic liturgy in I Cor. 11:23-26 shows that the church was already interpreting Jesus' death and its celebration in the eucharist as the establishment of a new covenant between God and his people. It would be fully consonant with his stress on Jesus' mission as one of transforming love, if indeed this Fourth Evangelist is interpreting the "new covenant" as the "new commandment" to love one another which is the legacy bestowed upon his own in the world.

That the commandment to love one another forms Jesus' followers into a community and provides it its identity in the world is clearly indicated in 13:35: "By this love you have for one another, everyone will know that you are my disciples" (JB). Not just *possession* of the commandment (which in any case is not unique to the Christian community) but the manifest reality of the love it commands is to characterize Jesus' disciples.[17] When the true disciple is described as one who "abides in [Jesus'] word" (8:31), the evangelist is not thinking of adherence to doctrinal norms (as is the author of the Pastorals when he speaks of holding to Jesus' word[s], e.g. I Tim. 6:3; cf. 4:6; Titus 1:9), but of "abiding" in Jesus himself and thus in Jesus' love. These are the themes of 15:1 ff. where Jesus is presented as the true vine and those who belong to him as its branches. Just as branches bear no fruit unless they remain in the vine, so apart from Jesus his followers can do nothing (vss. 4-5). But where they "abide" they are fruitful, and this is the sign of true discipleship (vs. 8). The evangelist is very explicit about the life force of this

---

[16] The connection between the new commandment and the new covenant is worked out in some detail by Brown, *The Gospel According to John*, pp. 612-14. Cf. Michel, "Das Gebot der Nächstenliebe," p. 76, n. 2.

[17] Cf. the remarks of Michel, "Das Gebot der Nächstenliebe," p. 78, and Bultmann, *The Gospel of John*, p. 528.

vine and the fruit of its branches being *love:* "Just as the Father has loved me, so have I loved you: abide in my love" (vs. 9). Jesus has remained faithful to his mission to the world by keeping the Father's commandments and remaining in his love, and in like manner his disciples are to remain faithful in their discipleship by keeping the Son's commandments and remaining in his love (vs. 10; cf. 14:15, 21, 23-24).

The meaning of the love command is further detailed in 15: 12-17 which moves beyond the vine-branches metaphor without, however, quite leaving it behind (the disciples, we are told, were sent out to "bear fruit," vs. 16). Jesus' love for his own is once more stressed as the ground for their obedience to the commandment to love one another (vs. 12; cf. vs. 9; 13:15, 34). The highest and noblest form of this love, we are told in the next verse (vs. 13), is to give one's life for one's friends. This idea, like the love command itself, is not unique to Christianity[18] and may be formulated here in accord with some known proverb.[19] But Dibelius is not persuasive in his argument that vss. 13-15 do not fit well into the total context.[20] His point is that vs. 13 represents a "heroic" view of love not otherwise characteristic of this Gospel which views love not in an "ethical" but in a "metaphysical" perspective—as constituting the Father's unity with his Son and the Son's unity with his own.[21] He holds, moreover, that except in 10:11 and 11:50 (and perhaps also 3:16) this evangelist does not interpret Jesus' death as a sacrifice for others,[22] and since there is no explicit mention of *Jesus'* death in connection with 15:13, the meaning there is quite a general one.[23]

[18] Brown, *The Gospel According to John,* p. 664, quotes Plato, "Only those who love wish to die for others" (*Symposium* 179B), and Bultmann, *The Gospel of John,* p. 542, n. 4 lists Tyrt. 6.1 ff. and the Anthol. Lyr. Gr. I. 9-10 (Diehl) as examples.

[19] So Bultmann, *The Gospel of John,* p. 542, n. 7; Brown, *The Gospel According to John,* p. 682; above all M. Dibelius, "Joh. 15, 13: Eine Studie zum Traditionsproblem des Johannes-evangeliums," *Botschaft und Geschichte: Gesammelte Aufsätze,* I, ed. H. Kraft and G. Bornkamm (Tübingen: J. C. B. Mohr [Paul Siebeck], 1953): 204-20.

[20] He regards vss. 14-15 as a kind of "midrashic digression" prompted by the proverb of vs. 13 ("Joh. 15, 13," p. 206) and suggests that vs. 16 is a later gloss (p. 205, n. 3).

[21] *Ibid.,* pp. 208 ff.

[22] *Ibid.,* pp. 214 ff.

[23] *Ibid.,* p. 216.

Dibelius, however, has seriously undervalued the references in 3:16; 10:11; 11:50 to Jesus' death for others. These verses should not be regarded as exceptions, for in the context of each there is a clear emphasis on the death of Jesus as a life-giving event for his people (see 3:14-15, 17-21; 10:10, 12-18; 11:1-44). Moreover, Dibelius' sharp distinction between the "ethical" and "metaphysical" views of love is not true to Johannine thought, as chap. 13 shows especially well. In this Gospel there is a concern that the *meaning* of the love which unites the Father to the Son and the Son to his followers find expression in very concrete ways (13:12-26). The connection between love's "ethical" and "metaphysical" sides is further illustrated in 15:1-11 where, as we have seen, abiding in love (metaphysical) and bearing the fruit of love (ethical) are vitally interrelated.

It is inevitable, then, that the reader (ancient or modern) of this Gospel would interpret the saying of 15:13 in the light of the evangelist's conviction that Jesus' own death was the culmination ("It has been accomplished," 19:30) of his whole mission of love (3:16). But have we not been led to expect, by Jesus' teaching in the Synoptic Gospels, that love for *enemies* is "greater than" love for one's "friends"? Is not love's scope restricted here to a closed circle from whom one may expect love in return? [24] This question deserves special attention,[25] but for the moment it is enough to observe that the term "friends" in vs. 13 is simply another designation for the "branches" in the preceding metaphor where, in turn, the branches had been identified with Jesus' disciples (vs. 8). This is clear from vs. 14, "You are my 'friends' if you do what I command you." Friendship is not conditional upon obedience, however, but upon the Father's prior love: by abiding in his love one is both sustained and commanded. That has been the whole point of 15:1 ff. The reciprocity of God's action and man's response is presumed.

In vs. 15 a contrast is drawn between "friends" and "slaves," and thus further light is shed upon the meaning of friendship

---

[24] See, for instance, the complaint of Clayton R. Bowen, "Love in the Fourth Gospel," *JR* XIII (1933): 39-49. Also Wendland, *Ethik des Neuen Testaments,* e.g., pp. 112, 115.

[25] Below, pp. 143-48.

here. Once the disciples were slaves, now they are friends. Brown refers to the wisdom literature where the divine Sophia is said to inhabit men and make them God's friends.[26] Some commentators compare this verse with Gal. 4:1-7 and Heb. 3:5-6 where a distinction is made between "sons" and "slaves." [27] But much nearer at hand and more apt is the distinction made within this Gospel itself between sons and slaves, 8:31-36.[28] From that context it is clear that this evangelist may think of disciples as "sons" and that to be a son (in contrast to being a slave) means to be *free*. Similarly, in 15:15 we are told that to be friends (in contrast to being slaves) means to *know what the master is doing*. Barrett takes this as a reference to *understanding* God's will,[29] but knowledge in Johannine thought includes far more than that. The slave's ignorance is blindness in a comprehensive sense: not knowing what the master does means not knowing the master! [30] To be "friends," "sons," "disciples" means to know to whom one belongs and thus to be free—not just from ignorance of God's will, but from the thralldom of the world's darkness. To dispel this darkness and to bring light and life to men (to make "slaves" into "friends") is the whole point of the Son's mission.[31]

It is in these same terms that vs. 16 must be read: "You did not choose me, but I chose you and appointed you that you

[26] *The Gospel According to John,* pp. 682-83.

[27] E.g., C. K. Barrett, *The Gospel According to St. John* (London: S.P.C.K., 1955), p. 398.

[28] Bultmann refers to this, *The Gospel of John,* p. 543.

[29] *The Gospel According to St. John,* p. 398.

[30] Cf. Bultmann, *The Gospel of John,* p. 543.

[31] Spicq argues that, in vs. 15, "friends" = "confidants," those initiated "into the secrets of the divine life and into the realities which the Father has communicated to him." Thereby, "as apostles and leaders of His Church, they are entrusted with the secret of the mystery of the life of the Trinity, of God's charity, and of his providential plan for salvation in which they are called to collaborate." Consequently, Spicq is confronted with the problem raised long ago by St. Thomas: "If Jesus had made known everything to them, it would follow that the disciples would know as much as the Son." Spicq's answer is that the meaning of Jesus' words "is more intensive than extensive" (*Agape in the New Testament,* III: 45). But "knowledge" in John does not have the rationalistic-cognitive character ascribed to it by Spicq. It is to be related to *discipleship* and to *obedience,* not to the mystic apprehension of God's nature and plans. (With Spicq's comments compare those of Moffatt, *Love in the New Testament,* pp. 264-65.)

should go and bear fruit and that your fruit should abide . . ." (*RSV*). The choosing which Jesus does is the choosing of his own from out of the world. There is no evident intention here to contrast "the elect" and the "non elect," but only to contrast the life of believers with the life of those who remain enslaved to the world's claims. This is specifically indicated in vs. 19 ("I chose you out of the world") and by the fact that the whole next section (15:18–16:11) deals with the meaning and problems of being "friends" and "disciples" in a world to which God's people do not finally belong. In such a context, "election" to friendship must be regarded as the bestowal of freedom, not the withdrawal of it. Moreover, it is election to an active life of obedience, a call to bear love's fruit. Lest this principal point be missed, the love command itself is repeated—with emphasis[32]— in vs. 17.

The Farewell Discourses are concluded with Jesus' prayer to his Father (chap. 17), and the prayer itself is concluded with the earnest petition that the same love which constitutes the unity of Father and Son may move among God's people to make them one (vss. 20-26). Moreover, the departing Jesus here anticipates that insofar as the love he mediates abides in his followers, he himself will remain in them (vs. 26). As Brown notes, the promise implicit here can only be fulfilled through the Spirit's coming—which Jesus has also promised (14:16-20, 26; 15:26; 16:7-16, 22); so, as in Paul, the presence of the Spirit is the presence and power of love active within the community of faith.[33]

The Scope and Character of Love

Commentators offer widely divergent conclusions about the love ethic in the Fourth Gospel. On one side Rudolf Schnackenburg has described this evangelist as "a loyal guardian of Christ's inheritance" who, "illumined by the Holy Spirit," has given "added profundity to the commandment of love" and has raised it "to be the ruling principle of Christian morality throughout all

[32] Spicq, *Agape in the New Testament*, III: 47.
[33] *The Gospel According to John*, p. 781.

143

ages." [34] A quite contrary opinion is expressed by C. R. Bowen who finds this evangelist's view of love distinctly inferior: he teaches that God's love is conditional upon man's prior love of God [35] and by defining the greatest love as that bestowed on friends, "draws a circle that shuts most out." [36] In short, according to Bowen, this particular New Testament writer does not really understand either Jesus or the gospel.[37] A more moderate view is held by John Knox who acknowledges an *implicit* universalism in the teaching on love here, but who then suggests that the Fourth Evangelist departs from the "ethical universalism" of the Synoptic writers and the prophets and returns to the teaching of Leviticus where "love your neighbor" had meant "love those within your own group." [38]

Most recently the Johannine love ethic has come under attack by Ernst Käsemann who also finds here a severely restricted view of love's scope.[39] While Käsemann acknowledges that "John cannot conceive of love without selfless service and surrender." [40] he insists that the evangelist more characteristically thinks of love as a "communication" between persons, a mutual "self-disclosure," which "transcends even the sphere of ethical decisions." [41] Moreover, "the love of God cannot be connected with the love of the world," [42] and the Son's mission of love is *to* the world only in the sense that it is to gather the scattered elect of God together, out of the world. "The object of Christian love for John is only what belongs to the community under the Word, or what is elected to belong to it, that is, the brotherhood of Jesus." [43]

We must begin by stressing the essential correctness of Käse-

---

[34] *The Moral Teaching of the New Testament,* p. 329.
[35] "Love in the Fourth Gospel," p. 45.
[36] *Ibid.,* p. 42.
[37] *Ibid.,* p. 48—following P. Wernle.
[38] *The Ethic of Jesus,* pp. 95-96. See also Anders Nygren's discussion of the Johannine view, *Agape and Eros,* trans. Philip S. Watson (Philadelphia: Westminster Press, 1953), esp. pp. 153-55.
[39] *The Testament of Jesus,* p. 59.
[40] *Ibid.,* p. 61.
[41] *Ibid.*
[42] *Ibid.,* p. 62.
[43] *Ibid.,* p. 65.

mann's point that love in John is no mere emotion or ethical feeling. Bowen's complaint that this evangelist "is not in himself, properly speaking, an affectionate man at all, nor writes to kindle affection in his readers" [44] may or may not be true, but it really has no bearing on the Johannine conception of love. According to this conception love is first of all that which unites the Father to his Son and then the Son to his own who are in the world (17: 20-26, cf. 15: 9). This is not just a static unity between Father and Son, and Son and disciples; it is a living and moving unity. In the case of the relation between Father and Son the evangelist expresses the dynamic character of this unity by speaking of the Son's being *sent*, commanded to a mission. The relation between Jesus' *being sent* by the Father and his *oneness* with the Father is made very explicit in 17: 21-23, 25-26. Quite a wrong impression of Johannine Christology is gained if we focus exclusively on the references there to the unity of Father and Son. Equally emphasized is the Father's *sending* of his Son. The Christology of the Fourth Gospel, like that of most of the rest of the New Testament, is centered on Jesus' *function*, not his *nature*.[45]

Similarly, when this evangelist describes the relation of believers to Jesus as their *abiding* in him or in his love, he is not thinking of some sort of inert, mystical fusion with him, but of their "following," "serving," and "obeying" him as the Son "obeys" the Father. Again, the image of the vine and its branches is apt. Unity is given by a love which courses through the whole plant as its life force and enables the plant to bear fruit. Indeed, Jesus not only shows his followers the same love shown him by the Father; he also sends them out on a mission as he himself has been sent out (17:18).

Käsemann sees all this clearly, but like Dibelius he seeks to minimize the number and the significance of texts in the Gospel

---

[44] "Love in the Fourth Gospel," p. 41.

[45] Oscar Cullmann's statement is particularly applicable to the Fourth Gospel: "The Logos is the self-revealing, self-giving God—God in action. This action only is the subject of the New Testament. Therefore, all abstract speculation about the 'nature' of Christ is not only a useless undertaking, but actually an improper one" (*The Christology of the New Testament*, trans. S. Guthrie and C. Hall [Philadelphia: Westminster Press, 1959], p. 266).

145

which speak of Jesus' death as the giving of himself in love.[46] Moreover, he presumes a distinction between love expressed as self-surrender and love expressed as self-disclosure. But it is just this distinction which is overcome in the Johannine conception. By sending his Son into the world—where, after his death and resurrection, he returns to reign as the Spirit—the Father discloses himself *as* love and *in* love. This theme pervades the Gospel, and it must be borne in mind when we attempt to assess the meaning of 14:21, 23. These texts, it has been alleged, contradict the notion quite explicit in I John 4:19 that we can love only because God first loved us.[47] Here Jesus says, "He who loves me will be loved by my Father, and I will love him and manifest myself to him"; and again, "If a man loves me, he will keep my word, and my Father will love him, and we will come to him and make our home with him" (*RSV*). A similar statement is found in 16:27: "For the Father himself loves you, because you have loved me and have believed that I came from the Father" (*RSV*). It is important to observe, however, that the contexts from which these texts are drawn speak about the promised *return* of Jesus as the Paraclete, God's Spirit, and thus about the *continuing* love of God and the Son for those who belong to them. Such statements in no way contradict the fundamental declaration of the Gospel that God's Son *has already been sent* in love to men and that their seeing, believing, obeying—and "abiding in love"—is absolutely dependent upon the prior bestowal of light, life, and love.

It remains for us to consider the allegation that love in the Fourth Gospel is not Christian agape at its fullest and finest because God loves only his "own" and his own are only commanded to "love one another." It is quite true that nothing is said about loving "the neighbor" or "the enemy." As in the writ-

---

[46] Bornkamm, in criticism of Käsemann's book, also stresses the importance of Jesus' death in the Gospel and the significance—even if there is dependence upon a pre-Johannine formula—of 3:16 ("Zur Interpretation des Johannes-Evangelium: Eine Auseinandersetzung mit Ernst Käsemanns Schrift 'Jesu letzter Wille nach Johannes 17,'" *Geschichte und Glaube*, I, BEvTh 48 [München: Chr. Kaiser Verlag, 1968]: 114, 118-19). See also Wendland, *Ethik des Neuen Testaments*, p. 112.

[47] Bowen, "Love in the Fourth Gospel," p. 45. Cf. Nygren, *Agape and Eros*, pp. 152-53.

ings from Qumran the focus here is on love within the chosen community. On the other hand, and in contrast with Qumran ideas, there is *also* no mention in this Gospel of hating the enemy or avenging the wrongs which others may have perpetrated.[48] Moreover (contrary to Käsemann), the Son's mission of love *is* conceived of as a mission to the whole world, and thus "the world" itself is conceived of in this Gospel in a very non-Gnostic (perhaps, indeed, in a specifically *anti*-Gnostic) way. This is shown not only by the declaration that Jesus is "the Savior of the world" (4:42) and that God in his love sent his Son to save and bring life to the world (3:16), but also by the presentation of Jesus as "the light of the world" (8:12) and the one who "overcomes" the world (16:33) by the righteousness and judgment which inhere in his coming to it (16:8-11).[49]

We may even agree with Käsemann that, for John, "theologically and in principle" it has already been decided who is "chosen" out of the world for eternal life.[50] But it is very significant that this evangelist, at the same time (as Käsemann himself readily concedes), regards the discovery of just who the chosen are as something still to be accomplished in a practical sense. Does this not indicate that what has been decided "theologically and in principle" is—in John's view—that, by responding to the light and to God's proffered love which it represents, one is recipient of the Father's gift and command of love and brought from death to life? Thus, in 12:32 Jesus says, "and I, when I am lifted up from the earth, will draw all men to myself" (*RSV*), and in the same context, "While you have the light, believe in the light, that you may become sons of light" (vs. 36 *RSV*). The Johannine summons to "come," "believe," and "walk" in the light shows that the "predestinarian" aspects of the Gospel originate in a concern to stress the sovereign initiative of God in coming into the world in love; they do not originate in a conviction that some are forever excluded from true life.

[48] Schnackenburg, *The Moral Teaching of the New Testament*, p. 328.
[49] Apropos of this point and in criticism of Käsemann, see Bornkamm, "Zur Interpretation des Johannes-Evangeliums," pp. 118-20. Cf. also Mary E. Clarkson, "The Ethics of the Fourth Gospel," *AThR* XXI (1949): 113; Warnach, *Agape. Die Liebe als Grundmotiv*, p. 156, n. 1.
[50] *The Testament of Jesus*, p. 65.

147

If we are correct in concluding that the Fourth Evangelist regards God's love and the Son's mission of love to be extended to all who will receive it (him), then we must also acknowledge that the commandment to "love one another" need not be regarded in itself as *excluding* love for "neighbors" and "enemies." In fact it is hard to fit such terms into the framework of this writer's theology. In this Gospel the expression "one another" has an eschatological reference, not a narrow ecclesiastical one. Once again the contrast with the Jewish sectarian enclave at Qumran is illuminating. There, as Brown points out, "love is a duty consequent upon one's belonging to the community," but in John "Jesus' love for men is constitutive of the community." [51] In the latter instance it is not so easy to talk about "enemies" or about love for mankind in general.

Moreover, the love command in John is given to a community which needs to find its own identity and maintain its own integrity in the midst of a hostile world. The crisis faced by the disciples as Jesus prepares to depart matches the crisis of faith for every later generation within the church, including John's own: What is to be the distinguishing mark of Jesus' followers and what will enable them to be faithful and effective in their mission in the world? Seen in this perspective, love for "one another" is neither a softening nor a repudiation of the command to love the neighbor, but a special and indeed urgent form of it. [52]

The Johannine Epistles

Although the Johannine epistles probably were not written by the Fourth Evangelist himself, they obviously stand within the theological jurisdiction of the Fourth Gospel. Their relationship to the Gospel may indeed be compared with the relationship of

[51] *The Gospel According to John*, p. 613.
[52] Cf. Michel, "Das Gebot der Nächstenliebe," p. 78; Bultmann, *The Gospel of John*, pp. 528-29.

the Pastoral epistles to the letters of Paul,[53] although theologically (and probably also historically) they stand much closer to the evangelist than the Pastorals do to Paul. II, III John are too brief and have too particularized concerns to yield many data relevant to our study of the Johannine love ethic, but I John is a rich field for investigation in this connection.

Many of the evangelist's teachings on love are found also in I John: God's love for man is the basic fact of man's existence (3: 1; 4: 7-8, 10, 16, etc.); that love is made manifest in the sending of his Son into the world to bring life through his own death (3: 16; 4: 9-10); the presence of the Spirit represents God's own abiding with men and makes possible man's abiding in him (3: 24; 4: 13); this mutual "abiding" involves man's keeping of the commandment(s) God has given (3: 24), and that means, essentially, to "love one another" (2: 7-11; 3: 10, 11-18, 23; 4: 7, 11-12, 20-21; 5: 2). Of course, there is nothing in I John comparable to the powerful portrayal of love's serving we have found in the footwashing scene of John 13; but the *conception* of love as expressed in a service like Jesus' is present here where there is reference to "walking" in the same way Jesus "walked" (2: 6) and opening one's heart in love to the needy brother (3: 17). Moreover, the author of I John has his own way of expressing the unity love establishes between God and his people: we are God's beloved *children*, "born of God" (see 2: 28-29; 3: 1-10; 4: 4-6; 5: 4, 18), an idea which is not foreign to the Gospel (e.g. John 1: 12-13; 3: 3-8), but which is by no means as prominent there as here.[54]

In I, II John as in the Gospel, there is an alternation between references to the "commandments" (plural: I John 2: 3, 4; 3: 22, 24; 5: 2, 3; II John 6) and the "commandment" (singular: I John

---

[53] H. Conzelmann, " 'Was von Anfang war,' " *Neutestamentliche Studien für Rudolf Bultmann, BZNW* 21, 2nd ed. (Berlin: A. Töpelmann, 1957): 201.

[54] Therefore the judgment of Schrenk (*ThD* II: 554-55) that I John lacks "the profound christological basis of loving as He loved, which is so prominent in the Gospel (Jn. 13:34; 15:12)" is too harsh. Besides the reference in I John 2:6 to walking as Jesus walked, we may note 3:3 (to be pure as he is pure); 3:7 (to be righteous as he is righteous), and 3:16 (we ought to lay down our lives as he laid down his). Cf. Bultmann, *Die drei Johannesbriefe, KEK* 14 (Göttingen: Vandenhoeck & Ruprecht, 1967): 32, n. 6; G. Eichholz, "Glaube und Liebe im 1. Johannesbrief," *EvTh* IV (1937): 423.

2: 7, 8; 3: 23; 4: 21; II John 4, 5, 6). Here in the epistles this alternation seems quite deliberate, as if the author were consciously
reflecting upon the relationship between the many commandments and the one great command.[55] This deliberateness is especially evident in II John 5, 6. The Father's commandment (vs. 4)
is identified as the commandment to "love one another" (vs. 5);
but then such love is in turn defined as "walking according to his
[sc. God's, vs. 4] *commandments*" (vs. 6a; cf. "walking in [the]
truth," vs. 4). Immediately, however, the singular is again employed, "This is *the commandment* . . . , that you walk in it [sc.
love]" (vs. 6b). There is an equally close juxtaposition of the
singular and plural in I John 3: 22-23. As in II John 6 the possessive pronoun "his" stands with the plural "commandments" (vs.
22) and the reference is to the commandments of God (vs. 21).
Once more, however, the plural changes to the singular (now the
possessive pronoun is retained): "And this is his commandment
. . ." (vs. 23 *RSV*). In this instance, in contrast with II John 5-6,
the reference to one commandment turns out to be more than a
mention of loving one another. We are in fact presented with *two*
commandments, or, rather—since the writer's reference to a
single commandment seems so deliberate—with a double commandment: to believe in Jesus Christ and love one another (vs.
23). This is the first mention of faith (believing) in I John, and
it is an important reference because of the connection drawn between faith and love: as in Paul (especially Gal. 5: 6) the point
here is that faith expresses itself in love. As Bultmann observes,
the same connection is implicit in 3:16 where Jesus' sacrificial
death for the brethren is made the basis of their responsibility
to give themselves for one another.[56] Again later the object of
believing is said to be "the love which God has for us" (4:16),
and also in this context there is emphasis on the command to
love one another.

It is tempting to see in I John 3: 23 the transformation of Jesus'
own double commandment to love God and the neighbor into
the church's exhortation to believe in Jesus Christ and then
love one another. But Jesus' double commandment is much more

[55] So Schrenk, *ThD* II: 554.
[56] *Die drei Johannesbriefe,* p. 64.

directly in mind in 4:20-21: "Should some one claim that he loves God but is hating his brother, he is false; for the one who does not love his brother whom he has seen certainly cannot love God whom he has not seen. Indeed, this commandment we have from him, that the one who loves God should love his brother also." There is a polemical edge to these words. Here, as throughout I John, the author has in mind certain Christians who proudly profess to enjoy a privileged relationship to God, special, direct knowledge of him. Among these persons the commandment to love God has apparently been converted into the proud claim that they *do* love God and has been divorced from any meaningful sense of being loved by God and thus commanded by him to love the brother. Such errors are combatted in 4:10-11 where true love is identified as God's love for us, not ours for him, and where love for one another is identified as the imperative consequent upon the divine love. The argument is further bolstered by the appeal to Jesus' own double commandment of love to God and man which we have seen in 4:21. The thought is continued in 5:1-2 where, using imagery typical of this epistle, the writer insists that love for the parent (God) necessarily involves love for the children (God's people). This is the only New Testament passage outside the Synoptic Gospels where we can be fairly sure of a direct reference to the Great Commandment with equal stress on each of its parts. The Fourth Gospel, for instance, not only lacks any reference to the Great Commandment, but also avoids any reference to man's loving God.

A further distinctive feature of the love ethic in these epistles is the author's hesitance to describe the love command as "new." In the Gospel, as we have seen, the commandment is called "new" because it is brought by the one in whom the new age has been instituted; the light, life, and love to which the world is summoned are already present. This idea is certainly also alive in the epistles: "What I am writing to you, and what is being carried out in your lives as it was in his, is a new commandment; because the night is over and the real light is already shining" (I John 2:8 *JB*). This is quite an acceptable interpretation of the evangelist's reference to the "new commandment" given by Jesus before his return to the Father (13:34). One gains the impression, however, that left to his own the present writer would prefer to speak of the love command as something "old." In this he may be influenced once more by a polemical concern; the errant teachers are accused of being too "progressive" (see II John 9) and of not "abiding" in the traditional teachings. There would be point, then, in stressing the *traditional* nature of the commandment to love one another:[57] "Beloved, I am writing to you no new commandment, but an old commandment which you had from the beginning; the old commandment is the word which you have heard" (I John 2:7 *RSV;* cf. II John 5). The reference is not to the Old Testament origin of the commandment, as Moffatt claims,[58] but to its place in the historical tradition of the church since its institution by Christ—as Conzelmann especially has shown.[59]

In these epistles there is no explicit mention of love for the "neighbor" or for one's "enemies." As in the Fourth Gospel, the focus seems to be upon love for "one another." In I John, however, the term "brother" is also employed in connection with the love command (2:9-11; 3:10-18; 4:20-21); this is never the case in the Fourth Gospel. Significantly, the term "brother" has been substituted for "neighbor" in the reference to Jesus' Great Commandment at 4:21: one is to love God and one's "brother." Does this mean that here in the epistles, at least, there is a *deliberate* restriction of the scope of love to relationships within the church itself? Many presume that all the references here to "the brother" are references to one's fellow Christian;[60] if so, the love ethic in I John would indeed be even more emphatically intramural than in the Gospel. But Schnackenburg and Bultmann both contend that, at least in some passages, the word "brother" is synonymous with "neighbor," and that the love command in

---

[57] *Ibid.,* p. 33; also Schnackenburg, *Die Johannesbriefe,* 3rd ed., Herders Theologischer Kommentar zum Neuen Testament," 13 (Freiburg: Verlag Herder, 1965): 111.

[58] *Love in the New Testament,* p. 293.

[59] " 'Was von Anfang war,' " esp. pp. 195-99; also Michel, "Das Gebot der Nächstenliebe," p. 79; Schrenk, *ThD* II: 555; Spicq, *Agape in the New Testament,* III: 105; Bultmann, *Die drei Johannesbriefe,* p. 33.

[60] E.g., Moffatt, *Love in the New Testament,* pp. 281-82; C. H. Dodd, *The Johannine Epistles, MNTC* (New York: Harper & Bros., 1946), p. xlvi; Spicq, *Agape in the New Testament,* III: 105; von Soden, *ThD* I: 145.

I John is quite definitely intended to pertain to one's relationships with his fellow *man* as well as his fellow *Christian*.[61] The evidence used to support this conclusion is worth noting.[62]

1. The references in 2:9, 11 to certain persons "hating" their brothers must be to those whose false Christianity is repeatedly attacked in this epistle, those who are blinded by the darkness and remain in it. It is unlikely that this writer would think of them as "Christians" or "fellow Christians"—indeed, they would belong to "the world" which stands in radical opposition to the faithful community (3:13). Thus, when it is said that such a person "hates his brother" the term brother is being used in a general sense to mean "fellowman." No common faith binds the hater and the hated together. Given this context, the word "brother" in vs. 10 must also have this meaning: "He who loves his brother [= his fellowman] remains in the light."

2. The comment of 3:13 that the world "hates you" is addressed to the "brethren," in this case (as in III John 3, 5, 10) a description of the Christian community. In the following verse the conduct of this Christian community is sharply contrasted with that of the world. "But *we*," the author says with emphasis (ἡμεῖς), "*we* know that we have already passed from death into life because we love the brethren" (vs. 14). The emphatic contrast with "the world's" conduct (hating Christians) would make little sense if the author were only speaking about loving those within one's own group. Moreover, in this same context the singular, "brother," is used in connection with the author's appeal to the story of Cain and Abel: Cain hated his brother and murdered him (vs. 12); anyone who hates his brother commits murder and is alienated from true life (vs. 15). Here again the term seems to have a broader application.

3. In 4:20 the severity of the criticism leveled against the person who claims to love God while he goes on hating "his

---

[61] See Schnackenburg's important excursus on this subject, *Die Johannesbriefe*, pp. 117-21; cf. Bultmann, *Die drei Johannesbriefe*, esp. pp. 34-35, 59; and most recently H. Schlier, "Die Bruderliebe nach dem Evangelium und den Briefen des Johannes," *Mélanges Bibliques en hommage au R. P. Béda Rigaux*, ed. A. Descamps and R. P. André de Halleux (Gembloux: J. Duculot, 1970), p. 243.

[62] Here I am following in general the arguments of Schnackenburg, *Die Johannesbriefe*.

brother" makes it probable that the writer has in mind the same gnostic outsiders who had been castigated in 2:9-11. Again, therefore, brotherly love means love of one's fellow human beings who—unlike God—are quite visible. Consequently, when the double commandment of the Synoptic tradition is invoked in vs. 21, but using the word "brother" instead of "neighbor," the conclusion to be drawn is not that this writer is thereby limiting love's scope. The more accurate conclusion is that, for this writer, the term "brother" can be used as a synonym for "neighbor," and that in I John there is indeed some specific acknowledgment of one's responsibility to love all men. As in the Gospel, it is affirmed that God has sent his own Son on a mission of love to "the world" and that he is "the Savior of the world" (4:9, 14).[63]

We have already noted that the author of I John, like the Fourth Evangelist, regards God's love as the basic fact of man's existence. But this writer goes even farther than the evangelist in portraying love as the all pervasive characteristic of God's being and acting: "God is love" (4:8, 16). It would be a mistake to impute to this author a concern to "define" God's metaphysical nature, although in isolation the affirmation that "God is love" might appear to be such a definition. Rather, as Dodd has shown, the author's meaning is that God's loving is not just one of his activities, alongside his creating, ruling, judging, etc., but that "all His activity is loving activity. If He creates, He creates in love; if He rules, He rules in love; if He judges, He judges in love." [64] Again in opposition to Gnostics who claim a direct, special knowledge of God, this writer insists that it is precisely in and through God's acting in love that he is known—in no other way. His decisive act of love was the sending of his Son who "laid down his life for us" (3:16 RSV; cf. 4:9, 14, 15-16a), so that the confession of Jesus Christ as God's Son is absolutely essential if one would appropriate God's love into his own life (e.g. 4:15; 5:1-12). It is clear, however, that "believing" in Jesus Christ means something far more for this writer than a formal declaration of faith; it means obeying the commandment(s): the true knowledge of God is inseparable from complete obedience to him

---

[63] See Schnackenburg, ibid., pp. 233, 242-43.

[64] The Johannine Epistles, p. 110; cf. Bultmann, Die drei Johannesbriefe, p. 71; Schnackenburg, Die Johannesbriefe, p. 232.

(2:3-6). Indeed, those who keep the commandments identify themselves as God's children (cf. 5:1-3) and "abide" in him just as he "abides" in them (3:24; 4:13). In this connection our author speaks also of the gift of God's Spirit, and like Paul he associates the Spirit's presence with the operation of love in the life of believers. Bultmann points out that the reference in 3:24a to keeping the commandments and thus abiding in God is parallel to 4:12 where God's abiding in us is said to be conditional upon our loving one another; and in each instance the Spirit's presence is said to be the sign of this "abiding" (3:24b; 4:13). Thus, love is not conceived as some innate possibility latent in human nature, but as a *gift* from God who is himself "love" and acts in love.[65] The ethical appeals of this epistle are in effect appeals to appropriate and actualize in one's own life the gift God offers.

When this writer refers to the appropriation and actualization of God's love in the lives of believers, he speaks about the "perfecting" of love (2:5; 4:12, 17-18). The *RSV* translates the first of these references: "Whoever keeps his word, in him truly love for God is perfected." This would mean that "perfect love" is man's love for God expressed in his obedience to God's word, and this idea would by no means be alien to the writer's thought (see, for instance, 4:8). But it is more likely that the reference here is to God's love for man (see the translations of *NEB* and *JB*). While man's love for God is sometimes mentioned (4:21; 5:2; cf. 4:20; 5:1) the author's emphasis is upon the divine love (3:1, 16; 4:9-11, 16, 19), and the response of men to this love is not conceived to be their "love for God" in a direct sense, but their love "for one another" (3:16b; 4:11, 21, etc.).[66]

The second passage which mentions "perfect love" shows that it is indeed *God's* love which is so described: "No one has ever gazed upon God; if we love one another God abides in us and *his love* has been perfected among us" (4:12). Here "perfect

---

[65] Bultmann, *Die drei Johannesbriefe*, p. 65.

[66] Bultmann (*ibid.*, p. 31) also mentions this writer's polemic against the idea that man can love God directly, and also takes this as a reference to God's love. Dodd, on the other hand, sees a reference to man's love of God (*The Johannine Epistles*, p. 31, following the Moffatt translation).

love" refers to God's love for men which, in their loving one another, has found its completion. This accords with the point of the preceding verse ("Beloved, if God so loved us, we also ought to love one another," *RSV*) and provides a fully intelligible meaning for 2:5: "keeping the word" means "keeping the commandments" (2:3). These are summed up in the one commandment to love the brother (2:7-11).

The third passage which refers to "perfect love" carries us farther: "Love has been perfected with us when we come to have confidence at the day of judgment, because as he is even so are we in this world. Love harbors no fear; instead, perfect love dispels fear, because fear has punishment in view. The fearful person has not been perfected in love" (4:17-18). The surrounding verses speak of God's love for man which enables one to abide in love (in God) as God's love is expressed in one's relationships with others (vss. 16, 19). In contrast, where God's love is not received and expressed, it has not reached its "goal" in man's life,[67] and the fear of final judgment rules where love ought properly to be at work. The appropriateness of Spicq's comment (in his discussion of 4:10-12) is borne out by the further remarks about "perfect love" in 4:16-19: "the love which is manifested to us by the sending and death of his Son bears fruit and reaches its perfection when Christians effectively love one another. Fraternal love would be the final outcome of the diffusion of charity which Christ transmitted to men." [68] These passages, then, do not adumbrate some doctrine of human perfection, nor do they focus on man's love for God as the supreme religious affection.[69] In keeping with the writer's concern throughout, they speak of the divine love which is extended to men in Christ —preeminently in his death—and seeks its completion in man's obedient response to the commandment, "Love one another."

This commandment to love one another, already prominent in the Fourth Gospel where it is presented as Jesus' farewell legacy to his followers, is now one of the major themes in I John. Now

---

[67] Cf. Bultmann, *Die drei Johannesbriefe,* p. 76; Eichholz, "Glaube und Liebe im 1. Johannesbrief," pp. 425-26.

[68] *Agape in the New Testament,* III: 136.

[69] Moffatt rightly rejects this second interpretation, *Love in the New Testament,* pp. 302-6.

in the course of his opposition to gnostic teachings this writer sees the love command as an essential ingredient of the Christian tradition which the church has had "from the beginning." Like the evangelist he speaks of the Christian life as an "abiding" in God and in his love; but once (II John 9; cf. I John 2:27) he speaks also about "abiding in the teaching of Christ"—remaining loyal to the traditional doctrines, especially, perhaps, the doctrines about Christ himself,[70] but including the one great command to love. A polemical concern and an emphasis on loyalty to the Christian tradition are also present in the Pastorals, as we have seen. But in those epistles traditional theological ideas and ethical instructions simply stand side by side, and there is little reflection on the theological basis for the Christian's practical conduct. In these Johannine epistles, however, theology and ethics are so closely joined that they are very nearly identified. The Christian is called to "believe" in Jesus Christ and to "love" the brother (3:23); in 1:5 the Christian tradition is summed up ("This is the message we have heard from him and proclaim to you . . .") in a theological statement ("that God is light and in him is no darkness at all," *RSV*), while in 3:11 it is summed up ("For this is the message which you have heard from the beginning . . .") in a practical command ("that we should love one another," *RSV*). This commandment gives content to the more general ethical implication already drawn from the initial summary—that one should "walk in the light as he is in the light" and thus be joined into the *koinonia* of God's people (1:7).[71]

In summary and conclusion we must emphasize that the love ethic here is closely related to the writer's Christology. Jesus' death is regarded as a demonstration of God's love and thus an example for men: "By this we know love, that he laid down his life for us; and we ought to lay down our lives for the brethren" (3:16 *RSV*; cf. 4:10-11). But, as in the Fourth Gospel, the point is not just that brotherly love should be "like" the divine love. Rather, the love expressed among men is to be the

---

[70] Bultmann, *Die drei Johannesbriefe,* p. 108.

[71] Wendland particularly stresses the identification of theology and ethics in the Johannine literature: "Here every separation between salvation and commandment, Christology and ethics, is completely abolished" (*Ethik des Neuen Testaments,* p. 111).

extension, the completion—the "perfection"—of God's own love. According to this conception God's love for us and our love for one another are the two segments of *one* grand continuum of love. This is the meaning of the statement, "We love, because he first loved us" (4:19). Is Spicq correct, then, when he describes love as "the divine nature participated in to varying degrees . . . by the believers," [72] so that their love for one another "wells up spontaneously from their divine nature, just as the love of their Father does . . . ?" [73] This goes too far. In I John "abiding" in God's love means *receiving* his love and *obeying* his commandment to love. Neither concept is compatible with a conception of fusion into the divine nature and a "spontaneous" life of love. True enough, brotherly love is said to be the sign that one "has passed out of death into life" (3:14; cf. John 5:24), but nothing suggests that once this passage is made, death and darkness are banished, and love holds sway without challenge. The opposite is implied, for this epistle is full of exhortations to make God's love visible in one's life, and all these are directed to those who have been "anointed by the Holy One" (2:20, 27) and "know the truth" (2:21). Their receiving of God's love has not molded them into his nature but has drawn them under his command and in that way brought them from death to life.[74] They must continue in his love by constant obedience as they encounter the particular claims of love in their daily affairs. These practical demands of love are never far from the writer's mind; thus, the statement that we ought to lay down our lives for others as Christ laid down his for us (3:16) is immediately given a concrete application (vss. 17-18): "But if a man has enough to live on, and yet when he sees his brother in need shuts up his heart against him, how can it be said that the divine love dwells in him? My children, love must not be a matter of words or talk; it must be genuine, and show itself in action" (*NEB*).

---

[72] *Agape in the New Testament*, III: 104; cf. p. 123.
[73] *Ibid.*, p. 129.
[74] Correctly, Nygren, *Agape and Eros*, p. 148.

V
THE LOVE COMMAND AND
CHURCH ORDER

Our study so far has shown how Jesus' love command was received and interpreted by the Synoptic evangelists, how Paul in his preaching emphasized the christological-eschatological dimensions of the "controlling love" present to faith, and how the Fourth Evangelist focused on the "new commandment" to love one another. We have seen, moreover, that in the Pauline and Johannine "schools," as also in the Synoptic Gospels, the love command was often applied to quite practical and urgent concerns, for instance Christian unity, church discipline, the church's

159

witness and identity in the world. Such practical, ecclesiastical concerns are particularly at the fore in the New Testament writings we have yet to consider. We shall see how the love command is increasingly employed as a principle for the creation and maintenance of church order. In I Peter, Revelation, and Hebrews, the church is facing suffering and seeking to define the meaning of its faith and the scope of its love in terms of its hope of deliverance from tribulation. The brevity of James, Jude, and II Peter, as well as the specialized problems with which they deal (moral laxity, apostasy, apathy within the church), make it particularly difficult to assess the meaning of the love command for their authors. But closely related to these books in time and in theological temper are the writings of the so-called "Apostolic Fathers," some of which were themselves once regarded as canonical by some Christians. It will be helpful, therefore, to look also at these as we trace the increasing tendency to use the love command as a rule for ecclesiastical governance.

Love Amid Suffering

I Peter

Our best evidence indicates that I Peter is by an anonymous Christian writing in Rome or Asia Minor at the end of the first or at the beginning of the second century, during a time of great stress for the Christian church.[1] Whatever one's conclusions with respect to its literary and preliterary history,[2] our canonical

---

[1] For discussions of the problems of authorship and date, see esp. F. W. Beare, *The First Epistle of Peter*, 3rd ed. rev. (Oxford: Basil Blackwell, 1970, pp. 28-50, 212-16, 226-27; W. G. Kümmel, *Introduction to the New Testament*, trans. A. J. Mattill, Jr. (Nashville: Abingdon Press, 1965), pp. 296-99, and J. N. D. Kelly, *A Commentary on the Epistles of Peter and of Jude*, HNTC (New York: Harper & Row, 1969), pp. 26-34. I find Beare's arguments the most compelling with respect to date. While assignment of I Peter to the reign of Domitian is not impossible (A.D. 81-96), it seems more probable that it reflects the situation under Trajan (*ca.* A.D. 110).

[2] E.g., does I Peter make use of a baptismal homily or liturgy? See Kümmel, *Introduction*, pp. 294-96; Beare, *The First Epistle of Peter*, pp. 25-28, 220-26; Kelly, *A Commentary*, pp. 15-26.

I Peter is a conjoint exhortation-declaration to stand fast in the true grace of God amid the present tribulations (5:12). With patience and with humility believers are to remain steadfast in their confidence that there is meaning in their suffering for Christ, and that they have been born anew to a sure hope for a greater glory to come. The theme of obedience in the midst of present affliction is particularly prominent in 4:12 ff., whereas the earlier paragraphs, as often noted, speak somewhat more generally of suffering and of the Christian's moral responsibilities. It is in the earlier chapters (1:1–4:11) that most, and the most significant, of the exhortations to love appear.

I Peter 4:7-11; 1:22

The first part of the epistle (and perhaps of an originally independent baptismal homily or catechism employed here) is concluded in 4:7-11. This concluding paragraph opens with a reference to the imminent parousia and closes with a doxology; in between there is a series of exhortations concerning the believer's eschatologically qualified and doxologically oriented life in the world. The initial appeal is standard in such contexts: "Keep sane and sober for your prayers" (vs. 7b RSV; cf. e.g. I Thess. 5:6 ff.). But the chief appeal comes in vs. 8 introduced by the emphatic, "Above all . . . ." The cardinal imperative of the Christian life is to love one another fervently, with total devotion. The emphasis placed here upon the love command makes it certain that for the author (or final redactor) of I Peter this command is to be the chief guide for that "doing good" which is so pervasive a concern in the epistle (2:14, 15, 20; 3:6, 17; 4:19).[3] We might expect in this context a reference to Jesus' Great Commandment or at least to the love command of Lev. 19:18, but there is no use, direct or indirect, of either of these anywhere in I Peter. Nor have we, in this particular passage, any explicit christological grounding of the love imperative—though we shall see that such is quite prominent elsewhere in the epistle.

[3] The identification of these two is explicit in I Clement 33:1.

THE LOVE COMMAND IN THE NEW TESTAMENT

Instead, in the last clause of vs. 8 we hear echoes of two Old Testament texts which speak of the "covering" of sins, Ps. 31:1 (LXX; Eng. tr., 32:1) and—especially—Prov. 10:12. Thus, we are told, "love covers a multitude of sins" (*RSV*).

The form of I Peter 4:8*b* is closer to the Hebrew text of the proverb than to the LXX version, and the Hebrew proverb quite evidently intends to say that, while hatred brings strife, love "conceals and passes over faults in silence." [4] But how is this thought being applied in I Peter? Calvin's interpretation represents one possibility: wherever, within the community of faith, one truly *loves* the brother, one will forgive that brother's faults and thereby cover over his sins. Thus, "each one seeks to preserve the honour of the other." [5] But the earliest commentators usually presume a different meaning: that where brotherly love is active in the life of the church, there God's *own* mercy and love will be extended to those who themselves walk in love rather than hatred. This interpretation fits the eschatological context of I Peter 4:8 and is probably the correct one: "at the coming judgement his readers will receive mercy for their own sins . . . provided in the meantime their mutual love does not falter." [6] In the following verses some practical instances of love's work within the community are indicated: hospitality and the constructive employment of spiritual gifts for one another. Here, in contrast to Paul and the author of the Pastorals, *all* Christians are called "stewards" of God's grace (Paul had used the term specifically of apostles, I Cor. 4:1; in Titus 1:7 it describes a bishop), and the concept of "stewardship" is employed with reference to the constructive caring for one another in love which this writer sees as the chief distinguishing mark of the eschatological people of God.

The centrality of the love imperative for this writer's view of the Christian life is confirmed by many other passages in I Peter,

---

[4] Kelly, *A Commentary*, p. 178.

[5] *Calvin's Commentaries*, XII, trans. W. B. Johnston (Grand Rapids: Eerdmans Publishing Co., 1963), p. 304. If Calvin's interpretation is correct, there could be a parallel in *Test. XII Patr.* Joseph 17.2: "Love one another, then, and with patience hide one another's faults" (cited by Moffatt, *Love in the New Testament*, p. 241—who himself rejects this meaning in I Peter).

[6] Kelly, *A Commentary*, p. 178; cf. Spicq, *Agape in the New Testament*, II: 361.

beginning already with 1:22. Conversion itself can be viewed as a commitment to "brotherly love" which is thus the content of one's "obedience to the truth [= the gospel]." Luther asks, "To what end should we now lead a chaste life? To be saved by doing so?" And he answers, in commentary upon this verse and quite in accord with its meaning: "No, but for the purpose of serving our neighbor." [7] This call to brotherly love is associated with and dependent upon one's "having been purified" (1:22) in the holiness of God to which he has been called (1:15-16), an association of ideas present even in the pre-Pauline liturgical traditions (cf. I Thess. 3:12-13 [8]). Moreover, as in the church's catechetical tradition used by Paul in Rom. 12:9-10, so here "brotherly love" (φιλαδελφία) is commended as a form of Christian *agape* (both Greek terms are used in vs. 22) and there is concern for the *genuineness* of Christian obedience to the love command.[9] One is to love "from the heart," that is, unreservedly, persistently, fervently. This is both demanded and made possible because the believer has been "reborn" in faith and to a new and living hope (1:3-5, 21). The obedience which is required in this new life is given its definition by the holiness of God himself. It is no accident that the first scriptural citation in I Peter is of Lev. 11:44-45 (in 1:16): "You shall be holy for I am holy." This is the general summons under which all the subsequent commands, especially the appeals to love, are assembled and interpreted, much as Matthew had epitomized the summons to love in the charge to "be perfect" as God is perfect.[10]

I Peter 2:16-17

The succinct exhortations of 2:16-17 also deserve consideration: "Live as free men, yet without using your freedom as a pretext for evil; but live as servants of God. Honor all men. Love the

---

[7] *Luther's Works*, XXX, ed. J. Pelikan and W. A. Hansen (St. Louis: Concordia Publishing House, 1967): 41.

[8] Cf. Spicq, *Agape in the New Testament*, II: 346.

[9] The adjective "genuine" which is used with "brotherly love" in I Peter 1:22 (*RSV*: "a sincere love of the brethren") had been used twice by Paul, both times to describe *agape*: Rom. 12:9; II Cor. 6:6.

[10] See above, p. 53.

brotherhood. Fear God. Honor the emperor" (*RSV*). Only in vs. 16 does the concept of freedom appear in I Peter, and here in a way which recalls Paul's comment on freedom in Gal. 5:13. As in Galatians the new life in Christ is described as a life in freedom, and the possible misuse of freedom is considered. Paul, using a military metaphor, had warned that freedom should not become a "staging area" for the flesh; the present writer changes the metaphor and thus also slightly alters the meaning: freedom should not be used to "mask" evil, that is, as an excuse for allowing evil to be done. Here, too, as in Galatians, Christian freedom is described, paradoxically, as slavery. But whereas Paul had spoken of using one's freedom to bind oneself in loving service to *others* and then in support had cited Lev. 19:18, this writer speaks of being bound in service to *God*, and there is no mention (in vs. 16) of love or neighbor love, and no citation of Scripture.

But vs. 16 should be read as an introduction to vs. 17,[11] and in this following verse it becomes apparent that also for the author of I Peter bondage to God involves the practice of love in one's life. The structure of vs. 17 is chiastic: there are four imperatives, the first and last employing the same verb ("honor"). This chiastic structure throws into special prominence the middle injunctions: "Love the brotherhood. Fear God." Such an arrangement also suggests the vital interrelationship of these two central imperatives, and that the responsibilities to love the brethren and to fear God have to be discharged in the midst of the secular and civil orders.

The commands to "love the brotherhood" and "fear God" form a distinctive but recognizable version of the double commandment of the Synoptic tradition: the essence of obedience is to be rightly related to God and to one's brother.[12] "Fear" is used here in its comprehensive, Old Testament sense of awe, reverence, covenant love. In the other part of this formulation the verb "to love" is used with reference to one of its forms, "brotherly love" (as in 4:8 ff.; 1:22). But unlike Paul, whose references are always to love for "the brother," this writer uses the more abstract concept of the "brotherhood" (also in 5:9; I Clem. 2:4; Hermas,

---

[11] Spicq, *Agape in the New Testament,* II: 354.
[12] Cf. *ibid.,* p. 356.

Mand. VII, 8:10; nowhere else in the New Test.). If, on the one hand, it is clear that an important connection between loving the brotherhood and fearing God is present here, it is, on the other hand, equally clear that the Christian's relationships to "all men" and to the emperor are of a different sort. To the world at large and to the civil order the Christian owes honor and respect, but not the kind of love which makes for Christian brotherhood or the kind of reverence due God alone. In contrast stands the Old Testament proverb, "Fear God and the emperor, son" (24:21, LXX), and the injunction of Plutarch, "Honor the emperor and worship him as the image of God who saves all things" (Themistocles 27). I Peter does not command "fear" of the emperor; moreover, the "honor" due him is of the same order as the "honor" due to all men.

In what, precisely, does this "honor" due to "all men" consist? Spicq argues that all four admonitions stand under the heading of "respect" and that "love" here is one particular kind of respect, "honor" and "fear" other kinds. Thus, he suggests, in the command to love the brotherhood "the accent is on reverence and service rather than love." [13] But Spicq's approach ignores the context in which vss. 16, 17 stand. The topic is one's relation to the civil authorities and the charge is to be subject to them (vs. 13). The ground for this is that they have been commissioned by God to support the good and punish the evil within the social order (vs. 14). It is God's will that the Christian community comport itself in an exemplary way as regards morality and law (vs. 15). In such a context, then, the reference to freedom (vs. 16) may also have special meaning: though you are free men, you are not free *from* honoring the structures which hold society together. You are free *for* the service of God, and that service ("fearing" him, loving the brotherhood) does not at all preclude respect for outsiders and for civil authority (vs. 17). Indeed, the Christian's life of obedience takes shape *within* a broad social context.

While the chiastically arranged exhortations of vs. 17 are understood to be compatible, they are not viewed as varied modes of love (in the sense of "respect") but as varied—and distinct—

[13] *Ibid.*, p. 355.

modes of the service of God (vs. 16). To fear God and love the brethren is primary. But "all men," including the emperor himself, have a relationship to God, and their life also is to be affirmed. It would seem quite legitimate to identify the "all men" of vs. 17 with "the Gentiles" of vs. 12 for whom this writer holds out the hope of ultimate inclusion within the people of God. To "honor the emperor" means to obey the laws which serve society; to "honor all men" means to respect their place within the structures of this social order and to care for their eventual entry into that "brotherhood" where God's love rules.

I Peter 2:18–3:12

Here we have a "code of household responsibilities" parallel to those in Col. 3:18 ff. and Eph. 5:21 ff. and, like them, somewhat adapted by the author of the epistle to express his own special concerns and emphases. Thus, the opening charge to Christian slaves to obey their (presumably non-Christian) masters, even when unjust and brutal punishment is meted out, becomes the occasion for a brief excursus upon the meaning of unmerited suffering (2:18-25). We may suppose that the original addressees could have readily likened their own troubled position as Christians in a non-Christian world to the plight of Christian slaves owned by hostile, nonbelieving masters. To them the word of I Peter is that evil should not be resisted but endured in patience and with a firm trust in God. The appeal is supported by a reference to the exemplary and redemptive suffering and death of Christ. Their Lord himself had borne the reviling of nonbelievers with patience and with an unwavering trust in the ultimate justice of God's own judgment; Christians should follow in his steps (2:21-23). The redemptive meaning of Christ's death is also stressed, however (vs. 24). Jesus the suffering servant (cf. Isa. 53) has taken upon himself our sins and healed our wounds. Thereby he has enabled us to "die to sin and live to righteousness" (another characteristically Pauline idea present in I Peter; cf. Rom. 6).

The concept of nonresistance present in 2:18-25 is very likely dependent upon the tradition which Matthew and Luke have

166

associated with Jesus and which had already left its impress upon Paul's ethical appeals. But in Matt. 5, Luke 6, and Rom. 12 where this tradition is also at work, the teaching on nonresistance of evil is coupled with positive appeals to "love" the enemy and to show active goodwill to one's persecutors. This positive note is muted in I Peter 2:18-25; it is only indirectly present in the injunction to slaves to "be subject" even to the overbearing master (vs. 18).[14] Unquestionably, the emphasis is upon the *passive* response to evil, upon obedience, patience, suffering, trust. A more distinctly positive note is sounded, however, in the concluding section of this household code, 3:8-12. Now the whole Christian community is addressed and admonished to retain its identity by maintaining unity, sympathy, brotherly love, compassion, and humility (vs. 8). Further, Christians are charged not to meet evil and reviling in kind, but with "blessing" (vs. 9). This is supported with a citation from Ps. 34 (LXX: vss. 13-17; Eng. tr.: vss. 12-16) which not only assures the faithful that God will heed the prayers of the righteous and turn from those who do evil, but also, indeed primarily, stresses the active doing of good and seeking for peace (vss. 10-12).

Two features of 3:8-12 require special attention. First, the concept of *loving one's enemies* is implicit here when the command is given to "bless" one's "revilers" (vs. 9). The positive note which was muted in 2:18-25 is now clearly sounded. Is this because now the subject is life *within* the church, whereas earlier the perpetrators of evil had been outsiders (the non-Christian slavemaster, Jesus' nonbelieving opponents)? This is possible, for 3:8 undoubtedly focuses on the Christian community itself. Moreover, it is at least questionable whether Christians experiencing the reality, or even the threat, of physical persecution, would have found the call to "love" the enemy very relevant. In their relationships with "the world" perhaps the only avenue open to love was passive nonresistance and measured respect (cf. 2:17), whereas within the church itself contentious brethren

---

[14] Beare is probably correct that the "respect" (literally, "fear") mentioned in 2:18 refers to one's fear *of God* by which all conduct is to be governed (1:17; 2:17), not some kind of "respect" for the master (*The First Epistle of Peter*, p. 147; although in this context these two should probably not be too strictly separated.

could be actively enfolded in love. It is also possible, however, that the injunction of 3:9 to bless one's revilers quite intentionally moves us beyond the narrower concern of vs. 8: love is to be manifest within the church, and *also* in the Christian's relationships with those outside the church. This juxtaposition of commands is often encountered in Paul's letters, as we have seen, for instance in Rom. 12:9 ff. and—most succinctly—at I Thess. 5:15: "See that none of you repays evil for evil, but always seek to do good *to one another* and *to all*" (*RSV*).

A second important feature in 3:8-12 is the basis upon which the exhortation to bless one's revilers stands. Believers "*have been called* to this [way of life]" (vs. 9). In view of what has gone before in the epistle, the reference to having been "called" must be a reference to the Christian's baptism and entry into a new life of obedience: he is to be "holy" as the one who *called* him is holy (1:15-16), and as a believer he belongs to God's own people who have been "*called* . . . out of darkness into . . . light" (2:9). It is safe to say, then, that the point of 3:9 is that blessing those who do one evil is a part of the new life of obedience in love to which one has been called, just as the promise of his own future blessing by God is a part of the "living hope" to which he has been born.[15]

Revelation and Hebrews

John of Patmos who wrote our canonical Revelation and the anonymous author of Hebrews must also confront the problems

---

[15] In contrast to Kelly (*A Commentary*, p. 137), I hold that the εἰς τοῦτο ("for this") in 3:9 looks *backward* (to the idea of blessing those who revile you) rather than forward (to one's own future blessing by God). I think this is shown by the parallel in 2:21, which is much closer to 3:9 than 4:6 to which Kelly appeals. But taking εἰς τοῦτο as looking backward does not leave us with the meaning Kelly alleges: "Bless your insulters (for you were called to bless them) so that you may in turn secure a blessing." This exegesis arbitrarily isolates the being "called to bless them" from the call to obedience inherent in the "new birth," the "ransom," and the "purification" which baptism represents (1:3, 18, 22) and which is such an important theme in the first part of this epistle. In fact, what we have in 3:9 is an imperative ("Bless your insulters") founded on an indicative ("You have been called to this" as part of your call to a new way of life).

of Christians living in troubled times. One does not ordinarily think of turning to Revelation for discussions of or admonitions to love, for it is well known that the seer shows only antipathy toward the Roman state and any who collaborate with it. He speaks of the uncompromising anger of God against all who submit to the pressures to worship Rome (14:9-11) and speaks of the vengeance which God wreaks on those responsible for the martyrs' deaths (6:10; 19:2). He conceives of the state itself only as an evil power constantly opposed to God's truth and God's people (e.g. 13:5-7a). Nowhere in this apocalypse is there the slightest hint that the Roman state has any legitimate function whatever (contrast Rom. 13:1-7; I Peter 2:13-17). Nevertheless, love is still hailed as a characteristic of the Christian life, indeed the vital element, the *sine qua non,* of Christian existence. When the Ephesian congregation is charged with having given up the love it had at first, the meaning is that they have fallen away from faith itself and need now to make a complete about-face (2:4-5). Love is not just one quality among others, but the very heart of their faithful endurance.[16] This is confirmed when the Christians of Thyatira are commended for their "love and faith and service and endurance" (2:19). In both these passages attention is centered upon the interior life of the Christian community, and love is identified with the believer's faithfulness to the gospel and his serving of the brethren.

The love which is to flourish within the church has its origin in Christ's own love for his people revealed in his death for them. The doxology which opens the series of seven letters undoubtedly employs liturgical formulas, but its significance for an understanding of the writer's own thought is not diminished thereby. He has, after all, chosen these words and given them a prominent place: "To the one who loves us and has delivered us from our sins by his blood and made us a kingdom, priests to his God and Father, to him be the glory and power for ever and ever. Amen" (1:5b-6). However, we do this writer an injustice if we concentrate only upon his words about the deliverance from sins already accomplished for us in Christ's death. In this

---

[16] See Moffatt, *Love in the New Testament,* p. 237; Schnackenburg, *The Moral Teaching of the New Testament,* p. 382.

apocalypse Jesus is not only presented as "the lamb who was slain" (e.g. 5: 6; 13: 8) but as "the one who lives," who has passed from death to life (e.g. 1: 18; 2: 8). As the living, reigning Christ Jesus stands in the midst of his people (1: 13; 2: 1) and "loves" them. The present tense in 1: 5b is indeed significant: believers are constantly supported by Christ's love[17] which not only protects them (3: 9), but also reproves and chastens them (3: 19). It is perhaps going too far to claim that this writer's vision of the new Jerusalem is a vision "of the final actualization of the 'new' and eternal order of God's love . . . ," [18] but it is certainly true that his call to the church for continuing patient endurance and faithfulness is at its center a call to love.[19]

Finally, we must emphasize that the seer's call to endurance and faithfulness is a call to the *works* of love. These are the visible signs of the church's acceptance of Christ's love and of its obedience to him.[20] In 2: 4-5 the Ephesians are told that repentance and return to their earlier life in love must mean doing "the works you did at first" (*RSV*), and in 2: 19 love, faith, service, and endurance are all listed as the "works" which have characterized the faithful Christians of Thyatira. Such are the "works" which "follow" those who die in the Lord and at last give these saints blessed rest from their labors (14: 13). The faithful community is held together and bears its witness in the world by its "keeping God's commandments" (12: 17; 14: 12). While these are nowhere specifically summarized in the single commandment to love, it is clear that concrete deeds of love within the beleaguered congregations are the prime evidence and content of their patient endurance.

The congregations to which Hebrews was directed were also under pressure from a hostile world (see, e.g., 10: 32-34) and also had to face the attendant dangers of apathy and apostasy among their own members (e.g. 2: 1; 3: 12 ff.). The elaborate typology of this homily, which presents Christ as the great High

---

[17] Spicq, *Agape in the New Testament*, III: 2; Wendland, *Ethik des Neuen Testaments*, pp. 118-20.

[18] Warnach, *Agape. Die Liebe als Grundmotiv*, p. 173.

[19] *Ibid.*, p. 172. For related comments, see William Klassen, "Vengeance in the Apocalypse of John," *CBQ* XXVIII (1966): 300-311.

[20] Cf. Spicq, *Agape in the New Testament*, III: 5-6.

Priest and his death as the ultimate and decisive sacrifice for sins, should not be allowed to obscure the fact that the author's chief intention is hortatory; he offers a "word of exhortation" (13:22 RSV).[21] No passage better epitomizes his concerns than 10:19-25 which begins with an emphasis on Jesus' saving death (vss. 19-21) and proceeds to a series of admonitions perhaps deliberately formulated around the traditional Christian triad, faith, hope, and love: "Let us draw near with a true heart in the certainty faith affords . . . , hold fast the confession of our hope without wavering . . . , and be concerned for one another, for a ferment of love and good works" (vss. 22-24). One can "draw near" to God because of his faith that his life has been purified through Christ's sacrificial death (vs. 22), and he can remain faithful to the Christian way because he knows that God himself is faithful to his promise (vs. 23). The promise is that those who remain faithful in hope will attain at last to the heavenly city, the new Jerusalem which is to come (11:10, 16; 12:22; 13:14). For this writer, then, "faith" is closely identified with "hope" (e.g. 11:1), but the concept of hope does not exhaust the meaning of faith. Faith is also obedience, as the example of Abraham, especially, shows: "By faith Abraham obeyed when he was called to go out to a place which he was to receive as an inheritance . . ." (11:8 RSV). According to 10:24, the obedience of faith is "love" and the "good works" which follow from that. What this writer urges his readers to do for one another (to show concern for the "ferment of love" from which good works derive) he himself intends to do for them by his own exhortations.

As in I Peter and Revelation so in Hebrews Christian love is viewed in terms of its visible deeds within the community. The "good works" of love include a serious and constant attention to the common life of believers so that they may be mutually encouraged and admonished in view of the impending eschaton (10:25). A parallel passage shows further how and why this

---

[21] When A. C. Purdy describes this author as a "liturgist" who makes only slight use of love imagery "because it was not relevant to his priestly analogy," and whose chief concerns are God's majesty, purification from sin, "a sense of awe in worship," forgiveness, and fellowship with God (IntB XI: 711-12), he is neglecting the pervasive hortatory style and intent of this homily.

work of brotherly love is to proceed (though the word "love" itself does not appear): "See to it, brothers, that no one among you has the wicked, faithless heart of a deserter from the living God; but day by day, while the word 'Today' still sounds in your ears, encourage one another, so that no one of you is made stubborn by the wiles of sin. For we have become Christ's partners if only we keep our original confidence firm to the end" (3:12-14 NEB). This writer exhibits a special concern for "pastoral care" within the church which, significantly, is to be the function of the whole community, not just of selected members or officials.[22] Their love is to find expression in their "serving the saints" (6:10) which, particularly in times of stress for the church, should include such practical kindnesses as hospitality,[23] care of the brethren who are in prison,[24] and ministration to those who have been ill-treated (13:1-3).

Goguel dismisses the ethic of Hebrews in less than a page contending that this writer "has a completely negative conception of redemption," [25] and Bultmann argues that here the imperative is not truly founded on the indicative because salvation is conceived as totally in the future.[26] These judgments, however, are too harsh. Although the accent does fall on the purification from and forgiveness of sins which Christ has effected and upon the hope for entrance into the new Jerusalem, the believer's receipt of the benefits of Christ's passion and death and his clinging to the authenticity of God's promise allow him to live *already* as a citizen of the heavenly city (12:22-24).[27] If faith is the mode of this citizenship and hope its right, then love is its badge and proof. Love's service of the saints is in fact regarded as the service of God himself (6:10), and one cannot rightly "consider"

[22] See Michel, *Der Brief an die Hebräer*, KEK, 10th ed. (Göttingen: Vandenhoeck & Ruprecht, 1957), p. 232.

[23] A standard part of Christian parenesis, as we have seen (above, p. 106). There is an excellent discussion of this in Moffatt, *The Epistle to the Hebrews*, ICC (New York: Charles Scribner's Sons, 1924), pp. 224-25.

[24] We may recall Lucian's account of the church's care of Peregrinus (above, pp. 17-18).

[25] *The Primitive Church*, p. 486.

[26] *Theology of the New Testament*, II, trans. K. Grobel (New York: Charles Scribner's Sons, 1955): 168.

[27] See Conzelmann, *An Outline of the Theology of the New Testament*, trans. J. Bowden (London: SCM Press, 1969), pp. 312-13.

in faith the meaning of Jesus and his sacrificial death (3:1) apart from a diligent "considering of one another" in a community where love is constantly at work (10:24).[28] To "consider" Jesus means to consider his continued faithfulness even while suffering, and to know that because he shared the tribulations of human existence (2:9-18; 4:15) he qualifies as the "pioneer" of true faith (12:2). As in I Peter, Jesus' suffering is presented as exemplary for Christians. Jesus "learned obedience through what he suffered" (5:8 *RSV*), and so his people are to be obedient (in love) in the midst of their suffering.

Conclusion

I Peter, Revelation, and Hebrews were probably all written at the end of the first or beginning of the second century and directed to congregations struggling to maintain their identity and their witness in the midst of tribulation and danger. Each writer, in his own quite distinctive way, seeks to interpret and apply the church's doctrinal, catechetical, and liturgical traditions for churches where suffering or the possibility of suffering is a fact of life. In all three the word is to remain faithful to the church's teaching and to cling steadfastly to the hope of salvation which does not disappoint. Moreover, we have seen that all three of these writers emphasize the practical ethical demands incumbent upon Christians in troubled times, and view them basically in terms of the command to love.

The accent on love is clearest in I Peter even though Jesus' Great Commandment is never specifically invoked nor the injunction of Lev. 19:18 ever cited. In fact, the word "commandment" does not once appear, nor, for that matter, the word "law." Thus, although there are enough authentically Pauline themes present here to warrant the description of I Peter as, in one sense, a "deutero-Pauline" letter,[29] the love command is not identified as the epitome of the law; Paul's polemical stance

---

[28] Moffatt points out that the same verb (κατανοεῖν) is used of heeding Christ (3:1) and one another (10:24), *The Epistle to the Hebrews*, p. 146.

[29] Wendland, for instance, discusses the ethic of I Peter under the heading of "Deutero-Pauline Writings" (*Ethik des Neuen Testaments*, pp. 101-4).

toward the law need be retained no longer. On the other hand, as in Paul's letters love is here linked implicitly—and once, even fairly explicitly (1:21, 22)—with faith and hope. To be "born anew to a living hope" (1:3 *RSV*) means to be called to a new life of holiness, to "doing good." And that means, to be called to love which is the essence of obedience and faithfulness. The imperatives in I Peter are closely related to the indicatives: the love command inheres in the reality of the believer's new birth (1:3, 23), in his having been ransomed from his old ways (1:18) and purified (1:22), in his having "tasted the Lord's kindness" (2:3), and having received his mercy (2:10). He has been called out of darkness into the light and into the company of God's people (2:9-10). Within this brotherhood of faith and hope love is summoned to life and to its deeds of service (1:22; 2:17; 3:8-12; 4:8-10; cf. 5:5). Christ's own redemptive suffering and death make this new life possible (1:18-21; 2:24-25) and are at the same time exemplary of the patient endurance and trust which should characterize Christians during the time of their "exile" in the world (2:21-23).[30]

We have seen that Christ's love and his reigning presence in the embattled church is also the basis upon which John of Patmos encourages his readers to remain faithful in love and to produce the works of love. Similarly in Hebrews Christ's sacrificial death enables the believer to come with faith into God's presence and to receive the hope of salvation. As for Abraham the venture of faith involves a life of obedience, understood here as serving love. Where love serves the brethren God himself is served and the authenticity of the promised salvation is confirmed (6:9-12).

In I Peter, Revelation, and Hebrews we find the love command being interpreted for Christians who need encouragement to remain committed in their faith, confident in their hope, and loyal to one another even in the midst of suffering and adversity. It

[30] Contrast Goguel (*The Primitive Church*, pp. 485-86) who believes that I Peter represents a "decline towards moralism" because the indicative and imperative "are simply placed side by side" and because "the action which has been done for believers has not saved them, but made them fit to save themselves." But in his discussion of the ethic of I Peter, Goguel ignores the significance of 2:21-24 and the dialectical relationship between the indicative and imperative which emerges there.

is not surprising that Christ's own suffering is sometimes held before them as an example of faithfulness (I Peter, Hebrews) as well as the decisive event of redemption. It is also understandable that in such times of stress for the church the primary force and relevance of the love command would be seen to be within the Christian community itself. These three writers, like the Fourth Evangelist in the Farewell Discourses, are concerned for the maintenance of the church's authentic witness in a hostile world. Particularly under such conditions the rule and reality of brotherly love give the afflicted community its identity and its hope.

The Yoke of Grace

James

The parenetic tract of James is a loosely arranged collection of traditional admonitions designed to provide practical moral guidance. The author believes that Christians are in constant danger of being corrupted by worldly standards and values (1:27). If one is a "friend" of the world he cannot be a "friend of God" (4:4). Truly to "love God" (1:12; 2:5) means to resist the allure of one's base worldly desires (1:13-14). The author's other and more famous formulation of this idea is: "faith without works is dead" (2:14 ff.).

Although the phrase "works of love" is not used, it is clear that charitable deeds are among the works for which a man of faith is responsible. "True religion," it is claimed, means not only avoiding worldly enticements but, in its positive aspect, ministering to those in need, of whom "orphans and widows" are typical (1: 27).[31] Again, there are several warnings in James about the destructive power of an evil tongue, for instance in 1:26: "A man may think he is religious, but if he has no control over his tongue, he is deceiving himself; that man's religion is futile" (NEB).

---

[31] See Spicq, Agapè dans le Nouveau Testament, I: 202-3.

A loose tongue is associated with a quick temper (1:19). Both of these are condemned, with the additional remark that "a man's anger does not produce the righteousness of God" (1:20). Behind this negative statement there is of course a positive idea, but it is not that "*love* produces the righteousness of God." Rather, it is only the preceding maxim that one should not speak against others too hastily. These verses also show under what aspect the writer conceives of *righteousness*. He thinks of it not as God's *gift* but as God's demand, and that in a very particular moral sense. "Producing righteousness" depends on purging oneself of wickedness (vs. 21) and is possible where the gospel ("the implanted word," vs. 21, "the word of truth," vs. 18) is received and obeyed. This is indeed a saving gospel (vs. 21), but receiving it does not mean just believing it, but performing the works it requires. Faith alone does not save, only faith which leads to works (2:14-17).

The author also includes within his moral teaching a commendation of mercy: "For judgment is without mercy to one who has shown no mercy; mercy triumphs over judgment" (2:13 RSV). The reference here is apparently to a forgiving spirit, and there are parallel exhortations in 5:9 ("Do not grumble, brethren, against one another, that you may not be judged; behold, the Judge is standing at the doors," RSV) and 4:11-12 ("Do not speak evil against one another, brethren." "There is one lawgiver and judge, he who is able to save and to destroy. But who are you that you judge your neighbor?" RSV).[32] Elsewhere the term "mercy" is associated with practical deeds of peace and gentleness, those virtues which issue from true Wisdom. Earthly "wisdom" engenders jealousy and strife and promotes disorder (3:14-16), but the divine Wisdom "is first pure,

[32] Forgiveness is explicitly mentioned only once, in 5:15 with reference to God's forgiveness of the sins of the sick brother on whose behalf the elders offer prayer (vs. 14). The theme is implicit in 5:19-20 which promises that whoever suceeds in bringing back into the fold a wandering brother will himself profit by his deed. As in I Peter 4:8, there is an allusion to Prov. 10:12, but without the specification that sins are covered by one's *love*. Cranfield hears in 3:9-12 an echo of Jesus' teaching on love for one's enemies (*Romans 12-13*, p. 50), but the text itself makes only the negative point that cursing men is sinful: "From the same mouth come blessing and cursing. My brethren, this ought not to be so" (vs. 10 RSV).

then peaceable, gentle, considerate, full of mercy and good fruits"
(3:17).

There is little in James that is either specifically or distinctively
Christian, whether in respect of the content of the admonitions
or of their grounding. Neither eschatological nor christological
sanctions for the ethic are prominent here; the mention of the
expected return of the Lord and the last judgment is hardly
more than a formality (5:7 ff.), and the saving work of Christ
is never mentioned. Yet Christian obedience is not simply identified with keeping the Old Testament law. For this writer only
the ethical demands of the law are significant, not its ritual demands. "Religious" service is not cultic action but moral action
(1:26, 27); to approach God with clean hands means to approach
him with a pure heart, in full sincerity and with humility (4:
8-9). Thus while it is true that this ethic has a nomistic structure,
the author understands that the Christian has been given a new
kind of law to follow. The phrase "new law" is not used by him
(we meet that first in Barn. 2:6 [33]), but the concept of a new
Christian law is clearly present when he speaks about "the perfect law" (1:25), "the law of liberty" (1:25; 2:12), and "the royal
law" (2:8).

The reference to "the royal law" in 2:8-9 is of considerable
importance for our study because in conjunction with this phrase
there is a direct quotation of the love command of Lev. 19:18:
"If indeed you are performing the royal law, according to the
Scripture, 'You shall love your neighbor as yourself,' you are
doing well. But if you are being partial you are committing sin
and are convicted by the law as trespassers." James is the only
New Testament writer besides the Synoptic evangelists and Paul
to make specific use of the text from Leviticus, although (as in
Paul) it is quoted by itself and not as part of a double commandment. Here, indeed, it is explicitly commended as authoritative
because it is scriptural, not because it is a command from Jesus.[34]
The vast majority of interpreters regard this verse as evidence
that the author of James believes the love command to be the

[33] See below, pp. 192-93.
[34] Correctly, Spicq: "[James] speaks of fraternal charity in Old Testament terminology, referring to the authority of Moses and not to the authority of Jesus Christ" (*Agape in the New Testament*, II: 7).

summary statute of the whole Torah and thus constitutive of what he now chooses to conceive of as a new kind of law.[35] Before we make a judgment on this, however, the immediate context of the verse in question must be considered.

The central point of 2:1-12 [36] is that, within the church, no partiality should be shown or any special privileges accorded in respect of persons. Specifically, the author criticizes the tendency to give deference to the wealthy man when that means neglecting the poor brother. Whether the rich man mentioned in vss. 2-4 is presumed to be a Christian or a nonbeliever who happens into a Christian assembly is uncertain.[37] But it is also immaterial to the point of the passage, which is emphasized in vss. 1, 5-6a: the poor brethren in the church should not be victims of discrimination, but should be honored as persons "rich in faith and heirs of the kingdom" (RSV), the people of God's own choosing. The wealthy, on the other hand (now nonbelieving rich persons are in mind), are guilty of economic exploitation and political and religious harassment of the Christian poor (vss. 6b-7). Then in vss. 8-9 the admonition to honor the poor man is supported by appealing to the law itself: if, in fact, one is intending to perform "the royal law," he will do well to heed the injunction to love his neighbor, and that excludes favoring some persons over others.[38]

---

[35] E.g., Spicq, ibid., pp. 7-9; Moffatt, The General Epistles: James, Peter and Judas, MNTC (New York: Harper and Bros., n. d.), p. 35; idem, Love in the New Testament, p. 232; Warnach, Agape. Die Liebe als Grundmotiv, p. 145, n. 1; Michel, "Das Gebot der Nächstenliebe," p. 80; Gutbrod, ThD IV: 1081; Joseph B. Mayor, The Epistle of St. James, 3rd ed. (London: The Macmillan Co., 1913), pp. 89-91; Bo Reicke, The Epistles of James, Peter and Jude, AB (Garden City, N. Y.: Doubleday and Co., 1964), p. 29; C. Leslie Mitton, The Epistle of James (Grand Rapids: Eerdmans Publishing Co., 1966), pp. 89-91; Goguel, The Primitive Church, p. 493; Wendland, Ethik des Neuen Testaments, p. 109.

[36] Vs. 13 is a separable maxim only loosely connected with the paragraphs to which it has been attached.

[37] On this question, see, most recently, Roy B. Ward, "Partiality in the Assembly: James 2:2-4," HThR LXII (1969): 87-97.

[38] Some commentators, however, believe that the reference to Lev. 19:18 is not the author's own contribution to the discussion. They hold that he seeks to refute any attempt to use the love command as an excuse for showing partiality to the rich. See, e.g., James Hardy Ropes, The Epistle of St. James, ICC (New York: Charles Scribner's Sons, 1916), p. 197. But such an interpretation is strained, for it is hard to believe that Lev. 19:18 would have occurred to anyone to be a suitable defense for the deferential treat-

Unquestionably, the love command is invoked here in the interests of Christian brotherhood, and love of neighbor is understood to be an important aspect of Christian obedience. But is *more* than this involved? Does this writer identify the love command as the very *essence* of the Christian ("royal") law? If so, we could readily agree that James like Paul is "in his own way an 'apostle' of love." [39]

The continuation of the discussion in vss. 10-12, however, should caution us against any firm judgment of this kind. In vs. 10 the point is made that failure to keep any one part of the law, any one of its multiple commands, means that one is guilty of breaking the law as a whole. There is no such thing as a "partial trespasser." This is illustrated in vs. 11 by an appeal to two of the statutes of the Decalogue: if one observes the prohibition against adultery but violates the prohibition of murder he is still a transgressor of the law. Applied to the situation at hand the meaning would be: Even if you keep all the (other) commandments of the law, but, by showing partiality to the rich, neglect the one commandment to love your neighbor (the poor brother), then you are in fact guilty under the whole law. Thus, if we take into consideration this continuation of the argument, it would appear that the commandment of Lev. 19:18 is regarded as one among many which are to be kept by the faithful Christian. In itself it does not constitute or even summarize the essence of the "royal law." [40] This phrase designates "the whole law" with its

---

ment being condemned. An even less defensible version of this interpretation is offered by B. S. Easton who holds that vs. 8 represents, in diatribe style, *the objection itself*, which the author then goes on to refute (vss. 9-12) by holding that any claimed obedience to Lev. 19:18 would be vitiated by disobedience of the command in Lev. 19:15—that preferential treatment of any group should be eschewed (*IntB* XII: 38). But this is certainly too forced. Objections cited by authors of diatribes are usually clearly indicated to be such, e.g. by Paul in Rom. 6:1, 15; 7:7, 13; Gal. 1:10; 3:21; I Cor. 15:35, and by James himself in 2:18: "But some one will say . . ." (*RSV*).

[39] Wendland, *Ethik des Neuen Testaments*, p. 109.

[40] Commentators who support this interpretation are M. Dibelius, *Der Brief des Jakobus*, KEK, 8th ed. ed. H. Greeven (Göttingen: Vandenhoeck & Ruprecht, 1956), pp. 132-35; H. Windisch, *Die katholischen Briefe*, HNT, 3rd ed. ed. H. Preisker (Tübingen: J. C. B. Mohr [Paul Siebeck], 1951), p. 15. I do not find the counterargument of Schnackenburg to be convincing; indeed even he is willing to say only that it is "not certain" the love com-

various commandments (vs. 10). Because partiality violates one of those, it violates the whole.

This interpretation is perhaps confirmed by the fact that—as most commentators agree—the three phrases, "royal law," "perfect law," and "law of liberty," are used synonymously in James. The latter expression (used as the argument of 2:1 ff. culminates, vs. 12) is found first among the Stoics, then in Hellenistic Judaism, whereas the Jews frequently referred to the *whole* law of Moses as "perfect" in contrast with the laws of the heathen (cf. Ps. 18:8 [LXX; Eng. tr. 19:7]; Ps. Aristeas 31, etc.). There are also precedents, especially in Hellenistic Jewish literature, for speaking of a "royal law." [41] It is doubtful whether we should expect any one of these phrases, in and of itself, to yield profound clues to the ethical thinking of James.[42] Rather, they

---

mandment is viewed as one among many (*The Moral Teaching of the New Testament*, p. 351, n. 10).

[41] See especially the materials assembled by Dibelius, *Der Brief des Jakobus*, pp. 133-34.

[42] Spicq, for instance, attempts this: "The simple adjective 'royal' marks a considerable evolution of the precept of love stated in Leviticus 19; indeed it 'Christianizes' it. James is the first and very reliable exegete of the thought of his 'brother' Jesus" (*Agape in the New Testament*, II: 8-9).

I am also unconvinced by the arguments of Dan Otto Via, Jr. who holds that James uses the phrase "law of liberty" with a quite particular meaning. It shows that he conceives of the law not as an external power but as something which corresponds to one's "internal nature" (Via here follows Goguel, *The Primitive Church*, p. 492). Thus, it allows for varying responses in different contextual situations, and "James is consciously trying to develop this concept" ("The Right Strawy Epistle Reconsidered: A Study in Biblical Ethics and Hermeneutic," *JR* XLIX [1969]: 261-62). Via supports this contention by appealing to 4:11-12: "Do not speak evil against one another, brethren. He that speaks evil against a brother or judges his brother, speaks evil against the law and judges the law. But if you judge the law, you are not a doer of the law but a judge. There is one lawgiver and judge, he who is able to save and to destroy. But who are you that you judge your neighbor?" (*RSV*). According to Via (following Gutbrod, *ThD* IV: 1082), James means that, "while the law requires love, it is not composed of specific commandments"; therefore love's demands must be contextually perceived and no one dare judge his neighbor's moral decisions (*JR* XLIX: 261). But this is surely an overly subtle exegesis of the passage which, taken as it stands, simply means: one should not slander his brother, for if he does he sets himself over against the requirement of the law to *love* the neighbor (see Dibelius, *Der Brief des Jakobus*, pp. 210-11; Mitton, *The Epistle of James*, p. 166). There are parallel admonitions at 2:13; 3:10, and 5:9.

are largely "decorative and suggestive," [43] used to characterize the whole Christian message of salvation[44] which is also referred to in James as "the word" (1:22-23), "the word of truth" (1:18), and even "the implanted word" (1:21).

While this writer surely understands love of one's neighbor to be a vital component of the Christian life, he hardly deserves to be called "an 'apostle' of love." His exhortations proceed not from a declaration of God's gift and demand of love but from his conviction that the "royal" and "perfect law of liberty" is the embodiment of the divine "Wisdom." This Wisdom is the essence of God's gift, to be sought and received by faith and then exhibited in an upright life: "If any one of you lacks wisdom, let him ask God who gives to all men generously and without reproaching, and it will be given him. But let him ask in faith, with no doubting . . . ." "Who is wise and understanding among you? By his good life let him show his works in the meekness of wisdom" (1:5-6; 3:13 RSV). There is indeed some similarity between the qualities ascribed to Wisdom in James 3:17 ("pure, . . . peaceable, gentle, considerate, full of mercy and good fruits, harmonious, sincere") and those ascribed to love in I Cor. 13:4-7.[45] But this only shows further the differing theological orientations of Paul and James. Paul's ethic develops from his gospel that love is the controlling and sustaining power of salvation (the new age) already inaugurated in Christ's death and resurrection. The ethical teaching of James stands in the wisdom tradition of Hellenistic Judaism.[46] Obedience is not viewed as one's acceptance and expression of Christ's love but as perform-

[43] The expressions are so described by Ropes (*The Epistle of St. James*, p. 199); but I think Ropes goes too far when he denies that James sees any distinction between the true Christian law and an older less perfect one.

[44] In this much, at least, Schnackenburg and I agree (*The Moral Teaching of the New Testament*, p. 350).

[45] Johnston, *IntDB*, K-Q, p. 175; Mitton, *The Epistle of James*, pp. 139-40; Reicke, *The Epistles of James, Peter and Jude*, pp. 42-43. J. A. Kirk has especially stressed the parallelism of 3:17 and Paul's list of the fruit of the Spirit, Gal. 5:22 ff. ("The Meaning of Wisdom in James," *NTS* XVI [1969]: 26-28).

[46] On the affinities between James's thought and the Wisdom tradition, see, e.g., Ropes, *The Epistle of St. James*, pp. 18-21, 139-40, 243-50. Ropes, however, is correct that the *literary form* of James is that of the diatribe, not that of wisdom literature (*ibid.*, pp. 16-17). See further Kirk's article cited in n. 45, esp. pp. 32-38.

ance of the new law. This is called "royal," "perfect," and the "law of liberty" because its commandments are understood to be exclusively ethical and to require concrete moral deeds. When it is held that "pure religion" is helping those in need (1:27), the point is not to exalt the love command as normative for all ethical action, but that religion finds its true expression in the moral life, not in the cultic. Similarly, responsibility for clothing and feeding the needy "brother or sister" (2:15-16) is not mentioned as an application of the love command in particular, but to illustrate the point that faith apart from works cannot save (2:14, 17).

Jude, II Peter

The brief tract of Jude is an appeal "to fight hard for the faith which has been once and for all entrusted to the saints" (vs. 3 JB). The author senses a present threat of doctrinal error and perverse morality (vs. 4), and he seeks to combat these by the sheer force of his appeal to faithfulness, not by any particular theological argument. The rhetoric of his polemic overshadows the actual content of his teaching. Even so, when the point of his appeal is summed up in conclusion, the traditional Christian triad of faith, hope, and love is prominent: Christians are to build themselves up in faith (with prayer), keep themselves in the love of God, and wait for the coming mercy of the Lord Jesus Christ which brings eternal life (vss. 20-21). The imperatives respecting faith, prayer, and hope are expressed by the use of present participles; the charge to remain "in the love of God" employs an aorist imperative and thus receives a certain emphasis.[47] Those who have been called are "beloved in God the Father and kept for Jesus Christ" (vs. 1 RSV), and by remaining loyal to Christian teaching they are to continue in that love. The reference may well be both to God's love and to the love which is to characterize the Christian's own life.[48]

---

[47] Spicq, *Agape in the New Testament*, II: 373.
[48] Cf. Spicq, *ibid.;* Windisch, *Die katholischen Briefe,* p. 47.

II Peter is directly and massively dependent upon Jude,[49] and like the earlier tract is concerned with doctrinal error in the church, specifically in this case, loss of hope for the return of Christ (3:1-4).[50] The references to love in the opening and closing lines of Jude have no parallels in II Peter, and conversely II Peter's one direct exhortation to love is without parallel in Jude. It occurs in 1:7 in the midst of several verses which provide a clear indication of this author's view of the Christian life. For him as for James "faith" in the sense of assent to doctrines is not enough. Moreover, like James he believes the Christian must avoid the corrupting influence of the world. Indeed, he goes farther than James when he views salvation as "escape" from the world and participation in "the divine nature" (1:4). That this is accomplished finally through the "divine power" itself is clear enough (1:3-4), but it is also insisted that faith in God's promise must be confirmed by the believer's own zealous deeds (1:10-11; 3:14).

The importance of Christian moral zeal is particularly stressed in 1:5 ff. where it is said that faith needs to be "equipped" (the verb is the same one employed for "outfitting" the chorus in a Greek drama) that it may issue in the "sure knowledge"[51] of Christ which is active and fruitful (vs. 8). Thereby one maintains the moral cleanliness granted him at his baptism (vs. 9) and assures himself a place in "the eternal kingdom" (vs. 11). In commenting on this passage, J. N .D. Kelly refers to the "programme of eight virtues which [Christians] must cultivate, starting with 'faith' and ending with 'love'. . . ."[52] In this case one could compare the dictum of Ignatius, "Faith is the beginning, love the

[49] See Kümmel, *Introduction*, p. 303. Few scholars any longer question II Peter's dependence on Jude, although Reicke has recently suggested that the two are independently dependent on common traditions (*The Epistles of James, Peter and Jude*, pp. 189-90).

[50] See E. Käsemann, "An Apologia for Primitive Christian Echatology," *Essays on New Testament Themes*, trans. W. J. Montague, Studies in Biblical Theology, 41 (London: SCM Press, 1964), esp. pp. 169-78.

[51] The Greek word used is ἐπίγνωσις, apparently intended to distinguish true knowledge (γνῶσις supplemented by "self-control," etc., vss. 5-6) from the false "knowledge" of the gnostic teachers II Peter opposes.

[52] *A Commentary*, p. 305. Spicq (*Agape in the New Testament*, II: 375) and Windisch (*Die katholischen Briefe*, p. 86), among others, also reckon with an eight-member list.

culmination" (Ign. Eph. 14:1), as many have, and perhaps also Paul's reference to "faith active in love" (Gal. 5:6). But perhaps it is more accurate to regard the concept of "faith" as standing somewhat apart from the rest of the list in II Peter 1:5 ff. Then the remaining seven virtues, beginning with the all-inclusive Greek ideal of *aretē* and ending with *agape,* will describe the kind of "works" which faith must produce if it is to have effect.[53] In any case, it is important to notice that, in contrast with Paul's meaning in Gal. 5:6, these qualities are not viewed as *expressions* of faith but as *additions* to it, apart from which faith is not sufficient.

There seems to be no strict ordering of the terms in this list, apart from the opening reference to "faith" and the closing references to love. "Virtue" is an all-inclusive term (see the *JB* translation, "goodness") while "knowledge" picks up the slogan of the writer's theological opponents. This must lead to "self-control," not to the "licentiousness" of which he accuses those Gnostics (2:2). "Steadfastness" corresponds with another concern of II Peter, that Christians remain firm in their hope for the parousia, while "godliness" is again a more general term for religious devotion and moral seriousness. In II Peter as in the Pastorals, "godliness" [54] is an important ethical concept (1:3; 3:11).

The last two items in the list, "brotherly love" and "love" (φιλαδελφία, ἀγάπη), are surprising. On the one hand, they are not so directly related to the occasion for II Peter as are some of the other terms here, and on the other hand they appear nowhere else in this tract.[55] The position of *agape* at the end of the list does give it a certain emphasis, and its position alongside "brotherly love" may suggest that the writer is thinking of love in both its narrower and broader dimensions. Beyond this there is little to be said about his view of love or its deeds. Here—again we may compare the Pastorals—love is one virtue among several.[56] God's own love receives only the barest, and at that

[53] Cf. A. R. C. Leaney, *The Letters of Peter and Jude,* The Cambridge Bible Commentary (Cambridge: At the University Press, 1967), p. 108.

[54] Greek εὐσέβεια. See above, pp. 129-30.

[55] The verb ἀγαπᾶν occurs once, but with a negative meaning, loving evil gain (2:15).

[56] Both Spicq (*Agape in the New Testament,* II: 375-77) and Michael Green (*The Second Epistle General of Peter and the General Epistle of*

indirect, mention: his "forbearance" has delayed the eschaton
to give more time for repentance (3:9, 15). The Christian's moral
duties are not seen to be grounded in a new life already granted
him or in a new age already coming, but solely in one's hope for
eventual escape from the world, entry into the eternal kingdom,
and ultimate union with God. To this end the Christian must remain zealous in equipping his faith with morality.[57]

The Apostolic Fathers

Many of the interpretations and uses of the love command we
have found in Hebrews, Revelation, James, Jude, and I, II Peter
are also present in the Apostolic Fathers which also date, variously, from the end of the first through the middle of the second
century. What character and functions do the exhortations to
love have in these writings?

References to "faith and love" are especially numerous in the
letters of Ignatius, the martyred bishop of Antioch (early second
century).[58] For him faith and love constitute the "whole" of the
Christian life to which nothing is superior (Ign. Sm. 6.1). They

---

Jude, Tyndale New Testament Commentaries [London: The Tyndale Press,
1968], pp. 70-71) find great meaning in the concept of love in II Peter 1:7,
but both must resort to an unwarranted harmonization of this passage with
passages from other writers, notably Paul and John.

[57] Some commentators (e.g., Spicq, *Agape in the New Testament,* II:
374-75; Green, *The Second Epistle General,* p. 66) believe that the imperatives of vss. 5 ff. are anchored in the indicative of vs. 4—one's participation
in the divine nature. But such a view is possible only if one ignores the
obvious appropriation here of the *Hellenistic* hope for one's escape from the
world and ultimate metamorphosis into the being of God. See the excursus
on this in Windisch, *Die katholischen Briefe,* p. 85; also Käsemann, "An
Apologia for Primitive Christian Eschatology," pp. 179-80. Obviously, the
readers of II Peter have not yet escaped from the world, and until they
do they are not yet transformed. Such apotheosis is counted among the
"promises" (1:4) they are to hold fast.

[58] Bultmann also acknowledges the importance of these themes in the
Ignatian letters ("Ignatius and Paul," *Existence and Faith: Shorter Writings
of Rudolf Bultmann,* ed. and trans. S. M. Ogden [New York: Living Age
Books, 1960], pp. 275-76). See also Jean Colson, *Agape (Charité) chez
Saint Ignace d'Antioche* (Paris: Éditions S. O. S., 1961), which, however,
offers little more than a collection of the passages where Ignatius speaks
about love.

represent the "beginning (ἀρχή) and "end" (τέλος) of life; where they are joined together in unity "God is," and all other good things follow (Ign. Eph. 14.1). In such contexts "love" seems to have reference to the believer's total commitment to the God of Jesus Christ. Just as faith is the "windlass" so love is the "way" which bears one up to God (Ign. Eph. 9.1; cf. 9.2; 15:3; Ign. Mg. 1.1).

Ignatius emphasizes with equal force, however, the importance of love as that which should bind Christian brethren together into a community of care and concord. He sees a reciprocal relationship between one's relationship to God and his relationship to the brethren. On the one hand, "conformity" to God demands respecting and loving one's Christian brethren (Ign. Mg. 6.2); on the other hand, it is this Christian unity in love which allows true communion with God to take place (Ign. Eph. 4.1, 2; cf. 5.1). Correspondingly, the meaning of God's grace is not properly understood if one's life does not show forth the fruits of love— concern for widows, orphans, all the distressed; for prisoners and exprisoners, for the hungry and thirsty (Ign. Sm. 6.2). Finally, then, faith, love, and harmony are the marks of that hope in which the church awaits the return of its Lord (Ign. Phld. 11.2).

The conception of the church as a community of love which pervades the Ignatian letters is also apparent in Barnabas, who twice addresses his Christian readers as "children of love [and peace]" (9.7; 21.9) and in Hermas, who envisions a day when God's church shall be "one body, one mind, one Spirit, one faith, one love . . ." (Sim. IX, 18.4; cf. 17.4). But there is special stress upon the importance of love within the church in I Clement (ca. A.D. 95). For Clement as for Ignatius, the brotherly love within Christ's body is conceived as an expression of the divine love by which the believer is lifted up to magnificent heights and united with God (49.4-5). Even more than Ignatius (whose preoccupation with the meaning of his own martyrdom dominates his letters), Clement is concerned lest the church fail to manifest this love in its life, and be dismembered by strife and schisms (e.g. 46.5 ff.).

Concord (e.g. 21.1; 30.3; 34.7; 60.4; 61.1; 62.1 ff.; 63.2, 4; 64; 65.1) and humility (e.g. 2.1; 13.1, 3; 16.1, 17; 21.8; 30.8; 38.2;

48.6; 56.1; 59.3) [59] are, along with love, repeatedly urged upon the readers. This writer has his own "hymn to love" (49.1-6), clearly dependent upon I Cor. 13 but nonetheless impressive for the emphasis it places on the importance of love in the Christian life. Not only does love lift us up and unite us to God (vss. 4, 5*ab*), it covers sins, bears everything, is not haughty, and promotes concord (vs. 5*cd*). In I Clement as in Ignatius love is seen to operate in good deeds (I Clem. 33.1; 34.2) as the members of Christ's body care for one another: "Let the strong care for the weak and let the weak reverence the strong. Let the rich man bestow help on the poor and let the poor give thanks to God, that he gave him one to supply his needs; let the wise manifest his wisdom not in words but in good deeds; let him who is humble-minded not testify to his own humility, but let him leave it to others to bear him witness; let not him who is pure in the flesh be boastful, knowing that it is another who bestows on him his continence" (38.2). Thus the "whole body" will be "preserved in Christ Jesus" as each is "subject to his neighbor" (38.1). Here, it should be noted, "neighbor" is used specifically in reference to fellow Christians. Moreover, the relationship of love which binds Christian neighbors together is closely identified with mutual "subjection," each member "knowing his place" in relation to others and acting accordingly. Paul's teaching about the varying functions of the members of the body is of course behind this, but a new twist is given it here in I Clement. The church is now likened to an army under command from the Lord (37.1). Under this "Emperor" there are various ranks, in order: generals, prefects, tribunes, centurions, right on down to the ordinary soldier (37.2-3). These are great and small, and when they all do their duty, there is unity and concord (37.4-5).

In keeping with this conception of the church as God's army Clement seems to prefer military to legal terminology when referring to the regulations which should govern the church's life: "Let us then, men and brethren, engage in our service with complete earnestness under [God's] faultless order [προστάγμασιν]"

---

[59] On the theme of humility in I Clement, see Robert M. Grant, *First and Second Clement*, The Apostolic Fathers, 2 (New York: Thomas Nelson & Sons, 1965): 34-35.

(37.1).[60] The hymn to love opens with an appeal to those who "have love in Christ" to follow his "orders" (παραγγέλματα, 49.1), and in the next chapter those are called "blessed" who "keep God's orders[61] [προστάγματα] in the harmony of love" (50.5). Once before the Corinthian church had been ruled by the Lord's orders (2.8), and then humility, peace, zeal for good works, and concern for one's neighbor had characterized their brotherhood (2.1-7). But now divisions have arisen among them, and Clement avers that "everyone has abandoned the fear of God and lost the eyes of faith, and neither walks in the way of his orders[62] nor conducts himself in accordance with his duty toward Christ" (3.4). One of the concluding summary appeals is typical of the whole epistle. Those who take Clement's advice will have no regrets: "For as God lives, and the Lord Jesus Christ lives, and the Holy Spirit, the object of faith and hope for the elect, the man who with humility and eager gentleness obeys without regret the righteous orders[63] of God, this man will be listed and enrolled in the number of those who are saved through Jesus Christ . . ." (58.2). While love is clearly one of the most important regulations for the church's life, the legal term "commandment" (ἐντολή, as in Matt. 22:34 ff., par.; Rom. 13:9; John 13:34, etc.) is used only once: the Lord Jesus spoke of mercy, forgiveness, and kindness, and this "commandment" should be obeyed (13.2-3).[64]

Elsewhere in the Apostolic Fathers references to the "commandments" of God are more frequent, especially in Hermas where a whole series of commandments are enjoined (Mand. I-XII). The first of these is to believe that God is one and that he demands righteousness. The rest spell out what righteousness demands, such as being at peace with all (II, 3), giving without

[60] Grant's translation, ibid., p. 64.

[61] Here I have altered Grant's translation (ibid., p. 82) to show that the same term is used for God's "orders" as in 37.1.

[62] I have again altered Grant's translation (ibid., p. 21). See n. 61.

[63] Once more I have changed Grant's translation (ibid., p. 91) from "commandments" to "orders."

[64] Even references to God's law are lacking in I Clement, although the plural, "laws of God," occurs in 1.3 (whether the text reads νόμοις or νομίμοις θεοῦ is uncertain). See also the use of νόμιμος in 3.4 and νομοθετεῖν in 43.1.

discrimination to those in need (II, 4-6), and patience (V, 1 ff.). In Hermas as in the Pastorals and II Peter, love is listed among the virtues which the faithful Christian should strive to cultivate in his life. These are faith, the fear of the Lord, harmony, words of righteousness, truth, and patience. The good deeds which "follow" from these all bear the stamp of love's concern for others: caring for widows, orphans, and all brethren who are in need; hospitality; not resisting evil; gentleness; poverty; preservation of the brotherhood, etc. (Mand. VIII, 9-10). Other lists of virtues, now personified, are offered in Vis. III, 8.3-7 (two listings) and Sim. IX, 15.2. The number and names of the virtues are somewhat varied in these three lists, but in each case faith and love are emphasized by being placed, respectively, at the beginning and at the end.

The love command itself, indeed in its double formulation to love God and the neighbor, is most prominent in the Didache. This Christian manual in its present form dates from the middle of the second century, but much of its material can be traced back many decades into Jewish and Christian parenetic traditions. Among the earlier materials incorporated into the Didache is the famous "Two Ways" teaching which opens the whole book. There is a "way of life" and a "way of death," and the way of life is summed up in the double commandment to "love the God who made thee" and "thy neighbor as thyself." To this is added the "Golden Rule" in its negative form (1.2). Jesus' authority is not invoked here, and it is even questionable whether the formulation is dependent upon the Synoptic tradition.[65] But the exegesis of the command clearly relies upon Jesus' teachings about loving one's enemies (1.3).

In the parallel material incorporated into the Epistle of Barnabas, the commandments to love God and the neighbor are both present but not formulated into one (19.2, 3, 4, 5), and there is no reference to loving one's enemies. In Barn. 19.5 we meet an

---

[65] See Köster, cited above, p. 17, n. 8; also Robert A. Kraft, *Barnabas and the Didache*, The Apostolic Fathers, 3 (New York: Thomas Nelson & Sons, 1965): 137-38. I am more inclined than Kraft, however, to regard the conjunction of Deut. 6:5 and Lev. 19:18 as a formulation of Jesus himself. Moreover, as Kraft observes, there is reason to think that the final editor of the Didache did reckon with the Synoptic formulation (*ibid.*, pp. 138-39).

189

interesting version of the command to love the neighbor "as thy-self." Barnabas has, "more than thy own life," an interpretation which may also be present at Did. 2.7.[66] The closest any other of these Fathers comes to conveying the double commandment is when Polycarp refers to the importance of faith, hope, and love and explains the latter as involving love toward God, *Christ,* and the neighbor (Polyc. Phil. 3.3*a*). This "triple commandment" to love constitutes the "commandment of righteousness" which is set over against all sin (3.3*b*). We may have here an echo of Matthew's emphasis upon the need for that "higher righteous-ness" which is defined in the love command.[67]

The concept of love found in the Apostolic Fathers has been severely criticized by Anders Nygren. Here, he claims, love is hailed as "the greatest human *achievement*" (his italics), "a meritorious work"; it is "no longer God's Way to man, but man's Way to God." [68] There is some truth to this charge. We have seen that love is listed among the virtues. Nowhere is it identified with the Spirit's presence as the power of the new age. It is also true that the performance of works of love (like almsgiving) is repeatedly commanded as a means of obtaining God's favor and forgiveness (e.g., I Clem. 50.5). Finally, Nygren is correct when he criticizes those who would read Barnabas' version of Lev. 19:18 ("love your neighbor *more than your own life,*" 19.5; cf. 1.4; 4.6) as an intensification of the original command. On the contrary, such an interpretation reveals that certain legal con-siderations are now being applied to the commandment: it *"has been re-thought in quantitative categories, and is intensified on this lower level"* (his italics).[69]

At the same time, we must insist that there are certain theo-logical dimensions to the love ethic in these Fathers which go

---

[66] On the textual problems of Did. 2.7, see Kraft, *Barnabas and the Dida-che,* p. 145.

[67] For a good discussion of this interesting passage from Polycarp, see William R. Schoedel, *Polycarp, Martyrdom of Polycarp, Fragments of Papias,* The Apostolic Fathers, 5 (New York: Thomas Nelson & Sons, 1967): 13-16.

[68] *Agape and Eros,* pp. 248, 259.

[69] *Ibid.,* p. 264. See also Goguel's comments on the Didache and his refer-ence to Did. 6.2 which commends full obedience, *or*—if that is impossible—"what you can" (*The Primitive Church,* pp. 494-95).

beyond any we have found in the canonical books of James or
II Peter. The commandments to forgive and to be merciful are
from Christ himself (e.g., I Clem. 13.1 ff.; Polyc. Phil. 2.3), and
his own life, suffering, and death provide an example of love
which those who believe in him can follow (e.g., I Clem. 2.1-8;
33.7-8; Polyc. Phil. 10.1; cf. 2.2). Moreover, the idea that one
serves Christ by serving his neighbor in love (Paul; Matt. 25:
31 ff.; I Peter 2:16-17) is still present here, for instance Herm.
Sim. I, 7-9: those who serve the Lord (οἱ δουλεύοντες τῷ κυρίῳ)
and have him in their hearts should do "the works of God"; by
spending their resources to care for the needy (widows and
orphans) they will be performing their services for Christ himself
(ἵνα ταύτας τὰς διακονίας τελέσητε αὐτῷ). Finally, Nygren[70] too
readily dismisses the note on which Clement's hymn to love concludes: "In love our Master received us; because of the love he
had for us our Lord Jesus Christ by the will of God shed his
blood for us . . . (I Clem. 49.6)." [71] This "indicative" motif is
present also in the opening line of the hymn: "Let him who has
love in Christ perform the commandments of Christ" (49.1).
Whether the phrase "in Christ" is construed with "love" (in
Christ we have love) or with "perform" (our obedience is in
Christ[72]), a christological context has been given from the very
start. Later in this hymn "God's elect" are said to "have been
made perfect in love" (49.5e), and in the chapter immediately
following the point is made that no one has such perfection in
love except as a gift from God (50.1-3; cf. 38.4).

Conclusion

The writings which have engaged our attention in this section
all reflect particular problems Christians of the late first and
early (to middle) second century were facing in the world and
within the church itself. Hope for Christ's imminent return has
faded, and with it has gone any significant sense of the church

[70] *Agape and Eros*, p. 248.
[71] R. M. Grant's translation, *First and Second Clement*, p. 81.
[72] So in Grant's translation, *ibid.*, p. 80.

as an eschatological community of the Spirit. Persecution and secularism threaten the church from without, heresy, apostasy, apathy, moral laxity from within. The importance of love in the Christian life is not forgotten and is sometimes impressively expounded, but in increasing isolation from a meaningful theological context and with increasing dependence upon the traditional formulations of Jewish and Christian catechesis. In spite of occasional references to blessing one's enemies, honoring all men, or striving for peace with everyone, attention is focused chiefly upon the place of love within the church itself. Ignatius, for instance, has nothing to say about loving or praying for one's persecutors, though he is quite preoccupied with his own impending martyrdom.[73] More and more the love command is applied as a *community regulation* by which unity, peace, and charitable service for the needy can be maintained.

The concern for the regulation and regularization of the Christian life (in both its personal and corporate aspects) is also apparent in the concept of a new "Christian law." Paul had referred once directly (Gal. 6:2), once indirectly (I Cor. 9:21), to "the law of Christ."[74] In James and in the Apostolic Fathers such a concept becomes formalized. James, as we have seen, speaks about the "royal law," the "perfect law," the "law of liberty." Similarly, Ignatius refers to the "law of Jesus Christ" (Ign. Mg. 2), and Hermas speaks of Christ's conveyance to men of a law he had received from the Father (Sim. V, 6.3). Barnabas is the first to employ the adjective "new," as he refers to the "new law of our Lord Jesus Christ" (2.6). While the phrase "law of love" does not occur in this literature, the love command is unquestionably regarded as a vital part (though not the whole) of this new law (cf. James 2:8ff.). Clement, for instance, refers to "the shackle of God's love" as he begins his hymn extolling the place of love within the church (I Clem. 49.2). The metaphor may hark back to Paul's comment that Christ's love "controls us" (II Cor. 5:14), although in I Clement, as we have seen, the emphasis falls on love's regulatory function in the church, not upon its being the power of the new age.

[73] See Bauer, "Das Gebot der Feindesliebe und die alten Christen,'" p. 42.
[74] See above, p. 100.

192

This regulatory function of the Christian law is appropriately conveyed by the image of the "yoke" (Did. 6.2; cf. Matt. 11:29-30), a metaphor also employed by Jewish writers with reference to the law.[75] The law must be *borne,* yet it is not represssive, but enables those who serve under it to work in harmony and with good effect. Although Barnabas emphasizes that the new law is *not* a "constraining yoke" (2.6), Clement accepts the metaphor and even christianizes it when he refers to the example of Christ's sacrificial death: "You see, beloved brethren, what an example has been given us! For if the Lord himself was so humble, what should we do who have come under the yoke of his grace?" (I Clem. 16.17).[76] Finally, then, for these writers, the love command is seen as the guiding law for God's people. It binds them together as one, enables them to do the "works of faith" (Herm. Sim. VIII, 9.1), and keeps them going straight in "the way of life." Because the new law has been conveyed in the words and deeds of Christ himself and leads to salvation, it is not really a burden at all, but can be received as the yoke of God's grace and therefore, in a certain sense, his gift as well as his demand.[77]

[75] See R. M. Grant, *First and Second Clement,* p. 39.

[76] Grant's translation, *ibid.,* p. 40.

[77] Lage Pernveden, *The Concept of the Church in the Shepherd of Hermas,* trans. I. and N. Reeves with M. Wentz, Studia Theologica Lundensia, 27 (Lund: CWK Gleerup, 1966), contends that the "indicative" aspects of the gospel are prominent even in Hermas (pp. 202 ff.). See also his discussion of "Paraenesis and Moralism," pp. 300-307. It is surely an over-simplification to describe *The Shepherd* as naïve moralism and to dismiss it out of hand. But Pernveden's own interpretation of Hermas is one-sided in the other direction.

CONCLUSION

Our investigation of the love command in the New Testament has now been completed. By respecting the integrity of the individual New Testament traditions and writers we have sought to understand the various ways in which the command to love was received, interpreted, and applied within the earliest church. We have found reason to believe that the love command was central to Jesus' own message and mission. Whether or not the Great Commandment as such was his own formulation, the exhortations to love God and the neighbor which it vitally coordinates and urgently presents are in keeping with what even the most cautious scholars agree to be most characteristic of Jesus' teaching.[1] The kingdom of God is the Rule of God's forgiving

---

[1] See, e.g., H. Braun, *Jesus: Der Mann aus Nazareth und seine Zeit*, p. 132.

194

and commanding love; Jesus' call to repentance and discipleship is a call to obey God's will, to manifest the reality and meaning of his kingship in one's life. The distinctiveness of the love command within Jesus' teaching was not that some new insight into "the nature of the good" had been achieved. Jesus was not the first to formulate the love command. But it was his distinction to have made that command central within the context of his proclamation about the coming Rule of God, the Rule of a divine Sovereign whose power is revealed in both his judgment and his mercy. The *urgency* of the command and the *concreteness* of the obedience it calls forth are emphasized in Jesus' parable of the Good Samaritan. The *meaning* of the love which is commanded is apparent in Jesus' repeated exhortations to refrain from judging others and—most of all—in his appeal to love the enemy. Here is a further distinction of Jesus' command to love. Love of enemies is not some "extended form" of brotherly love, or neighbor love. The love Jesus commanded, be it directed toward the "neighbor" or toward the "enemy," is understood in just one way: as active goodwill toward the other, as my affirmation of him as a person who stands or falls quite apart from what I think of him, as my acknowledgment of our common humanity and our common dependence upon One whose judgment and mercy is over all, and as my commitment to serve him in his need.

We have seen that the Jesus-traditions employed by Matthew and Luke, especially the versions of the Great Commandment which they have received and interpreted, and also their own particular interests and emphases, retain the love command and the call to works of love in a central place. Matthew views the love command as the key to the law's meaning and as the essential content of the "higher righteousness" which distinguishes Jesus' followers. Luke is especially concerned to contrast the Christian love imperative with the ethics of reciprocity extolled in the Hellenistic world, particularly stresses the need for love to find expression in concrete deeds of mercy and compassion, and consistently portrays the church as a community of love wherein the gospel of peace and reconciliation is powerfully present and formative. While both these evangelists view the love command as central to Jesus' *teaching,* neither of

195

them abstracts his teaching in general or the love command in particular from his ministry or his redemptive mission. He teaches with divine authority, his are imperial commands. Because in his own person God's Rule has broken in, his summons to obedience and to discipleship is interpreted—now in the light of the church's Easter faith—as a summons to *believe in him and in his redemptive work.* To love God and the neighbor is service of the Lord Christ himself.

In Paul's thought the teaching of the earthly Jesus has no place as such. The apostle's preaching is focused almost entirely upon the death and resurrection of Christ as the decisive eschatological event. Love is the power of the new age present and active in the working of the Spirit. Man's bondage to the old age, to his own past, to the finite claims of the world, has been broken—above all in Christ's death. In the cross, in Jesus' radical obedience unto death, and in God's gracious gift, the meaning of love is revealed. It means *caring* for the other—not because of who he is or where he stands in relation to oneself, but just because he *is,* and because he is *there.* It means *identifying* with him, with his needs, his hurts, his joys, his hopes, his lostness and loneliness. It means being willing to *risk taking the initiative in reconciliation,* and being willing, finally, to *give oneself* to him in service and support of his humanity. In Christ one is a recipient of such love and thereby becomes a participant in the new creation. By love he is freed—to love; for love is the meaning of his obedience and his life.

In the Fourth Gospel and the Johannine Epistles, as in the Synoptic Gospels, the love command is identified as a specific item of Jesus' teaching, indeed as its vital center. But now a step is taken which the Synoptic writers could have taken but did not take: the love command is interpreted not only as Jesus' rule for his followers, but in fact as the command under which the entirety of Jesus' own mission has been carried out. As the Father has commanded him, so he commands his disciples; as he has loved them to the uttermost, so they are to love one another. In the Johannine literature as in Paul's letters the priority of God's love is constantly stressed, Jesus' death is regarded as the decisive redemptive event, and the believer is viewed as one who has been brought from death to life and placed under the divine command to love as he has been loved.

Not only in the Synoptics, Paul, and the Johannine literature, but also in Colossians, Ephesians, and I Peter, the rule of love is presented as central to the gospel imperative. Moreover, the *power* of love's presence as gift and as demand is still emphasized in these writings, although, to be sure, in different ways and with different accents. In Colossians love is the power of the *Christ triumphant,* the life force of Christian community, the body of Christ. In Ephesians love's power is identified with the eternal purpose of God and the cosmic peace which he ordains and which has been made visible in the oneness of his church. In I Peter the power of love in the life of faith and hope is seen to derive from the exemplary and redemptive suffering and death of Christ. This writer, like the writers of Hebrews and Revelation where love has a similar though less prominent place, is heavily dependent upon the creedal, liturgical, and catechetical traditions to which he is heir. But even if the theological originality of these writers is somewhat less than that of the evangelists and Paul, their concern for the presence and operation of love in the Christian life is hardly diminished.

We must conclude, however, that not so much can be said for some other New Testament writers. In the Pastoral Epistles and II Peter, love is no longer seen as the *power* of the Christian life, rooted in the love bestowed through the redemptive event of Christ's incarnation, death, and resurrection, and expressed in a life already being re-created "in Christ." For these writers, love is one among numerous Christian virtues, one of the *practical requirements* of life in a church which hopes for and awaits the future Rule of God, but does not regard itself as already participating in it. We have also seen that the teaching about love, forgiveness, and the service of others which is prominent in James, does not, however, play a distinctive role there. Love is part of, but not the critical measure of, the "royal law" which the writer extols. Love and the deeds of love are defined with reference to the law and the counsels of Wisdom, not with reference to God's gift of love in Christ. Finally, we have found Nygren's judgment concerning the meaning of love in the Apostolic Fathers, especially in the letters of Ignatius and Clement,

197

to be too severe. Although one may note there a tendency to interpret and apply the love command simply as a rule or regulation for the life of the church, it is without question understood to be a significant part of the "new law of Jesus Christ." Love is a constituent aspect of the "yoke of grace" which has been laid upon believers to join them together in that common obedience and concord whereby the unity of God and of his purpose is made manifest.

Our findings, then, do not admit of any easy schematization of the New Testament love command. On the one hand, it is impossible to hold that the love command always and everywhere has a central place in the ethical teaching of the New Testament, or that it always and everywhere has an important theological grounding. On the other hand, it is equally impossible to trace a gradual dilution and restriction of the meaning of the love command beginning, say, with Jesus and following the "fate" of the commandment down into the second century. Moreover, we have had to recognize that the reception, interpretation, and application of the love command within the earliest church were always, in numerous significant ways, conditioned by the needs and possibilities of the given time and place. This in itself is not an unimportant conclusion. That the love command *was* received and that the church *did* struggle, sometimes at considerable cost, to interpret and apply it in newly meaningful ways, is testimony to three things. First, that it was regarded as a crucial part of the church's witness to Christ; second, that from the beginning the church understood the necessity of *interpreting* its meaning for new situations; and third, that the concern for *applying* it to these situations remained constantly alive.

Four Considerations

I have already cited the risks of attempting summary generalizations of the meaning of the love command in the New Testament. If this present study can contribute anything to an understanding of this commandment it will be primarily, I trust, in its attempt to articulate the meaning of particular texts and to identify the distinctive emphases of particular New Testament writers. At the same time I am not unaware of the lamentable gap which has continued too long between the work of biblical exegetes and Christian ethicists.[2] Finally, then, it may be helpful to formulate into a few compact sentences some of the findings of this study which would seem to merit consideration in contemporary discussions of Christian ethics.

I. The New Testament commendation of love is formulated in a *command* to love.

It is important, first of all, to recognize the significance of the fact that what we have in the New Testament is a *commandment* to love. Unfortunately, the meaning of the love command *as a command* has been too often neglected, or else improperly assessed. The question has been avoided entirely by Nygren, for instance. His summary conclusions regarding the Great Commandment are in keeping with the New Testament witnesses: the commandments to love God and the neighbor are inseparable yet distinguishable, the reference to self-love is not intended as a third command, and the love commanded for the neighbor includes also the enemy.[3] Yet nowhere in his discussion of these points does Nygren consider how there can be a *commandment* to love at all, especially if love be regarded as "real Agape, spontaneous and creative."[4] What does it mean to be *commanded* to love? Indeed, is it even possible for "real Agape," as Nygren has defined it, to be "commanded"?

These questions are not adequately handled simply by referring to the Jewish background of Jesus' teaching and the early church's catechetical traditions, although it is quite true that the moral teaching of early Christianity was heir to the Jewish legacy of law and commandments and the attendant conception

---

[2] Brevard Childs has some apt remarks on this in his *Biblical Theology in Crisis* (Philadelphia: Westminster Press, 1970), pp. 123-26.

[3] *Agape and Eros*, pp. 95-102.

[4] *Ibid.*, p. 102.

of man's responsibility to *obey*. It is equally true, however, that these very conceptions underwent significant alteration in the church, indeed doubtless already in the teaching of Jesus. For most of the New Testament writers the love command is not just one among numerous important statutes of the law, but the *decisive* and *central* commandment. And in the Pauline and Johannine traditions particularly the concept of obedience itself is radicalized in such a way that it no longer has reference to the believer's relationship to *the law*, but to the claim of God which is normatively encountered not in the body of the law but in the person and work of Jesus Christ. These points are not taken seriously enough when John Murray—to cite just one recent conservative interpreter—exegetes the Pauline statement, "Love is the fulfillment of the law" to mean that love *requires* that *all the statutes* of the law be obeyed.[5] Such a view, to employ temporarily Joseph Fletcher's distinction, regards the Great Commandment more as a "compendium" of all the laws than as a "distillation" of them whereby the intention of the law is "liberated."[6] Yet Fletcher's own formula needs correction, for it is insufficient to call the double commandment only a distillation of "the essential spirit and ethos of many laws. . . ."[7] More accurately, it is clearly regarded within the Synoptic traditions as the criterion and measure by which the law itself, with all its various commandments, is to be judged.[8] This criticism of the law is already at work precisely within those materials (for example, the exhortations about nonretaliation and love of enemies) which take us closest to Jesus' own teaching. If this be so, then the significance of love as a commandment has not yet been uncovered if we seek to define that in terms of its relation to the law, as both Murray and Fletcher do, although in quite different ways.

1. That the summons to love is formulated as a commandment indicates, first, that the summons to love arises not from within

---

[5] *Principles of Conduct: Aspects of Biblical Ethics* (Grand Rapids: Eerdmans Publishing Co., 1957), esp. pp. 192, 226-227.

[6] *Situation Ethics: The New Morality* (Philadelphia: Westminster Press, 1966), pp. 70-71.

[7] *Ibid.*, p. 71.

[8] Michel, "Das Gebot der Nächstenliebe," p. 62.

the natural affections of the one commanded, nor from within the natural attractiveness (lovability) of the one to be loved, but from a source *outside* the parties to the relationship itself. In biblical terms, the source of the commandment is God, and that means that the commandment remains even when the natural inclinations or attractiveness of the parties involved are changed. To formulate the summons to love as a commandment is to recognize that love in the Christian sense is *not* something "spontaneous," but something which must be repeatedly called forth and repeatedly obeyed. To be confronted with a *commandment* to love is to be reminded that the Christian life is no settled state but a *vocation,* a *being called,* a *being claimed.*

Immanuel Kant's discussion of the Great Commandment is still worth reading,[9] no matter what one thinks of the Kantian ethic as a whole. Kant at least understood very well that love in the New Testament sense is not dependent upon "aroused feelings." It therefore excludes the kind of perfectionist ethic which presumes to be guided by "a spontaneous goodness of heart, needing neither spur nor bridle nor even command," and which leads one to preoccupation with his own merit.[10] Still important also is Sören Kierkegaard's discussion of the subject.[11] Only when love is undertood as a duty is it truly free to be love in the Christian sense.

If one man, when another man says to him, "I can no longer love you," proudly answers, "Then I can also stop loving you": is this independence? Alas, it is only dependence, for the fact as to whether he will continue to love or not depends on whether the other will love. But the one who answers, "Then I *will* still continue to love you," his love is everlastingly free in blessed independence. He does not say it proudly—dependent on his pride; no, he says it humbly, humbling himself under the "shalt" of eternity, and just for that reason he is independent.[12]

[9] See *Critique of Practical Reason and Other Writings in Moral Philosophy,* trans. Lewis W. Beck (Chicago: University of Chicago Press, 1949), pp. 189-93.

[10] *Ibid.,* p. 192.

[11] See *Works of Love,* trans. David F. and Lillian M. Swenson (Princeton: Princeton University Press, 1949), pp. 20-36.

[12] *Ibid.,* p. 33.

2. Our first point can also be expressed by saying that it is man's *will* which is claimed by love, not his "emotions" or "affections." [13] Now this observation is sometimes misunderstood and misapplied, as I think it has been to some extent by Joseph Fletcher in his chapter, "Love Is Not Liking," [14] and farther on some qualification of the point will be suggested. But this much, at least, is true for most and perhaps all New Testament writers: love is not to wait upon some interior attitudinal transformation. Love in the Christian sense is not to be confused with filial or familial affection, for these can in no way be commanded. Love which can be commanded can only be—to use Kant's phrase— "practical love." [15] This is in keeping with the New Testament insistence that love is present where it is "active" in deeds of mercy and kindness, in the actuality of caring for and serving the neighbor. So love is an act of the will, not just some vague and generalized "disposition of the soul," feeling, or attitude.

3. We are brought now to a third point: to be thus commanded means to be addressed individually and concretely with the requirement to love, to be claimed for love and the works of love amid all the real possibilities and real limitations of one's own situation. The parable of the Good Samaritan, certainly in the Lucan setting, is at least in part an illustration of the way the love command summons concrete acts of obedience in response to encountered need. The appeal to "Go and do likewise" is central to the parable, and the point is not the theoretical one that one should henceforth adopt some less restricted and more broadly humanitarian view of who his neighbor is. It is the more immediately "practical" point that the "neighbor" is the *next person encountered,* and that obedience in love means serving *him.* This concrete call to service is the heart of Jesus' command to love the neighbor.[16]

[13] This point is often made by Bultmann, e.g. in *Jesus and the Word:* "Only if love is thought of as an emotion is it meaningless to command love; the *command* to love shows that love is understood as an attitude of the will" (p. 118).

[14] *Situation Ethics,* pp. 103-19.

[15] *Critique of Practical Reason,* p. 190.

[16] These points are made well by G. Friedrich, "Der Christ und die Moral," ZEE XI (1967): 285, and H. Braun, *Jesus: Der Mann aus Nazareth und seine Zeit,* p. 130.

The many passages in which Bultmann has emphasized the concreteness of love's demand and the situational context of obedience may indeed be interpreted as adumbrating a "situational ethic." In this case one would have to take seriously the kind of criticism of "Situation Ethics" typical, for instance, of Paul Ramsey: "A person is not fully in earnest about the Christian moral life if he is so concerned about the Christian compassion expressed and exhibited in individual actions case by case that he neglects the Christian compassion that must needs be expressed and exhibited in societal *rules of practice,* in law, and in social institutions." [17] Yet Bultmann's essential point in this connection seems to me quite in accord with the Christian insistence that love is a *command,* and thus not really in accord with attempts to formulate "situation ethics" into an ethical *theory.*[18] Bultmann rightly sees that the love command does not demand "general love of man . . . , based on an abstract or ideal value of man, but love of the real man with whom I am bound up, based on nothing but the fact that he *is* my neighbor, whom I understand as such only in loving." [19]

4. Finally, precisely because love is formulated as a command, we ought to be wary of converting it into simply a "criterion" or "principle" of ethical action, or into an epistemological tool whereby, in the actual case, the content of moral action is revealed. Bultmann is correct when he suggests that love *"understands my solidarity of connexion with my neighbour in each situation as it arises"* and discloses not some "concept" of the neighbor, but "each time" the neighbor himself. He goes too far, however, when he adds, "and thereby [love] discloses what I

[17] "The Biblical Norm of Righteousness," *Interpretation* XXIV (1970): 424. Ramsey's most extended critique of "Situation Ethics" and of Joseph Fletcher's views in particular is in his *Deeds and Rules in Christian Ethics* (New York: Charles Scribner's Sons, 1967), esp. chaps. VI, VII (pp. 123-225). For a discussion of Bultmann's work in particular, see James M. Gustafson, *Christ and the Moral Life* (New York: Harper & Row, 1968), esp. pp. 130 ff.

[18] On the difficulties of viewing the "new morality" as a method of ethics, see Ramsey, "The Biblical Norm of Righteousness," pp. 424-26 and Donald Evans, "Love, Situations and Rules," in G. H. Outka and P. Ramsey, eds., *Norm and Context in Christian Ethics* (New York: Charles Scribner's Sons, 1968), pp. 367-414.

[19] "To Love Your Neighbour," *Scot Per* I (1947): 50 (trans. by the Editor).

ought to do each time." [20] This appeal to love as a criterion, principle, or guide for use in making specific moral choices is particularly prominent in the writings of those who identify themselves with a "new morality." Joseph Fletcher thus speaks of a "strategy of love" [21] and of love's "selfless, calculating concern for others," [22] of an "agapeic calculus." [23] And Sydney Barr, who proposes to support the "new morality" approach from the New Testament, calls agape "the one enduring criterion for human relationships which never fails," [24] a criterion which provides "a specific and positive platform on which to stand" and "a significant key that can speak meaningfully [sic!] to any and every culture in any and every kind of world that may develop in the future." [25]

Now the problem here, from an exegetical point of view, is not that the Christian's obedience to the love command ought not to involve "figuring the angles" when confronted with complex moral choices.[26] On the contrary, we have seen that the New Testament itself reflects the church's constant endeavor to interpret the meaning of obedience within the various new circumstances it had to face. The problem is, rather, that there is a danger here of assimilating the "love principle" or "love criterion" so far into the decision-making process itself that it loses its force as the single command under which that whole process is to be constantly judged and redeemed. As Karl Rahner insists, the fundamental distinction of the love command is that it "cannot be performed or negotiated." And this is so because, as Rahner puts it, what love demands "is never simply present but

---

[20] *Ibid.*, p. 48. Cf. *Jesus and the Word*, p. 94: "If a man really loves, he knows already what he has to do." I see some tension between such remarks and Bultmann's insistence that love should *not* be regarded as "the material principle of an ethic. . . . It offers no principles of action in accordance with which, if I *know* them, I can then comport myself" ("To Love Your Neighbour," pp. 47–48).

[21] *Situation Ethics,* p. 151.

[22] *Ibid.,* p. 110.

[23] *Ibid.,* p. 115.

[24] *The Christian New Morality: A Biblical Study of Situation Ethics* (New York: Oxford University Press, 1969), p. 69.

[25] *Ibid.,* p. 105.

[26] This is the criticism of his "calculating love" which Fletcher acknowledges and seeks to turn aside, *Situation Ethics,* p. 116.

is always on the way to itself." [27] As a *command*, then, love stands over every particular requirement or set of requirements. This is what it means to say, as we have said, that love was understood in the Jesus-traditions as the critical measure of the law itself. And it is what Paul meant when he prayed that the Philippians might abound in love "with knowledge and all discernment" (Phil. 1: 9 *RSV*). Here love is not sought as a criterion of specific actions but as the context within which concrete choices must be faced, figured, and made.[28] I believe that Gene H. Outka's distinction between the love command as an "unqualifiedly general ethical principle" and the various "subsidiary" principles, norms, and rules to which it leads, is applicable to our New Testament evidence.[29] The earliest church constantly particularized the love command by formulating specific rules of practice for its life. But in general (although not without exceptions) the church avoided *reducing* the commandment to such rules or using these rules as if, collectively, they exhausted the meaning of the love command itself. The point here may be clearer if we proceed to a second consideration.

II. The Christian love command is the *sovereign* command of a *sovereign* Lord.

Not only in the Great Commandment, but wherever New Testament writers stress the centrality of the love command, one's love for the neighbor is vitally related to his relationship to God.[30] Man is understood as a creature of God, and his human-

---

[27] "The 'Commandment' of Love in Relation to the Other Commandments," *Theological Investigations, V: Later Writings,* trans. K.-H. Kruger (Baltimore: Helicon Press, 1966), p. 451.

[28] See my discussion of this passage in *Theology and Ethics in Paul,* pp. 235-37.

[29] See his article, "Character, Conduct and the Love Commandment" in *Norm and Context in Christian Ethics* (above, n. 18), esp. pp. 38-60.

[30] The Pastorals, James, and II Peter which admittedly do not stress the priority of God's love and of man's relationship to God, are no exceptions to this generalization. For these are the very same writings in which love is regarded simply as one command (James) or one virtue (the Pastorals, II Peter) among others.

ity is viewed as thereby subject to the creative and redemptive power of God. In Jesus' teaching the sovereignty of God is expressed in the proclamation of his coming Rule, and the sovereignty of God's claim is expressed in the call to repentance and obedience. In Jesus' teaching, eschatology and ethics go closely together, the proclamation of God's imminent Rule is coordinate with the promulgation of the commandment to love. Wolfhart Pannenberg's exposition of the meaning of Jesus' preaching of the Kingdom is essentially in keeping with the findings of our study: "God's love was revealed in the ways the presence of the Kingdom manifests itself before it comes in power." "The present announcement of the imminent Kingdom of God offers man a chance to participate in God's future rather than being overwhelmed by its sudden arrival and being conquered as an adversary of that future. This is the offer of salvation which reveals God's loving concern for man." [31] The sovereign priority of God's love is also stressed by Paul when he identifies Jesus' own death as the decisive event of redeeming love and when he identifies love with the gift of the Spirit as the power of the new age already present and effective. Again, in the Johannine literature love is regarded as the eschatological power by which the Father and the Son are united and in obedience to which the Son is sent on a mission of love to the world.[32]

1. When love is presented in the New Testament as the sovereign command of a sovereign Lord, then it becomes evident that it is the divine love alone which is regarded as the measure and meaning of love's claim. This truth is only obscured if self-love is included as a third commandment or in some other way made parallel with the commands to love God and the neighbor.[33]

[31] *Theology and the Kingdom of God* (Philadelphia: Westminster Press, 1969), pp. 64-65; cf. pp. 117-18.

[32] Hence, I believe Spicq is wrong to contrast the Pauline conception of love as "active *dynamis*" with a Johannine view of love as "above all a nature . . ." (*Agape in the New Testament,* III: 171). This leads Spicq to neglect the *missional* character of love as we find it in John, its formulation into a commandment calling for obedience, and to concentrate on love as aimed at a "reciprocal indwelling," a "communication of being and life . . ." (*ibid.,* p. 173).

[33] See, e.g., Fletcher's reference to "the three objects of love (God, neighbor, self)" and his contention that "all love is *amor sui*, self-love, i.e., all love seeks its own good," so that "if we love ourselves for God's sake

We cannot and need not find direct biblical support for the modern insight that genuine acceptance of others requires acceptance of oneself. Our experience is quite sufficient testimony to the validity of this insight. The concept of self-love in the New Testament is directed to a different aspect of man's experience, namely, that *preoccupation* with self sets one under the tyranny of finite claims and in thus alienating him from the divine claim denies the truth about his humanity and cuts him off from life. When, however, love is received as the command of a sovereign Lord, it is formed in response to and by the power of that prior gift of love which is present and active already in the Sovereign's creating and redeeming activity.

Accepted as a command inherent in a gift, love liberates one from bondage to himself and to the world. It is quite right to say that in the New Testament self-love is regarded as "the attitude of the natural man which must be overcome." [34] Likewise, encountered as God's gift and demand, love exercises a binding force over those whom it addresses. As Ramsey has pointed out, "An unbinding love would seem the least likely conclusion one would reach if he seriously regarded the freedom of God's love in binding Himself to the world as the model for all covenants between men. Could anyone who perceives that God in total love and total freedom bound Himself to the world possibly view the implications of this love as unbinding on men?" [35] In the Pauline view especially, the divine love is presented as a liberating power whereby, in response to love's claim, the believer is *bound* in love to the neighbor.

2. Further, if love is a sovereign command, then the claim it makes is without restriction or limitation of any kind. For one thing, the totality of love's claim means that not just deeds of love are asked for, but the *whole person* of the one under command. The point has already been made that the love command is addressed to the will, not to the emotions. But this should not

and the neighbor's, then self-love is right" (*Situation Ethics*, pp. 113-14). There is an excellent discussion of this whole matter in Paul Ramsey's *Basic Christian Ethics* (New York: Charles Scribner's Sons, 1950), pp. 98-103, cf. p. 162.

[34] Bultmann, *Jesus and the Word*, p. 116.

[35] *Deeds and Rules in Christian Ethics*, pp. 127-28.

be taken to mean that love is satisfied by formal obedience, simply by the performance of deeds designed to support and serve the neighbor. In the same way, the formula "love is not liking" [36] is apt to distract us from the fact that the biblical view of man allows no systematic distinction between the determination of one's will and the disposition of his being as a whole. Because it is a sovereign command, love demands the doer along with his deeds. "There is only one 'virtue' which asks man for himself—really himself wholly and completely—and this is the virtue of love and it alone . . . ," says Rahner, for the other commandments are satisfied with "certain tangible achievements or the omission of certain actions, concrete realities which therefore can be accomplished to the full and whose accomplishments can be checked." [37] Not so with love. Although the New Testament writers without exception refuse to consider the possibility that love is present where it is not concretely manifested, it is equally certain that—for most of them—the lover himself must be present in his deeds. This is the meaning of "radical obedience" as Bultmann has discussed it, that the doer does not stand beside his work but within it, "that it is possible for him to be in what he is doing." [38] Because deeds of love are deeds of service to the neighbor, the doer identifies both with his deed and with the neighbor who is served thereby.

The juxtaposition of the conception of love as obedience to a commandment with the conception of love as compassion achieved by Luke when he joins the parable of the Good Samaritan to the Great Commandment accords with the point we are making. Although love is response to a command and not to a personal feeling, where the command is obeyed lover and beloved are brought into a relationship which is by no means merely "routine." [39] And because the relationship has been transformed by the command to love, so inevitably is the one who hears and

---

[36] This is the title Fletcher gives to the chapter in which he expounds the proposition that "love wills the neighbor's good whether we like him or not" (*Situation Ethics*, pp. 103-19).

[37] "The 'Commandment' of Love," p. 451.

[38] "To Love Your Neighbour," p. 52.

[39] Cf. Pannenberg, *Theology and the Kingdom of God*, p. 118: "Creative love does not ask the beloved for his dependency but for his personhood. To relate to somebody as a person is no routine thing but an act of faith."

answers the summons transformed by love. As Pannenberg insists, "Love effects that unity among men which expresses itself in legal forms but which is always more than those forms. Love fills the legal forms with life and thus achieves true justice." [40] This is the point discovered finally by Ishmael in Herman Melville's novel, *Moby Dick*. Forced to share a room in the Spouter-Inn with pagan Queequeg, Ishmael finally decides that Christian charity demands he reach some accommodation with Queequeg's way of life. Subsequently, Ishmael discovers that his initial repugnance to the other has been transformed into real friendship, and he is led to remark on "how elastic our stiff prejudices grow when love once comes to bend them." [41]

Love's command is unrestricted also in the sense that it makes no distinctions respecting the objects of love. Love neither presupposes nor requires a response in kind. "This love does not inquire after the 'Why' and 'Wherefore' of love, but rather loves simply because it cannot do otherwise than love." [42] Because it stands under the sovereign command of a sovereign Lord there is no room for love to pick and choose its own desired objects. Kierkegaard is right when he comments that the one who truly loves has closed his eye respecting the neighbor's identity and "become only an ear for hearing the commandment." [43] Not even where New Testament writers specifically and emphatically command love to enemies is there any apparent concern to extend the definition of "neighbor" to include the enemy. Rather, the motive for loving even him is presumed to require no other basis than the sovereign command itself, and to involve nothing different from what love requires in any other case. Love of neighbor and love of enemy are not two kinds of love but one and the same. When, in the Great Commandment, God and

[40] *Ibid.*, p. 79. See also Pannenberg's discussion of the sense of solidarity and shared destiny by which lover and beloved are united, pp. 118-20. The phrase "caring justice" has been used by Paul Ramsey ("The Biblical Norm of Righteousness," p. 421), by which he apparently means the kind of "care-full love" which identifies with the griefs, grievances, and temptations of others who, like ourselves, are "creature[s] of flesh and blood whose fate it is to live always in the valley of the shadow of death" (*ibid.*, p. 429).

[41] *Moby Dick* (New York: Rinehart & Co., 1948), p. 53.

[42] Friedrich, "Der Christ und die Moral," p. 289.

[43] *Works of Love*, p. 57.

neighbor are set side by side as the object of love, it has already been affirmed that the idea of "neighbor" ought to be no less absolutely conceived than the idea of "God." [44] Again it is Kierkegaard who has provided a memorable summary of the point: "If there are only two men, the other man is the neighbor; if there are millions, each one of these is the neighbor. . . ." [45]

III. By the love command a *community* of love is called into being and summoned to responsible action.

The love command is addressed to individuals and calls for their direct response by means of concrete obedience in actual situations. But because it is a command to *love,* in summoning them to obedience it summons them to one another. [46] The formation of deeds of love is at the same time the formation of a community of love. Here it is possible only to indicate three of the many important ways in which this point may be developed.

1. The New Testament writers speak from within and to a Christian community. The very existence of such a thing as a New Testament is significant. That these varied writings of authors who lived and wrote at different times and places and under various conditions came to be exchanged, circulated, and finally joined together into a New Testament canon is testimony to the sense of *being a community* which underlies all they have written. Our whole investigation of the love command has focused on its reception, interpretation, and application—all of these by a community of faith, hope, and love which regarded itself as entrusted with the gospel of Jesus Christ.

Paul and John offer the most profound insights into love's work in forming community, but the theme runs throughout the New Testament. Love's "community" is understood to manifest itself at various levels. There is the community which occurs

[44] See Martin Rade, "Der Nächste," *Festgabe für A. Jülicher* (Tübingen: J. C. B. Mohr [Paul Siebeck], 1927), p. 78.

[45] *Works of Love,* p. 18.

[46] Correctly, Bultmann: "Love is not in the least a quality, a 'what' *to* man but a 'how' of his togetherness with others" ("To Love Your Neighbour," p. 49); thus "love is a way of togetherness understood only by him who understands himself in his connexion with others" (*ibid.,* p. 52).

between persons when love reaches across old barriers and overcomes old alienations. Such community in love is often illustrated in the Synoptic parables. There is also the wider community of those who understand themselves as "brethren for whom Christ died" and bound together by love's powerful gift and claim into the "body of Christ." And at least some of the New Testament writers are sensitive to the yet further work of love in guiding, perhaps we may say in "humanizing," the Christian's relationships with the non-Christian world.

The New Testament word—it is primarily Paul's word—which best describes love's work in calling a community of love into being is *reconciliation*. It describes the meaning of God's gift of love and of the command to love inherent in the gift. To be reconciled to God means to be reconciled with one another within the community of love, and the reconciled community itself is given the ministry of reconciliation. The community of love is thus a community which lives from love and under love's command. It does not exist from itself or for itself, but from and for God. That is, it is the creation of God's reconciling love and at the same time is summoned to be the instrument of such love.

2. When it is said that obedience to the love command means reconciliation and the formation of a reconciling community, then something further has also been said: love's community is not just the result or *consequence* of loving, but is itself the *embodiment* of love's power and of love's claim in history. What binds the community together and gives it its distinctive character is not the common obedience of its members to God's law. One might very well say this about the Jewish sectarian community at Qumran. But by contrast, the New Testament presumes a community which exists by virtue of God's love, and whose members believe that they are already participants in (or at least heirs of) a new life founded on love. Thus, most of the New Testament writers understand that obedience in love is not just a demand laid upon them but is, along with God's gift of love, one of the constitutive aspects of the new life itself.

A great deal of what New Testament writers say about love is representative of the community's understanding of itself as the manifest presence of God's love in the world and of its attempt to understand what it means concretely for Christians to *be* that kind of community. This helps to account for the fact that in certain places, and on the part of some writers more than others, there is an apparent preoccupation with love's task within the church. But it is important to remember that even when this is or appears to be the case, there is an operative presumption that the life of love *interior* to the Christian community has at the same time an *exterior* visibility and effect. Even if the earliest church did not always perceive it, the community's existence as the historical embodiment of love's power and claim, as a community whose very *life* is love, means that it is love's witness in the world. And how must the witness to love be borne? How must love be commended? By its *operation*, by its *being* love, by its *manifestation* as care and concern for the other, whoever he may be. Finally, then, as *reconciliation*.

In our day the Christian community has a far different status and bears a far different relationship to society than in the first several centuries of its life. For one thing, it can no longer live in expectation that the world with its societal orders and structures will "soon"—although this word meant different things already for first and second-century Christians—come to an end as Christ returns in full power and glory. The church in our day is required to understand itself as an "eschatological community" which, however, has a continuing existence within history, and therefore it is obliged to have certain institutional features and forms. Moreover, in most parts of the world, the Christian community is no longer a persecuted minority. It has wealth and power, and its members occupy important positions within the social, economic, and political structures. It is no longer easy (if it ever was really easy) to distinguish between the church's interior life and its relationship with "the world." The line between church and world is very often difficult to perceive, and sometimes one wonders whether it is there at all.

This new relationship between church and world means, first, that the Christian community has vast new opportunities and responsibilities to embody love's gift and claim. The love command, as we have seen, does not summon the community to live for itself but for God and for others. Further, as a sovereign command of the sovereign Lord love calls for radical obedience and lays one's whole life under its claim. It is the Christian himself who bears love's gift and command, and he bears it therefore, and must seek to be obedient to it, wherever he goes, whatever the sector or the sphere within which he moves.[47] I believe it is this fact which not only allows but even requires that the church of our day be concerned for embodying the power and doing the works of love in ways which are relevant to the existing social, political, and economic structures. Because of its particularized eschatological expectation and social position, the earliest church was not required and in fact was unable to apply the love command in this way. But in principle, because the love command summons *community* into being, its call to reconciliation is no different where social institutions are involved than where it is a matter of individuals only. Oscar Cullmann is quite correct in pointing out that "as soon as centuries are reckoned with, it must necessarily be acknowledged that more just social structures also promote the individual change of character required by Jesus. A reciprocal action is therefore required between the conversion of the individual and the reform of the structures, even though the former must remain the principal factor in the life of the Christian."[48] Indeed, I believe we should go even farther than this and, in view of the nature of love's claim, insist that love is *only* authentic where it awakens the individual to the fact of his responsibilities within the whole complex web of interpersonal and interinstitutional relationships within which he is called to be obedient.[49]

[47] Henri-Marie Féret, O.P., has some suggestive remarks on the church's witness to love in the world, formulated specifically in terms of the new understanding of mission expressed in and subsequent to the Second Vatican Council. "In contrast with those times when brotherly love was usually practiced only among Christians . . . while the 'missionaries' in the old sense undertook practically alone to spread the Good News of God's presence in Jesus beyond the visible boundaries of the Church, today all Christians will have this mission to reveal the Gospel to these spiritual groupings, without having to go outside the framework of their daily lives" ("Brotherly Love in the Church as the Sign of the Kingdom," *Opportunities for Belief and Behavior,* Concilium: Theology in the Age of Renewal, 29 [New York: Paulist Press, 1967]: 27).

[48] *Jesus and the Revolutionaries,* trans. G. Putnam (New York: Harper & Row, 1970), p. 55.

[49] Cf. Pannenberg, *Theology and the Kingdom of God,* pp. 79-80: "The Kingdom of God, far from being merely a formalistic idea, is the utterly concrete reality of justice and love. But let no one think the Kingdom of

The new opportunities and responsibilities of obedience thrust upon the Christian community in the modern world unquestionably complicate the decision-making process. Moreover, the modern "diaspora" of the church in the world involves a great risk—the risk that the community will lose its identity as a community under love's command and as the embodiment of love's power and claim. In that case the reconciliation of the world would be dissipated into mere accommodation to the world.

3. The point presently under discussion is phrased quite deliberately so as to speak of the *community* which love summons into existence as the embodiment of love's gift and claim in the world, and of the *responsibility* which this involves. My concern, finally, is to stress the complexity of the ethical responsibilities to which the community is summoned, particularly in our day, and that the community brought forth by God's love itself provides the context within which moral choices must be examined and made. The community formed by love is not automatically conformed to love. The works of love do not erupt spontaneously from its life. To be commanded to love means to be called not just to "decision" in the profound sense about which existentialist philosophers and theologians often speak. It means also to be called to all sorts of specific "decisions."

It has not been the intention of this study to offer a catalog of specific actions love requires or prohibits in our day. Nor has it been our objective to summarize or evaluate all the particular applications of the love command present in the New Testament itself. The importance of the New Testament for contemporary Christian ethics does not consist in its provision of specific solutions to the ethical problems of every subsequent age. It is clear enough that the moral complexities faced by the earliest Christians belonged to their own time, not to ours. Their answers are not automatically, and sometimes not at all, transferable to our situation. Rather, what is most important for us is an understand-

---

God is therefore primarily concerned with the subjective behavior of individuals, rather than with the institutions of social life." "Subjective behavior and social institution must never be separated. Subjective behavior is related always to social institutions and, in most instances, is the enactment of the social forms of life." "Justice and love are relevant not only to the individual but, primarily, to the structures of human interaction."

ing of what the theological bases were upon which the earliest church's ethical teaching was founded and the way it went about interpreting and applying its gospel in daily life.[50] The former has in a sense been the focal point of our study. With respect to the *way* the earliest church went about the task of decision-making, we have no better witness than the apostle Paul. His letters provide us considerable data not only about the moral problems confronted by the Christians under his care, but also about Paul's own typical ways of dealing with those problems. We do not find in Paul's dealings with his churches the promulgation of a casuistic ethic, a series of rules, norms, or principles systematically arranged so as to provide reference points from which the proper action may be deduced and applied for particular cases. He certainly does not employ the law in that way, and he makes no attempt to build any such structure on the love command. For him, as for the New Testament in general, the love command remains a *command* and is never reduced to a "criterion" or "principle" in the casuistic sense. Occasionally in this study I have spoken about a "love ethic," but only in the loosest sense to refer to a particular writer's interpretation of the love command. In the strictest sense, there is no "love ethic" in Paul or anywhere else in the New Testament. Not only is every ethical *system* foreign to these writers; more significantly, the love command stands over every "ethical system" and, as we have observed already under II above, thereby subjects every such system to the sovereign judgment and mercy of God.[51]

[50] Here I am in agreement with the position worked out by James M. Gustafson in his excellent article, "The Place of Scripture in Christian Ethics: A Methodological Study," *Interpretation*, XXIV (1970): 430-55.

[51] Gustafson's statement that "biblical theology and ethics . . . are not exclusively a theology and an ethic of love" is obviously meant to include both Old and New Testaments and is supported, quite properly, by a reference to the "variety of theological and ethical themes in the Scriptures themselves . . ." (*ibid.*, p. 451). My intention is to say that, even though with few exceptions love is the central theme of exhortation in the New Testament, even *there* one should not speak of a "love ethic" in the formal sense. This means further, that when Gustafson's statement, "love cannot become the single principle used to judge events and actions even within Scripture" (*ibid.*) is applied to the New Testament alone, it remains true—but for the reason I have given above: in the New Testament love never loses its character as a sovereign command.

How, then, does Paul approach practical matters of conduct? We find him, time and again, seeking to be informed by every possible datum available—the facts of the situation at hand, the teaching of Scripture, some word of the Lord, the practice of Christians generally, the ethical wisdom of the ages, or even— once, anyway (I Cor. 11:14)—"nature itself." Without too much difficulty one can see in Paul's constant struggle to find the concrete ways in which the one excellent way of love should be manifest, that "process of disciplined theological reflection" which Brevard Childs has commended as a way for doing ethics in our own day. It should be a process, Childs continues, "that takes its starting point from the ethical issue at stake along with all its ambiguities and social complexities and seeks to reflect on the issue in conjunction with the Bible which is seen in its canonical setting." [52] In similar fashion James Gustafson speaks of the importance of maintaining "a dialectic between more intuitive moral judgments and both scriptural and nonscriptural principles and values . . . ," "a dialectic between principles of judgment which have purely rational justification and which also appeal to the tradition expressed in Scripture and developed in the Christian community." [53] It is the *community* context for Christian decision-making, presupposed, I believe, in the remarks of Childs and specifically mentioned by Gustafson, which was axiomatic for every New Testament writer. In summary of his own position, Gustafson writes further: "The vocation of the Christian community is to discern what God is enabling and requiring man to be and to do in particular natural, historical, and social circumstances. Its moral judgments are made in the light of that fundamental ought or demand." [54] With reference to New Testament thought there is just one additional word to be interjected here, but it is a crucial one. The Christian community in the context of which moral judgments are made understands itself as from the beginning the creation of God's love and the recipient of his command to love. Formed by that command, its call to responsible action is thereby a summons to be conformed to God's

[52] *Biblical Theology in Crisis*, p. 131.
[53] "The Place of Scripture in Christian Ethics," p. 451.
[54] *Ibid.*, p. 455.

love. The community does not stand under a bare "ought, or demand," but specifically under the command to love.

IV. The command to love is, simultaneously, also a call to repentance and a proffer of forgiveness.

Our final thesis is in a sense a recapitulation of the preceding ones. The gospel by which the community is formed and commanded is, according to the faith of the earliest church, a gospel which frees us from the past, sets us to a task in the present, and gives us a hope for the future. It is the forgiving and redeeming power of God whereby, in faith, we are opened up to life. The love command integral to this gospel is therefore never abstracted from the call to repentance and the proffer of forgiveness. These particular terms are present chiefly in the Synoptic Gospels and in the traditions they have employed, but the view of man's relationship to God which they presume is characteristic also of Paul, John, and some other New Testament writers. Paul, for instance, even as he stresses man's accountability to God and God's sovereignty in judgment, proclaims also the sovereignty of God's grace and the redemptive power of God's reconciling love. Faith as obedience means, for Paul, man's acknowledgment of his dependence upon God's redemptive as well as creative power, and man's constant reaffirmation of that dependence by the giving of himself in love to the neighbor, wholly and without reserve.

It has already been indicated in various ways that, because the love command is regarded as the expression of the sovereign love of God, it therefore exercises a sovereign claim. There is no limit to what it demands of the one who is open to hear it, no limit to the radius within which it is to be obeyed, no limit to the time in which its demands are in effect. The place and time for obedience in love are always *here* and *now*; the *kairos* of God's redeeming love is also the *kairos* of his commanding love. Therefore, obedience to the command of love is not self-fulfilling; that is, because of what love is and requires there can never be anything like cumulative achievement when it comes to love's claim. Hence, one must not cease being ready to forgive and, as Paul says, one is always a debtor as regards love.

Is it not, then, an intolerable burden to be asked to bear when we are asked to bear and obey this command to love? No one can claim to love God and neighbor with his whole heart, mind, soul, and strength, for in the nature of the case, since love is not an achievement which can be measured and preserved, what is demanded by love will be demanded again and again. "Love today is . . . what it should be today only if it acknowledges that it is something of which more will be demanded tomorrow." [55] Therefore, to hear the love command is to be called to repentance. In and of itself the love command "does not tell [a man] what love is; but it makes him conscious that he does not know it because he *does not love.*" [56] Yet because the infinite demand of love formulated into this commandment has its origin and context in the infinite love of God, the one under command knows that he stands not only under judgment, but under grace. The command discloses not only the depth of man's sin and the seriousness of his alienation from true life, but also the depth of God's forgiving love and the seriousness of the divine purpose to save.[57]

Perhaps, after all, there is no better way to describe the Christian love command than to apply to it the phrase from Clement of Rome, the "yoke of grace." For when, in the earliest church, the love command was accorded its most distinctive formulation and application, it was being interpreted as a sovereign claim born of the sovereign love and righteousness of God, operative already in history as the redeeming power of the new age. It stood, therefore, not as the base principle of some new ethical system or as a moral geiger counter for the detection of the good in individual cases. Rather, it stood and stands in judgment over every ethical system and over every moral choice. And it stands there also as the sign and way of God's own redemptive purpose and power.

[55] Rahner, "The 'Commandment' of Love," p. 452; cf. Rahner's further remark that "a carefully checked and measured love which basically closes itself to any greater love simply ceases to be love" (p. 453).

[56] Bultmann, "To Love Your Neighbour," p. 51.

[57] Cf. Bultmann, *ibid.*: "Love is therefore only possible on the basis of faith which seizes the *forgiveness of sins* offered in the Word of God and in this forgiveness knows itself to be loved and freed for love" (p. 54).

APPENDIX

New Testament Words for Love

It is well known that the predominant and most important word for "love" in the New Testament is ἀγαπᾶν/ἀγάπη. Moreover, the renown and the influence of Nygren's book, *Agape and Eros*, has all but universalized the impression that the word itself (a) was practically "invented" by Christianity and (b) is really the only notable word for love in the New Testament. As a matter of fact, Nygren himself made no such sweeping claims, and his justifiably famed book does not include any close philological study of love terminology in antiquity and earliest Christianity. While that is not the purpose of the present volume, either, it is important to review the philological situation in order to gain some perspective on the overall New Testament usage.[1]

I

The verb ἀγαπᾶν occurs 141[2] times in the New Testament, more often employed by the Fourth Evangelist (36 times) than by any other single writer,[3] though it is missing entirely from Acts, Ephesians, I Timothy, Titus, and Philemon. The noun ἀγάπη is present 116 times, most frequently in the Pauline letters.[4] The noun is never used in Luke-Acts or in James, leaving Acts as the only New Testament writing in which neither the verb nor the noun is employed.[5] Apart from the Pauline and deutero-Pauline letters the noun is most often found in the Johannine materials (Gospel, 7 times; Letters, 21 times).

Considerable attention has been paid the fact that, while the verb is attested in classical Greek from Homer on down, there is no certain instance of the noun ἀγάπη prior to its occurrence in the LXX (20 times). Even an alleged second-century A.D. occurrence in a pagan document is questionable,[6] leaving as the first certain instance

---

[1] Important studies of the terminology for "love" in classical and Hellenistic Greek sources have been published by Ceslaus Spicq, notably in his *Agapè: Prolégomènes à une Étude de Théologie Néo-Testamentaire*, Studia Hellenistica, 10 (Louvain: E. Nauwelaerts, 1955), hereafter cited as *Prolégomènes*, and in his three-volume *Agapè dans le Nouveau Testament: Analyse des Textes* (1958-59). Valuable as Spicq's studies are for the materials there assembled and for numerous specific insights, his overall methods and exegesis have been shaped to a disappointing extent by apologetic interests. The slender but important monograph by Robert Joly, *Le vocabulaire chrétien de l'amour est-il original? Φιλεῖν et Ἀγαπᾶν dans le grec antique* (Bruxelles: Presses Univ. de Bruxelles, 1968) ably refutes Spicq's contention that ἀγάπη words are "Christian" in quite a special sense, and provides good examples of how this view leads Spicq to overly subtle exegesis.

[2] Statistics are from R. Morgenthaler, *Statistik des Neutestamentlichen Wortschatzes* (Zürich: Gotthelf Verlag, 1958), p. 67.

[3] There are, in addition, 30 occurrences of the verb in the Johannine letters.

[4] 47 times in the indisputably authentic letters (Rom., I and II Cor., Gal., Phil., I Thess., Philem.); to which add: Eph., 10; Col., 5; II Thess., 3; Pastorals, 9.

[5] The adjective ἀγαπητός ("beloved") occurs once in Acts, in the letter sent from Jerusalem to Antioch (15:25, describing Barnabas and Paul).

[6] In a prayer to Isis, Oxyrhynchus Papyrus XI. 1380, line 109: ἀγάπην θεῶν. This was the reading of the original editors (B. P. Grenfell and A. S. Hunt, eds. & trans., *The Oxyrhynchus Papyri*, Part XI [London: Egypt Exploration Fund, 1915], pp. 190-220), and it has been supported by, among

of ἀγάπη in "secular" Greek an epigram from the third century A.D.[7] Moreover, its employment in the LXX hardly prepares one for the way it comes later to be used by Christian writers, for there it usually refers to the conjugal love between man and woman (II Kings 13:15 [RSV: II Sam.]; Song of Solomon 2:4, 5, 7; 3:5, 10; 5:8; 7:6; 8:4, 6, 7 [bis]; cf. Jer. 2:2). This meaning is retained in the New Testament only in the traditional parenesis at Col. 3:19 (paralleled by Eph. 5:25 where, however, this agape between partners in a marriage is said to be analogous to the agape between Christ and his church). However, also in the LXX, in Wisdom, the noun begins to take on a more "theological" character, applied to the relationship between God and his elect people (3:9) and to the relationship of the obedient man to Wisdom (6:18).[8]

From this it would appear—and the point has often been made—that ἀγάπη is exclusively (or almost exclusively) a biblical word and, at that, a word relatively uncommon in the LXX. From the LXX it is then borrowed by earliest Christianity and invested with significantly new meaning.[9] Warnach goes so far as to suggest that ἀγάπη

---

others, A. Deissmann, *Light from the Ancient East*, trans. L. R. M. Strachan from 4th German ed. (New York: Geo. H. Doran Co., 1927), pp. 75-76, n. 3; the revisers of the Liddell-Scott *Greek-English Lexicon* (Oxford: At the Clarendon Press, 1940), p. 6; James Moffatt, *Love in the New Testament*, pp. 10-11; C. H. Roberts, "ΑΓΑΠΗ in *The Invocation of Isis* (P. Oxy. xi. 1380)," *Journal of Egyptian Archaeology*, XXXIX (1953): 114; and R. E. Witt, "The Use of ΑΓΑΠΗ in *P. Oxy.* 1380: A Reply," *JThSt* XIX (1968): 209-11. This reading has, however, been rejected by many others, including E. Stauffer, *ThD* I: 38 (who, however, accepts the reading ἀγάπην in line 28 of the same papyrus), G. de Manteuffel (cited by Stauffer, *ibid.*, and n. 88), and Stephanie West, who follows C. H. Roberts ("ΑΓΑΠΗ") in rejecting Manteuffel's revised reading of line 109, but proposes an alternate reading of her own, ἀγαθὴν θεόν ("An alleged Pagan Use of ΑΓΑΠΗ in P. Oxy. 1380," *JThSt* XVIII [1967]: 142-43; and "A Further Note on ΑΓΑΠΗ in P. Oxy. 1380," *ibid.*, XX [1969]: 228-30). Spicq discusses this problem in his article "Le Lexique de l'Amour dans les Papyrus et dans quelques Inscriptions de l'Époque hellénistique," *Mnemosyne*, ser. IV, VIII (1955), esp. pp. 30-31.

[7] Cited in Bauer, *A Greek-English Lexicon of the New Testament*, p. 5, and Spicq, "Le Lexique de l'Amour."

[8] In II Kings 1:26 (RSV: II Sam.) and Sir. 48:11, some mss. read ἀγάπησις rather than ἀγάπη. In Jer. 2:2 ἀγάπη is bridal love, but applied metaphorically to the relationship of God and Israel.

[9] See, e.g., H. B. Swete, *An Introduction to the Old Testament in Greek*, rev. R. R. Ottley (Cambridge: University Press, 1902), p. 456. Also, P. Bonnard, who suggests that "no other Greek term owed so much to early Christianity" (art. "Love," in *A Companion to the Bible*, ed. J. J. von Allmen [New York: Oxford University Press, 1958], p. 243); and V. Warnach who speaks of the "specifically Christian character" of the word and de-

221

was for Christians in effect a *verbum arcanum*, a "holy word" formed by the Holy Spirit.[10] But more cautious judgments are in order. Even if the noun cannot be located in pre-Christian "pagan" sources, it *is* a "pre-Christian word" (*viz.* LXX, Hellenistic Judaism) and, at that, often used in a quite "profane" way. This in itself may indicate that, already by the time the LXX was produced, ἀγάπη had begun to be used as an ordinary word for love.[11] Moreover, there is ample evidence for the broad currency, prior to the Christian era, of the verb ἀγαπᾶν and a recent study by R. Joly has shown that, beginning in the fourth century B.C., even in "pagan" sources, the use of φιλεῖν steadily declined while the use of ἀγαπᾶν increased correspondingly.[12]

The issue, therefore, is not whether Christianity—or, more precisely, Judaism before it—has coined an absolutely new word, unsullied by previous "pagan" associations. Even if there are no pre-Christian "pagan" instances, the usual LXX associations are quite "secular." Nor is it possible any longer to contend that Christianity adopted the verbal form because it was such a nondescript, rarely used word that it could easily be given a special Christian content. The facts do not support this, as Joly's careful work has shown. A study of the love motif in early Christianity cannot proceed very far on an exclusively lexical basis. The meaning of love in the earliest Christian literature is not tied to semantics, but to the whole range of Christian beliefs about God, man, and the world.

II

It is, of course, significant that New Testament writers make no use at all, and seem intentionally to avoid, two other words for love available to them, στέργειν/στοργή (familial love, love of country, etc.)[13] and ἐρᾶν/ἔρως (passionate desire.)[14] This phenomenon has been noted often enough. Less attention has been paid, however, to the appearance in the New Testament of a number of other words for

---

scribes it as "an authentic revelation-word" (*Agape. Die Liebe als Grundmotiv*, p. 18).

[10] *Agape. Die Liebe als Grundmotiv.*

[11] Cf. C. C. Tarelli, "ΑΓΑΠΗ," *JThSt* I (1950): 64-67.

[12] See Joly, *Le vocabulaire chrétien de l'amour.*

[13] But Paul does use φιλόστοργος and ἄστοργος once each, and ἄστοργος is also used in II Tim. 3:3. See below, pp. 227-28.

[14] There are good discussions of these words, and some indications of why they were inappropriate as terms for love in a Christian sense, in Spicq, *Prolégomènes*, pp. 2-6 and 7-11 respectively. Cf. Moffatt, *Love in the New Testament*, pp. 35-39, 49-51.

love, all of them perfectly familiar in the literature and in the market places of the day.

Of these, by far the most frequent in the New Testament is φιλεῖν/ φίλος, the verb 25 times, the noun 29 times.[15] These words have to do with love between friends, a favorite topic of Greek philosophers and epigrammists.[16] This filial love was regarded as consisting of mutual respect, trust, care, and goodwill between virtuous men. It was thus the ἠθικὸν πάθος, a high and noble "ethical feeling" shared by two persons.[17] And it was precisely the *mutuality* of the love which gave the filial relationship, as understood by the Greeks, its distinctive aspect. Spicq cites as a "perfect" expression of both the excellence and the limitation of this Greek ideal, the inscription on the tomb of Darius, as recorded by Strabo (xv, 3, 8): φίλος ἦν τοῖς φίλοις—"He was a friend to friends." [18]

In the New Testament there is no concern at all for "friendship" as an ideal, no discussion whatever of the virtues or qualities which should characterize authentically filial relationships, according to the typical Greek models. The absence of such themes is particularly significant in view of the frequency with which they are taken up in Hellenistic Judaism, even in the LXX. Discussions of friendships are especially prominent in Sirach (6:5-17; 27:16-21; 37:1-6), and friends and friendship are often extolled in Jewish maxims (e.g., Sirach 22:20; 25:1; Prov. 17:9; cf. I Esdras 3:22; friendship was also a rabbinic topic, e.g., Baba Bathra I, *The Babylonian Talmud,* p. 82; Berakoth IX, *ibid.,* p. 397).[19]

New Testament writers do, however, employ φιλεῖν/φίλος, and most often in the everyday "secular" Greek sense. It is perhaps not surprising that most of these instances come in Luke-Acts, a work which has been recognized as having "the closest parallelism to secular writing." [20] On the other hand, seven of Luke's references to "friends"

---

[15] The noun φιλία ("friendship") occurs just once, Jas. 4:4, the verb φιλιάζειν never (although both are used in the LXX).

[16] For discussions of these terms and the Greek ideal of friendship in general, see Spicq, *Prolégomènes,* pp. 12-32; John Ferguson, *Moral Values in the Ancient World* (London: Methuen, 1958), pp. 53-75, and the other literature cited by these.

[17] Spicq, *Prolégomènes* pp. 64-65.

[18] *Ibid.,* p. 32, n. 3.

[19] The noun φιλία also appears in the LXX to refer to sexual passion, either within (Prov. 5:19) or without (Prov. 7:18) the marriage relationship. Cf. the use of ἀγάπη in Song of Solomon.

[20] Henry J. Cadbury, "Four Features of Lucan Style," in L. E. Keck and J. L. Martyn, eds., *Studies in Luke-Acts: Essays Presented in Honor of Paul Schubert* (Nashville: Abingdon Press, 1966), p. 87.

(singular or plural) are in parabolic materials (11:5-8 [three times]; 14:10; 15:6, 9, 29)[21] which regularly reflect the everyday life of peasant folk. Thus, references to their "friends" come naturally and are also present in rabbinic parables.[22] But then twice this evangelist links together "kinsmen and friends" (συγγενῶν καὶ φίλων, Luke 21:16; τοὺς συγγενεῖς αὐτοῦ καὶ τοὺς ἀναγκαίους φίλους, Acts 10:24), a formulation also found in Greek inscriptions and in Hellenistic Judaism (e.g., Philo and Josephus).[23] Twice also he refers to Paul's "friends," and in at least one of these instances the reference is to non-Christian friends ("the Asiarchs," Acts 19:31[24]); whether that is so at Acts 27:3 is disputed.[25] Moreover, Luke alone refers to the centurion's "friends" in the story at Luke 7:1-10 (vs. 6; contrast Matt. 8:5-13), and makes comment about Herod and Pilate overcoming their "enmity" and becoming "friends" with one another (Luke 23:12). Also, the saying "Make friends for yourselves by means of unrighteous mammon . . ." is only in Luke (16:9).

All three Synoptic Gospels employ the verb φιλεῖν to mean "kiss" in the betrayal narrative (Matt. 26:48; Mark 14:44; Luke 22:47), and this is again a usage attested in nonbiblical sources.[26] So also is the use of the verb to indicate a personal preference or liking for some specific thing or action, in the New Testament (as it so happens) used in polemical contexts. Thus, Rev. 22:15, a reference to those who "love" falsehood, John 12:25, in the Johannine version of Jesus' saying about "finding" (John: "loving") one's life and losing it, and

---

[21] Only in the case of the parable of the lost sheep is there a Synoptic parallel (Matt. 18:12-14), but without Luke's mention of the shepherd's calling together his "friends and neighbors" to help celebrate the lost sheep's recovery.

[22] E.g., 'Abodah Zarah I, The Babylonian Talmud, p. 14; Niddah X, ibid., p. 491; Pesikta Rabba 12.12, trans. W. G. Braude, Yale Judaica Series, XVIII (New Haven: Yale University Press, 1968): 237-38.

[23] Instances are cited by Michaelis, ThWB VII: 737, 739. Cf. Luke 14:12 where, however, τοὺς φίλους σου seems to be paired with "your brothers" (τοὺς ἀδελφούς σου) and τοὺς συγγενεῖς with "rich neighbors" (γείτονας πλουσίους): ibid., p. 740. See also Spicq, Agapè dans le Nouveau Testament, III: 92-93 (notes), who gives other examples from both classical and Hellenistic sources.

[24] On "Asiarchs," see the article by F. D. Gealy, IntDB, A-D, p. 259.

[25] Haenchen (Die Apostelgeschichte, p. 624, n.1), following Harnack, believes the expression τοὺς φίλους is surrogate for "Christians," but Spicq sees no necessity for interpreting it thus, since the term is not used elsewhere in Acts to mean "Christians," and since, when a substitute for "Christians" is chosen, it is "his own" (τῶν ἰδίων αὐτοῦ, 24:23): Agapè dans le Nouveau Testament, III: 95 and n.9.

[26] See, e.g., Bauer, A Greek-English Lexicon, p. 867; Liddell-Scott, Greek-English Lexicon, p. 1933.

John 15:19, Jesus' comment that the world would "love its own." This meaning is also present in the Synoptic polemic against the scribes and/or Pharisees who "love" to display their piety (Matt. 6:5), to take the best seats (Matt. 23:6; Luke 20:46), to make "salutations in the market places" (Matt. 23:7; Luke 20:46), etc. Thus, it is striking that the parallel woe at Luke 11:43 uses the verb ἀγαπᾶν, perhaps influenced by the preceding charge that the Pharisees *neglect* the ἀγάπη of God, vs. 42. The result is a sharpening of the polemic by means of ironic contrast. A comparable contrast is present in I John 2:15 where loving (ἀγαπᾶτε . . . ἀγαπᾷ) the world is set over against the love (ἡ ἀγάπη) of God.

Other New Testament passages exemplify the everyday use of φιλεῖν/φίλος to refer to close familial or parafamilial relationships: children's love for parents, and theirs for the children (Matt. 10:37 [27]) and the love of Christians for one another (Titus 3:15; III John 15). Spicq has shown how the formulations in Titus and III John, though adapted to a Christian context, have been influenced by secular epistolary conventions.[28] Hence, in these two cases φιλεῖν terminology is used where otherwise ἀγάπη words might have been expected. Finally, it is also a "secular" use of φίλος when the Jews warn Pilate that if he releases Jesus instead of Barabbas he will not be "Caesar's friend" (John 19:12).[29]

All the New Testament instances of φιλεῖν-φίλος adduced so far are perfectly in accord with extrabiblical usage, and the majority of occurrences are thus accounted for. But certain other New Testament texts are more distinctive.

1. In Jas. 2:23 righteous Abraham is called "the friend of God," and the background of this phrase is surely Septuagintal. Not only does Jewish wisdom literature extol "friendship" (φιλία) with God (e.g., Wisd. 7:14; cf. 8:18, friendship with Sophia) in a general way;

---

[27] It is often held that the Matthean form of this logion (whoever loves family more than Jesus is not worthy of him) is an interpretation of the Semitic idiom which is retained in Luke (14:26). See, e.g., J. M. Creed, *The Gospel According to St. Luke*, p. 194. Yet Matthew's form has a certain parallel in IV Macc. 2:10-12 where it is insisted that the law ranks above all of a man's closest relationships (to parents, wife, children, friends [φίλων, vs. 12]). Here (vss. 11, 12) the noun φιλία is used of both conjugal and parental love. In Matt. 10:37 ὁ φιλῶν . . . ὑπὲρ ἐμέ could well be translated: "who prefers . . . to me." A positive relationship of φιλία between Jesus and his followers is not necessarily implied here.

[28] *Agapè dans le Nouveau Testament*, III: 85-87, where parallels from secular letters are given.

[29] Some have contended that φίλος τοῦ Καίσαρος was even an official title (but see R. Bultmann, *The Gospel of John*, p. 663, n. 3).

the phrase "friends of God" is actually applied to the righteous (Wisd. 7:27) and, according to Philo's text of the LXX, Abraham is specifically singled out as one of these at Gen. 18:17.[30] (The Hebrew texts of II Chron. 20:7; Isa. 41:8; Jub. 19:9; 30:20 also speak of Abraham in particular as God's friend, although the LXX uses forms of ἀγαπᾶν in II Chron. and Isa.) The sole New Testament instance of the noun "friendship," Jas. 4:4, is occasioned by a desire to set over against one another as radically antithetical, "friendship with the world" and friendship with God.

2. In several New Testament passages one is genuinely surprised to find φιλεῖν used rather than ἀγαπᾶν. In Rev. 3:19 it is used of the divine love itself, "Those whom I love I reprove and chasten . . . ," a quotation from Prov. 3:12 which in the LXX uses ἀγαπᾷ! (The author of Hebrews retains ἀγαπᾷ when he cites the same text [12: 6].) Furthermore, Paul concludes a letter to the Corinthians with the warning, "If any one does not love [οὐ φιλεῖ] the Lord let him be accursed," I Cor. 16:22 [31]; and in John 21:15-17 φιλεῖν replaces ἀγαπᾶν the third time Jesus asks about Peter's love, and the disciple's answers invariably employ φιλεῖν. It is probable that the verbs are simply used synonymously here, although the point has been much discussed.[32]

3. In the context of Jesus' ministry and teaching the reference to him as "a friend of tax collectors and sinners" (Matt. 11:19; Luke 7:34) prepares the way for, even if it does not yet presuppose, significant new dimensions of meaning for the term φίλος. Luke also adds meaning to the term when he has Jesus address his disciples as "my friends" (12:4; not present in the parallel passage at Matt. 10:26 ff.).

4. But it is in the Fourth Gospel, the single writing in which the verb ἀγαπᾶν is most used, that the φιλεῖν/φίλος concept receives its

---

[30] E. Nestle, "Abraham, the Friend of God," *ExT* XV (1903): 46-47. See also W. E. Oesterley in *The Expositor's Greek Testament*, IV, ed. W. R. Nicoll (London: Hodder & Stoughton, n. d.), pp. 448-49; E. Peterson, "Der Gottesfreund: Beiträge zur Geschichte eines religiösen Terminus," *Zeitschrift für Kirchengeschichte*, XLII (1923): 161-202; and Spicq, *Agapè dans le Nouveau Testament*, III: 88-89.

[31] Contrast I Cor. 8:3 where Paul uses ἀγαπᾶν for one's love of God. At 16:22 he may be dependent upon a set formulation (cf. Spicq, "Comment comprendre ΦΙΛΕΙΝ dans I Cor. XVI, 22?" *NT* I (1956): 200-204, and C. K. Barrett, *The First Epistle to the Corinthians*, p. 396.

[32] The literature on this topic is cited by Spicq in connection with his own discussion, *Agapè dans le Nouveau Testament*, III: 225-37, to which may now be added O. Glombitza, "Petrus—der Freund Jesu. Überlegungen zu Joh. xxi.15 ff.," *NT* VI (1963): 277-85, and E. D. Freed, "Variations in the Language and Thought of John," *ZNW* LV (1964): 167-97.

most distinctive New Testament treatment.[33] Here it is used in speaking of God's love (for his Son, 5:20; for men, 16:27a; cf. Rev. 3:19), of Jesus' love for individuals (Lazarus, 11:3, 11, 36; an unnamed disciple, 20:2), and of the disciples' love for Jesus (16:27b; cf. I Cor. 16:22). Moreover, it is in this Gospel that Jesus declares his disciples to be "friends," no longer "slaves," and describes agape as laying down one's life "for his friends" (15:12-15).

III

Other New Testament words for love are much less frequent and also less significant. These remaining word groups may be said to connote, respectively, "brotherliness" (φιλαδελφία, φιλάδελφος), "hospitableness" (φιλοξενία, φιλόξενος), "benevolence" (φιλανθρωπία, φιλάνθρωπως), "family affection" (φιλόστοργος) and "cordiality" (φιλόφρόνως). In addition to these, notice should be taken of four words, each compounded with the prefix φιλ-, which occur exclusively in the Pastoral Epistles, and there only once each: φιλάνδρους and φιλότεκνος in Titus 2:4, and φιλήδονος and φιλόθεος in II Tim. 3:4. The total number of occurrences of these words, taken all together, is still only 21, and most of these are in epistolary parenesis. That is, they usually occur in contexts where a New Testament writer is patently drawing upon traditional materials in order to admonish his readers to fashion their lives in particular ways. Thus, Paul uses three of these terms together in Rom. 12:10-13 (φιλαδελφία, φιλόστοργος, φιλοξενία). Indeed, these verses may be regarded as Paul's exposition, in familiar parenetic terms, of what he means by the "genuine love" (ἀγάπη ἀνυπόκριτος) to which he has referred in vs. 9 immediately preceding. Such is to include a brotherly love of other Christians, akin to the affection which exists among members of the same family (τῇ φιλαδελφίᾳ εἰς ἀλλήλους φιλόστοργοι), and the practice of Christian hospitality (τὴν φιλοξενίαν διώκοντες). Outside of Christian writers "brotherly love" seems always to have referred literally to the love between blood brothers (e.g., Philo, On Joseph 218; IV Macc., esp. chap. 13), an affection natural to the family relationship, as Plutarch insists in his essay, "On Brotherly Love" (Moralia 478-92). In the New Testament, however, the term is always applied figuratively, to the bond of affection among "brethren" in the faith, a particular manifestation of agape. That Paul uses the adjective φιλόστοργος with it in Rom. 12

[33] Even aside from the disputed vss. 15-17 in chap. 21, for it is probable that the whole of that chapter is the addition of a later writer (so, e.g., Bultmann, The Gospel of John, pp. 700 ff.).

perhaps suggests that for him brotherly love among Christians is also "natural" to the "household of faith" (Gal. 6:10).[34]

The third term for love which Paul uses in Rom. 12 (φιλοξενία, vs. 13) designates "hospitality," the reception and entertainment of strangers. Though the importance of hospitality is stressed in the Old Testament,[35] this word group as such does not appear in the LXX. There are, however, ample instances in Greek literature, both classical and Hellenistic.[36] Within Christian circles, due principally to the missionary zeal which sent itinerant preachers and teachers out across land and sea, the practice of hospitality came to have exceptional importance.[37] It is therefore not surprising that, when New Testament writers, in their parenesis, begin enumerating practical duties of Christians, this one should be among them, as it is not only in Rom. 12:13, but also in Heb. 13:2; I Tim. 3:2; Titus 1:8; I Peter 4:9. In Hebrews (13:1, 2) as in Romans (12:10, 13) "hospitality" is linked with "brotherly love," and in I Peter (4:8, 9) as in Romans (12:9, 13) hospitality seems to be viewed as a particular instance of agape.

Apart from Rom. 12 Paul uses the term "brotherly love" only once, in I Thess. 4:9 where he declines to discuss it as such on the grounds that the Thessalonians have been "taught by God." [38] In I Peter 1:22 its close relationship to agape in the vocabulary of earliest Christianity is again apparent. Not only is the adjective "genuine" applied to it, as Paul had applied it to agape in Rom. 12:9, but the exhortation to "love one another earnestly" (ἀλλήλους ἀγαπήσατε ἐκτενῶς) immediately follows. A similar connection is explicit in II Peter 1:. where the noun occurs twice, and implicit in I Peter 3:8, the only New Testament instance of the adjective.

The idea of "benevolence" (φιλανθρωπία) is akin to that of hos-

---

[34] On Gal. 6:10, see above, pp. 101-2. Only in Rom. 12:10 does φιλόστοργος appear in the New Testament, though ἄστοργος is used in Rom. 1:31 and II Tim. 3:3, also parenetic contexts (vice lists). The character of φιλοστοργία as natural family affection is illustrated well in Plutarch's essay, "On Affection for Offspring," *Moralia* 493-97. On this word, see esp. Spicq, "ΦΙΛΟΣΤΟΡΓΟΣ (a propos de Rom., XII, 10)," *RB* LXII (1955): 497-510. Also C. E. B. Cranfield, *A Commentary on Romans 12–13* (*SJTh* Occasional Papers, 12 [Edinburgh: Oliver and Boyd, 1965]), p. 40.

[35] See J. Pedersen, *Israel: Its Life and Culture* (London: G. Cumberlege, 1926), I-II: 356-57; G. Stählin, *ThD* V: 19-20.

[36] See Liddell-Scott, *Greek-English Lexicon*, p. 1938; Bauer, *A Greek-English Lexicon*, p. 868; Stählin, *ThD* V: 17-19.

[37] See D. W. Riddle, "Early Christian Hospitality: A Factor in the Gospel Transmission," *JBL* LVII (1938): 141-54; Stählin, *ThD* V: 20-25; Harnack, *The Mission and Expansion of Christianity in the First Three Centuries*, trans. and ed. James Moffatt (London: Williams & Norgate, 1908), I: 177-80.

[38] On this passage, see above, p. 95.

pitality in both extrabiblical and biblical Greek. Diodorus Siculus, in telling of a man who invited passing strangers into his house to be entertained, describes the host as "benevolent" (φιλανθρώπως, XIII, 83), and Polybius speaks of the "hospitable and humane" nature of the Arcadian nation (IV, 20.1).[39] Thus, the use of this terminology in Acts (adverb, 27:3; noun, 28:2) conforms to secular Greek diction.[40] The only other New Testament instance of the word is Titus 3:4 where, coupled with the noun "goodness" (RSV, for χρηστότης), it describes God's divine mercy in sending his Holy Spirit in Jesus Christ to cleanse and save sinful men (vss. 5-7). Other examples of the linking together of the two words χρηστότης and φιλανθρωπία are to be found (e.g., in Philo and Josephus[41]), at least once precisely in relation to God: "Who has banished jealousy from His presence in His kindness and love for mankind" (χρηστὸς ὢν καὶ φιλάνθρωπος ὁ θεός, Philo, On Abraham 203).[42] There is, in fact, ample evidence for the use of the word "philanthropy" to describe the divine love,[43] and yet another passage from Philo, as Spicq points out,[44] is an instructive parallel to Titus. 3:4:

> What house shall be prepared for God the King of kings, the Lord of all, who in His tender mercy and loving-kindness [δι' ἡμερότητα καὶ φιλανθρωπίαν] has deigned to visit created being and came down from the boundaries of heaven to the utmost ends of the earth, to show His goodness [ἐπ' εὐεργεσίᾳ] to our race? (On the Cherubim 99)

In Titus the epiphany of God's "philanthropy" is also associated primarily with his "mercy" (and hence with his grace, cf. 2:11). In Diognetus (9.2) God's philanthropy is coupled with his agape. But the concept of a "divine philanthropy" apparently did not commend itself to earliest Christianity in general. In the New Testament it occurs only in Titus 3:4, and in the Apostolic Fathers only in Diognetus 9.2, the latter clearly dependent upon the former.[45]

[39] These references are Spicq's, Agapè dans le Nouveau Testament, II: 149, n. 3, where he also cites Heraclides of Pontus, Fragment III, 6: "benevolences to strangers."

[40] Henry J. Cadbury, "Lexical Notes on Luke-Acts," JBL XLV (1926): 201-2.

[41] Several passages, including some from other literature, are cited by M. Dibelius, Die Pastoralbriefe, p. 109, following Wettstein. Others are given by Spicq, "La Philanthropie hellénistique, vertu divine et royale," StTh XII (1958): 176, n. 1.

[42] Cited by Spicq, "La Philanthropie," p. 175, n. 2.

[43] Spicq's whole article, ibid., pp. 169-91, is devoted to the documentation of this point.

[44] Ibid., p. 176.

[45] For a general discussion of the concept of "philanthropy" in Greek literature, see Ferguson, Moral Values in the Ancient World, pp. 102-17.

The final terms worthy of note occur but once each in the New Testament. One of these, φιλοφρόνως, has to do essentially with cordiality and is therefore closely related to the concept of hospitality. Like the latter it is found often in classical and Hellenistic Greek sources, but in the New Testament only at Acts 28:7. There it is said that Publius of Malta "entertained" (ἐξένισεν) the shipwreck survivors for three days—an act of cordial hospitality.[46] In a typically parenetic context in Titus (2:4), "the young women" are exhorted to love their husbands and children, for which the terms φίλανδρος and φιλότεκνος are employed, both familiar from secular sources where, as in Titus, they are frequently linked together in parenetic contexts (e.g., Plutarch, *Moralia* 769 C).[47] In the vice list at II Tim. 3:2 ff., "lovers of pleasure" (φιλήδονοι) are contrasted with "lovers of God" (φιλόθεοι)—vs. 4. Neither of these words appears in the LXX, but both are found in classical and Hellenistic writers, and Philo, *On Husbandry* 88, draws exactly the same contrast between lovers of pleasure and of God as found in II Tim. 3:4.[48]

IV

This brief lexical survey of love terminology in the New Testament leads to several clear conclusions which may now be summarized.

1. The agape group is indeed the most frequent and important for New Testament writers when they speak about love. Agape words are particularly important in the Pauline letters and the Fourth Gospel.

2. Two common Greek concepts of love are avoided: στέργειν/στοργή (except for φιλόστοργος in Rom. 12:10) and ἐρᾶν/ἔρως.

3. Certain other familiar words for love are employed by New Testament writers in conformity with everyday, "secular" Greek usage. The chief of these are, respectively, terms for filial love (φιλία), humane or benevolent love (φιλανθρωπία), and cordiality (but only the adverb, φιλοφρόνως). The great majority of instances of these terms

---

[46] The two occurrences of the adverb in the LXX correspond to this, esp. II Macc. 3:9 where the high priest at Jerusalem extends a friendly welcome, but also IV Macc. 8:5 where it stands as a sign of, and invitation to, friendship (φιλία).

[47] Numerous other instances are cited by Deissmann, *Bible Studies*, 2nd ed., trans. A. Grieve (Edinburgh: T. & T. Clark, 1903), pp. 255-56, and Dibelius, *Die Pastoralbriefe*, p. 105. In the LXX φιλοτεκνία/φιλότεκνος occur, together, eight times in IV Macc. 14-16.

[48] Assuming (as G. H. Whitaker in his Loeb translation apparently also does) that Philo's contrasts are chiastically constructed: ἀποστρέφῃ καὶ φιλήδονον καὶ φιλοπαθῆ μᾶλλον ἢ φιλάρετον καὶ φιλόθεον.

used in the ordinary sense, without specifically "Christian" connotations, are in Luke-Acts.

4. In a few instances New Testament writers employ familiar Greek terms in ways which move them considerably beyond their usual "secular" meanings. This is particularly true of their use of the agape group, but also of their use of the term "brotherly love" (φιλαδελφία), which is always figurative, never literal as in non-Christian literature). The concept of hospitality (φιλοξενία) is also given new dimensions (in Christian parenesis), and so too, occasionally (and particularly in the Fourth Gospel), the concept of friendship. One New Testament writer conceives of a divine philanthropy (Titus 3:4), although for this conception there is precedent in both classical Greek and Hellenistic Jewish writers.

5. In parenetic contexts New Testament writers bring the concept of agape into especially close association with brotherly love, the latter usually being regarded as included in and a particular mode of the former (Rom. 12:9 ff.; I Peter 1:22; cf. 3:8; II Peter 1:7). Since "brotherly love," like agape, is used distinctively in the New Testament (above, 4), the relationship of these two words is particularly significant.

6. Although the concept of agape has a distinctive place in the New Testament, as the lexical statistics themselves show, one must not overlook those instances where agape terminology is employed in ways *not* distinctively "Christian." In Luke 11:43 the verb means nothing more than "to prefer," more specifically, "to desire vainly," and is equivalent to φιλεῖν which has the same sense in the parallel at Luke 20:46. The same general meaning of ἀγαπᾶν is present in I John 2:15, and in Col. 3:19 agape is simply the conjugal relationship though, presumably, Christian readers of Colossians would be able to see further and deeper dimensions to this agape than are present, e.g., in the LXX. Certainly, the writer of Ephesians saw these (5:25).

7. Whereas, as the parallelism of Luke 11:43 and 20:46 shows (above, 6), a Christian writer may on occasion use ἀγαπᾶν to mean nothing more than the "preference" which φιλεῖν also often denotes, more often New Testament writers enrich the concept of *philia* to mean what is ordinarily associated with agape. Instances of such are found in the Pauline letters (I Cor. 16:22), the Apocalypse (Rev. 3:19), and—especially—in the Fourth Gospel (e.g. John 5:20; 16:27a; cf. 21:15-17). In John 15:12-15 it is precisely in the midst of the admonition to "love one another" that agape and filial love are associated.

231

INDEX OF PASSAGES

232

INDEX OF MODERN AUTHORS

238